BLOOD, TOIL, TEARS AND SWEAT

D0953673

Blood, Toil, Tears and Sweat

The Speeches of

Winston Churchill

Edited and

with an Introduction by

DAVID CANNADINE

Houghton Mifflin Company • Boston • 1989

First American edition 1989
Speeches copyright © 1989 by Winston S. Churchill, MP
Introduction and selection copyright © 1989 by David Cannadine
All rights reserved

For information about permission to reproduce selections from
this book, write to Permissions, Houghton Mifflin Company,
2 Park Street, Boston, Massachusetts 02108.

Library of Congress Cataloging-in-Publication Data

Churchill, Winston, Sir, 1874–1965.
Blood, toil, tears, and sweat : the speeches of Winston Churchill
edited and with an introduction by David Cannadine. — 1st
American ed.
p.   cm.
ISBN 0-395-51744-3
1. Great Britain — Politics and government — 20th century.
I. Cannadine, David, date.   II. Title.
DA566.9.C5A5   1989   89-19939
941.082 — dc20   CIP

Printed in the United States of America

Q 10 9 8 7 6 5 4 3 2 1

Contents

PART TWO
Scorning and Warning 1917–1939

PART THREE
Mobilizing the English Language 1940

PART FIVE

Speaking with Different Tongues
1945–1955

Preface

During the last two decades of his life, Winston Churchill was widely acclaimed as 'the greatest Englishman of his time'. His death was mourned by millions around the world, and he remains to this day Britannia's most celebrated son. The flood of books and articles about him continues unabated, and the public appetite for more is both voracious and insatiable. Each year, hundreds of thousands of people from all over the world visit Blenheim, Chartwell, Bladon and the Cabinet War Rooms in London. The adjective 'Churchillian' and the noun 'Churchilliana' are now authoritatively accommodated between the covers of the new edition of the *Oxford English Dictionary*. Ships in the Royal Navy are named after him, as are cigarettes and public houses. His life is the subject of films, television series and even West End musicals. His books are still avidly and appreciatively read. His paintings command high prices in the salerooms. His most famous words have become immortal.

Yet there is no single-volume edition of his most important speeches, and the purpose of this book is to provide one. I am most grateful to Anne Boyd of Cassell for first suggesting this appealing project to me, and for her unfailing enthusiasm, encouragement and assistance thereafter. Mike Shaw of Curtis Brown has been both a tower of strength and a pillar of wisdom. I am also very heavily indebted to Dr David Reynolds, of Christ's College, Cambridge, for many memorable and illuminating conversations on the subject of Winston Churchill, and for his personal kindness no less than for his intellectual generosity. Clare Kudera provided invaluable research assistance at a crucial stage. But, once again, my greatest debt is to Linda Colley.

DNC
New Haven
New Year's Eve, 1988

IX

List of Illustrations

ACKNOWLEDGEMENTS

The publishers wish to thank the following for permission to reproduce illustrations:

Winston S. Churchill, MP, for photographs from the Broadwater collection: Plates 2, 3, 19 and 22

The Master, Fellows and Scholars of Churchill College in the University of Cambridge: Plates 6, 7, 8, 9, 10, 12, 13, 14, 15, 18 and 21

The Hulton Picture Library: Plates 1, 4, 5, 11, 17 and 23

Camera Press, London: Plate 16

Associated Press Photo: Plate 20

Introduction

WINSTON CHURCHILL was the most eloquent and expressive statesman of his time, truly both the master and the slave of the English language. Indeed, his extraordinary career may most fittingly be regarded as one magnificent and magniloquent monologue. Day after day, and often night after night, he poured forth words and phrases in tumultuous torrent and inexhaustible abundance – inspiring, exhorting, moving, persuading, cajoling, thundering, bullying, abusing and enraging. In private engagement or public appearance, Cabinet meeting or Commons debate, car or boat, train or plane, dining-room or drawing-room, bedroom or bathroom, his flow of oratory never ceased. Dozens of books, scores of articles, numerous state papers and countless memoranda bear what is literally the most eloquent witness to his unfailing verbal resource, to his prodigious rhetorical ingenuity and to his lifelong love of language. From the time of his election to the House of Commons in 1900, until his very last weeks as Prime Minister in 1955, Churchill was a man of whom it could quite properly be said that he never seemed at a loss for words.

Because he was essentially a rhetorician, who declaimed and dictated virtually every sentence he composed, most of his words were spoken rather than written. But some were more spoken than others. For it was as an orator that Churchill became most fully and completely alive, and it was through his oratory that his words and his phrases made their greatest and most enduring impact. With Churchill as with Gladstone, 'speech was the very fibre of his being'. During his own lifetime, more of his oratory was published in book form than that of any other political contemporary. The definitive edition of his speeches runs to eight vast volumes, containing well over four million words. And his most memorable phrases – not just 'blood, toil, tears and sweat', 'their finest hour', 'the few', and 'the end of the beginning', but also 'business as usual', 'iron curtain', 'summit meeting' and 'peaceful co-existence' – have become part of the everyday vocabulary

I

of millions of men and women. As Churchill himself once remarked, 'words are the only things which last for ever'. In his case, at least, this confident prediction has also become a fitting and incontrovertible epitaph.

I

Yet despite the unrivalled mastery of the spoken word which Churchill eventually achieved, he was in no sense a born orator. As a young man, it seemed inconceivable that he would ever impress as a public figure or excel as a public speaker. He was physically unprepossessing and uncharismatic, not much above five feet tall, with a hunched frame, a stooping walk, a weak upper lip, a delicate skin and a waistline which became self-indulgently expanded in middle age. He felt deeply his lack of an Oxbridge education – partly because it left him with an abiding sense of intellectual inferiority, and partly because it meant he 'never had the practice which comes to young men at university of speaking in small debating societies impromptu on all sorts of subjects'. Except for making a few brief remarks at social gatherings, he never mastered the art of extemporaneous public speaking. Most distressing of all, his voice was unattractive and unresonant, and he suffered from a speech impediment, part lisp and part stammer. As one candid observer noted early in his career, he was 'a medium-sized, undistinguished young man, with an unfortunate lisp in his voice . . . and he lacks face'.

The main reason why Churchill's oratory eventually took the particular form it did was that he had to overcome these debilitating disadvantages. He only mastered his chosen craft by 'hard, hard work', and by serving a 'long and painful apprenticeship'. He studied – and often memorized – the greatest orations of Cromwell, Chatham, Burke, Pitt, Macaulay, Bright, Disraeli and Gladstone. He knew his father's speeches off by heart, and deliberately emulated his dress and his mannerisms. He laboured heroically to overcome his lisp and his stammer, by visiting several voice specialists, by constant practice and perseverance, and by choosing unusual words and phrases so as to avoid the treacherous rhythms of everyday speech. He spent hours in front of the looking-glass, rehearsing his gestures and practising his facial expressions. Despite this monumental dedication, he was always afraid, in his early years, that he would blurt out some unpremeditated and inappropriate remarks in the Commons; and to the very end of his career he remained apprehensive before making any major speech, and

Introduction

was always on edge until he was satisfied that his words had not misfired.

Above all, he was obliged to lavish hours on the detailed construction of the speeches themselves. Whether delivered in the Commons, on the platform or at the microphone, Churchill's orations were neither the effortless effusions of an accomplished extempore speaker, nor the rambling remarks of someone thinking vaguely and incoherently aloud. They were formal literary compositions, dictated in full beforehand, lovingly revised and polished, and delivered from a complete text which often included stage directions. As such, they were meticulously constructed set-pieces, carefully planned from beginning to end, with ample documentation to support the case being made, and with the arguments flowing in ordered sequence, until the peroration was finally reached. Inevitably, this process occupied a great deal of Churchill's time. His first major speech in the Commons took six weeks to put together, and even during the darkest and busiest days of the Second World War, he was never prepared to shirk or skimp the task of composition. Although he sometimes made speeches which were unsuccessful, he hardly ever made a slovenly one.

To this extent, Churchill mastered the techniques of speech-writing and speech-making in ways that best compensated for his physical, temperamental and intellectual disadvantages. But he also fashioned a personal style which was essentially his own. He began by combining the stately, rolling sentences of Gibbon with the sharp antitheses and pungent wit of Macaulay, the two authors he had read so carefully during his days as a soldier in India. Among living orators, he was most indebted to Bourke Cockran, an Irish-American politician out of Tammany Hall, whose best speeches were even more eloquent than those of William Jennings Bryan. The resounding perorations which soon became such a marked feature of Churchill's utterances were modelled on those of the Younger Pitt and Gladstone, while for invective and vituperation, there was always the strikingly successful example of his father, Lord Randolph. To this exceptionally heady mixture, Churchill added his own personal ingredients: detail, humour and deliberate commonplace. The result, as Harold Nicolson noted, was a remarkably arresting 'combination of great flights of oratory with sudden swoops into the intimate and the conversational'.

In addition, Churchill was himself a true artist with words. For a self-educated man, no less than for a career politician, his vocabulary was uncommonly large. From the time when he was an otherwise

3

Introduction

unpromising schoolboy at Harrow, he took an almost sensuous delight in military metaphors, arresting alliterations, polished phrases, sharp antitheses and explosive epigrams. His speeches, like his paintings, were full of vivid imagery and rich colour. He loved short, strong, robust nouns: 'blood, toil, tears and sweat'. He relished evocative, assertive and often bookish adjectives: 'silent, mournful, abandoned, broken'. He became the master of the unexpected but apt choice of word, as in his description of the Mississippi as 'inexorable, irresistible, benignant', where the last, unusual adjective breaks the predictable alliterative pattern to great effect. Above all, he was unrivalled among his political contemporaries as a fertile maker of memorable phrases. His remark at the time of the General Strike, 'I decline utterly to be impartial as between the fire brigade and the fire', is one well-known example. And his later description of Russia as being 'a riddle, wrapped in a mystery, inside an enigma' is another.

The combined result of such remorseless determination, diligent application and consummate artistry was that Churchill very rapidly acquired the most rhetorical style of any statesman in British history. From department to department, from one crisis to another, from government to opposition, he took his glittering phrases with him, modifying and reworking well-tried word patterns to meet new circumstances. Consider his famous panegyric on the Battle of Britain fighter pilots in 1940: 'Never in the field of human conflict was so much owed, by so many, to so few' – a sentence of classic simplicity and seemingly effortless perfection. But it had been through many different permutations before reaching its final form. 'Never before', he observed at Oldham in 1899, 'were there so many people in England, and never before have they had so much to eat.' Nine years later, as Colonial Under-Secretary, he made this comment on a projected irrigation scheme in Africa: 'Nowhere else in the world could so enormous a mass of water be held up by so little masonry.' One of the reasons why his rhetoric flowed so easily and so splendidly in 1940, when Churchill was a titanically busy man, was that so many of the phrases and sentences were already there, just waiting to be used.

But they were also there because they exactly expressed his true personality. For Churchill's speeches were not just accomplished technical exercises in rhetorical composition, verbal ingenuity and public histrionics. He also spoke in the language he did because it vividly and directly reflected the kind of person he himself actually was. His own

4

extraordinary character breathed through every grandiloquent sentence – a character at once simple, ardent, innocent and incapable of deception or intrigue, yet also a character larger than life, romantic, chivalrous, heroic, great-hearted and highly coloured. As Asquith's daughter Violet noted, shortly after meeting him in the 1900s, 'There was nothing false, inflated or artificial in his eloquence. It was his natural idiom. His world was built and fashioned on heroic lines. He spoke its language.' In 1940, Vita Sackville-West was comforted by essentially the same thought: 'One of the reasons why one is stirred by his Elizabethan phrases is that one feels the whole massive backing of power and resolve behind them, like a great fortress: they are never words for words' sake.'

For all these reasons, Churchill's oratory soon became a remarkably well-tuned and well-practised political instrument. Indeed, considering that he never built up a regional power base in the country or a personal following at Westminster, that he changed his party allegiance twice, that his judgement was often faulty, that his administrative talents were uneven, and that his understanding of ordinary people was minimal, it is arguable that oratory was, in fact, his *only* real instrument. It enabled him to make his reputation as a young MP, to survive the vicissitudes of the First World War, to recover his position in the 1920s, to wage his solitary campaign against appeasement, to rally the forces of freedom during the Second World War, and to play the part of world statesman in the years which followed. At best, by sheer force of eloquence, he imposed his own vision, and his own personality, on men and on events. He expressed noble sentiments in incomparably eloquent speeches which possessed a unique quality of formal magnificence. For Churchill was not just speaking for the moment, however important that was: he was also speaking for posterity. The very existence of this volume is emphatic proof of how successfully he achieved that aim.

II

Nevertheless, despite the remarkable and transcendent qualities of Churchill's speeches, the fact remains that for much of his career they were ultimately ineffective, in that they did not enable him to achieve his supreme ambition of becoming Prime Minister. For all its undeniable brilliance, the very nature of his oratory actually made it harder for him to get to the top in public life. In part, no doubt, this was because his glittering phrases, his polished performances and his

Introduction

unconcealed delight in his own hard-won oratorical prowess provoked a great deal of envy in the great majority of lesser and duller men. It was also true that for most of his career his speeches frequently failed to persuade, and regularly offended and antagonized at least as much as they captivated and impressed. As one MP remarked in 1935, 'When the Rt. Hon. Gentleman speaks ... the House always crowds in to hear him. It listens and admires. It laughs when he would have it laugh, and it trembles when he would have it tremble ... but it remains unconvinced, and in the end it votes against him.' What were the defects of Churchill's oratory which meant that this appreciative but damning verdict held so true for so much of his public life?

Part of the problem was that the very luxuriance of Churchill's rhetoric, the disconcerting ease with which it was so readily mobilized in support of so many varied and even contradictory causes, only served to reinforce the view – which became widespread very early in his career, and which lasted to 1940 and beyond – that he was a man of unstable temperament and defective judgement, completely lacking in any real sense of proportion. It was not just that he constantly yearned for excitement and action, and that he exaggerated the importance of everything he touched. It was also that his rhetoric often seemed to obscure his reason, and that his phrases mastered him, rather than he them. Any policy, any scheme, any adventure which could be presented with rhetorical attractiveness immediately appealed to him, regardless of its substantive merits – or drawbacks. As Charles Masterman complained, 'he can convince himself of almost every truth if it is once allowed to start on its wild career through his rhetorical machinery'. All too often, he seemed to be guilty of the charge which Disraeli had levelled at Gladstone, of being merely 'a sophisticated rhetorician, inebriated with the exuberance of his own verbosity'.

A further difficulty was that, by their very nature, his Commons orations were dramatic, theatrical set-piece speeches, which were ill-suited to the essentially intimate, domestic, conversational atmosphere of parliamentary debate. As Clement Attlee once remarked, they were 'magnificent rhetorical performances, but ... too stately, too pompous, too elaborate, to be ideal House of Commons stuff'. They were an impressive exposition of his own views, they read superbly in *Hansard*, and they have captivated posterity; but they rarely reflected the mood of the House, they often contributed little or nothing to the debate itself, and they were sometimes completely out of place. On several occasions, this resulted in conspicuous parliamentary humiliation,

6

Introduction

when he failed to anticipate the mood of the Commons correctly, but was so tied to his text that he could only plough on inexorably towards disaster. Early in his career, Balfour poured scorn on Churchill's 'powerful but not very mobile artillery', and much later, Aneurin Bevan, using the same metaphor, complained that 'he had to wheel himself up to battle, like an enormous gun'.

In addition, Churchill's highly polished words often gave the very greatest offence and only reinforced another widespread criticism, that he was almost completely insensitive to the feelings of others. For his invective was (in Balfour's words) 'both prepared and violent,' something which his victims neither forgot nor forgave. Early in his career, in a pompous and patronizing speech, he dismissed Lord Milner, the darling of the British establishment, as 'a guilty Parnell'. In the late 1920s, he brutally described Ramsay MacDonald as 'the boneless wonder'. Soon after, he caricatured Gandhi as 'a seditious Middle Temple lawyer', a 'half-naked fakir'. In 1945, there was his notorious 'Gestapo' jibe at his Labour opponents in his first party political broadcast of the general election. And four years later, he mounted a swingeing attack on Cripps, the Labour Chancellor of the Exchequer, and his former colleague in the wartime coalition, in the aftermath of devaluation. As Attlee once remarked, 'Mr Churchill is a great master of words, but it is a terrible thing when the master of words becomes a slave of words, because there is nothing behind these words, they are just words of abuse.'

Much of Churchill's oratory was also implausibly pessimistic and apocalyptically gloomy. In lurid and vivid phrases, he depicted a succession of terrible threats to the very survival of the British nation and Empire: the Bolsheviks, the trade unions, the Indian nationalists, the Nazis, the post-war Labour governments and the atomic bomb. Each one was for him the most dire and deadly peril. And he described them in very similar language. 'On we go,' he thundered in 1931, when the danger was India, but it might equally well have been Germany, 'moving slowly in a leisurely manner, towards an unworkable conclusion, crawling methodically towards the abyss.' But it was not just, as Leo Amery remarked, that many of these speeches were 'utterly and entirely negative, and devoid of all constructive thought'. It was also that many of these menaces were at best exaggerated and at worst quite imaginary. By using phrases so similar to describe threats so varied and sometimes so implausible, Churchill effectively devalued his own rhetoric of alarmism by crying wolf too often. No wonder MPs did not

7

heed his warnings over German rearmament. They had heard it all before. It had become rather boring. Why should he be right this time?

While much of Churchill's oratory was too melodramatic and doom-laden, it was also too high-flown. However sincerely meant, it often sounded false, flatulent, bombastic, overblown. In the humdrum world of the inter-war years, and in the Socialist era of 1945–51, his rhetoric was too bright, too rich, too vivid, too exuberant. In the era of Lytton Strachey and George Orwell, the 'grand manner' just failed to convince. One woman, after hearing Churchill thunder at a public meeting, thought him 'a preposterous little fellow', 'detestable as anything except a humerous comic entertainer', with 'his folded arms, tufted forelock and his Lyceum theatre voice'. As the wireless began to supersede the political meeting, he became more than ever out of touch and out of date: as a broadcaster, he lacked the low-key, conversational style which was appropriate to the medium and also to the times. Not surprisingly, politicians like Baldwin and Attlee, who made a virtue of being down-to-earth and matter-of-fact, who were much more sensitively attuned to the mood of the nation, and who despised rhetoric and distrusted rhetoricians, often got the better of him – both in the country and in the Commons.

The fatal flaw in Churchill's oratory was that its defects were thus inseparable from its virtues, and were very much on the same Olympian scale. His speeches were meticulously prepared, but this meant they were ponderously inflexible. They often clothed noble sentiments in majestic language, but they could also ring hollow and sometimes gave great offence. They were endlessly inventive in their word-play, but this merely reinforced the widespread opinion that he was a man of unsound judgement and indiscriminate enthusiasms. For all their brilliance, polish and fireworks, they could bludgeon an audience into indifference or insensibility as easily as they could persuade it into admiration or acquiescence. But their greatest weakness was that they were essentially the speeches of a man completely self-absorbed and egotistically uninterested in the opinions of anyone else. 'He usurps a position in this House', complained George Lansbury, 'as if he had a right to walk in, make his speech, walk out, and leave the whole place as if God Almighty had spoken ... He never listens to any other man's speech but his own.' And if he was not prepared to listen to others, is it any wonder that, on many occasions, others were not prepared to listen to him?

Introduction

III

As Churchill's career unfolded, the balance between the strengths and weaknesses of his oratory shifted very markedly. During his early years, from his election to Parliament in 1900 until his resignation in the aftermath of the Dardanelles disaster in 1915, Churchill was learning his craft as an orator and trying to master the House of Commons. Inevitably, he made mistakes and suffered setbacks. His earliest speeches were crude in expression, and his attacks on Brodrick and Balfour – who were, after all, leaders of his own political party – were excessively violent. On one occasion, he actually broke down in the Commons in mid-sentence, having completely lost the thread of his words. On another, his first major speech as a junior minister, his remarks were fatally ill-tuned to the mood of the House. And some of his early phrases were so prolix, so antithetical and so polysyllabic, that it was sometimes impossible to understand what he actually meant. 'Terminological inexactitude' was both clever and funny; but to say that the London docks, 'which have already been called obsolescent, may have to be allowed to obsolesce into obsoleteness', was nothing but sheer rhetorical nonsense.

Nevertheless, Churchill's tireless application and flair for fine phrases soon brought real and important rewards. As a Tory back-bencher, he was constantly in the limelight, and after he crossed the floor his rise as a Liberal Minister was meteoric. As Colonial Under-Secretary, his speeches on the granting of self-government to the Transvaal were remarkable not only for their mastery of detail, but also for their breadth and generosity of view. As First Lord of the Admiralty he introduced the naval estimates in 1914, in a speech lasting over two hours, which was generally regarded as a masterpiece of lucid and cogent exposition. As Lloyd George perceptively remarked, 'the applause of the House' had become 'the very breath of his nostrils'. At the same time, he acquired a formidable reputation as a platform speaker, especially during the controversy surrounding the 'People's Budget' and the House of Lords constitutional crisis. In one particularly effective speech, he gave a memorable riposte to Lord Curzon's unfortunate claim that 'All civilization has been the work of aristocracies.' 'The upkeep of aristocracies', Churchill retorted, 'has been the hard work of all civilizations.'

The second phase of his career lasted from his return to power in 1917 until the outbreak of war in 1939. As a leading member of the

9

Introduction

Lloyd George Coalition he made memorable speeches introducing the army estimates in 1920 and in support of the Irish Free State Bill two years later. And as Chancellor of the Exchequer, from 1924 to 1929, his budgets were widely praised for their superb presentation and great sense of occasion. 'No one', Harold Macmillan later recalled, 'could withhold admiration for the wit, humour, ingenuity and rhetorical skill which he displayed.' But matters such as import duties on hops, road-fund grants and rating reform were both too complex and too arcane to be ideal subjects for his grandiloquent rhetoric, and there was a growing feeling that his style was becoming out of date. Above all, he carried with him a lengthening black-list of mistakes, misfortunes, misadventures and misjudgements – Tonypandy, Antwerp, the Dardanelles, Chanack, the General Strike – which no amount of oratorical skill could conceal or eradicate. As Neville Chamberlain put it in 1925: 'His speeches are brilliant, and men flock to hear him ... The best show in London, they say.' But he went on, 'So far as I can judge, they think of it as a show, and are not prepared at present to trust his character, still less his judgement.'

It was against this discouraging background that Churchill fought his two great oppositional campaigns of the 1930s, which showed him at his worst and then at his best as a speechmaker. From 1929 to 1935 he waged what Sam Hoare later called 'Winston's Seven Years War', against the Government of India Bill. It was a determined display of persistent and resourceful eloquence, but rarely can so much effort have been expended on a cause so completely misjudged. As Stanley Baldwin perceptively observed, Churchill's diehard opinions were essentially those of George III couched in the language of Edmund Burke. It was largely because of the hostility he aroused by this ferocious but futile campaign that his closely argued and powerfully documented speeches against the Nazi threat attracted much less notice than they deserved during the second half of the decade. As a sustained, one-man crusade, and as displays of parliamentary courage, they represent the summit of his oratorical achievement: but they were often delivered to a half-empty chamber. 'For five years', Churchill candidly lamented in 1938, 'I have talked to this House on these matters – not with very great success.'

Between 1939 and 1945, however, the Commons, the nation and the world were much more attentive. Throughout the 'Phoney War', Churchill made a succession of vigorous, fighting speeches as First Lord of the Admiralty, which gave a reassuring impression of resolute confidence and robust competence. But it was only when he became Prime Minister in the perilous circumstances which he had been waiting and hoping all his life to command, that his oratory fully caught fire. For this was authentically the hour of fate, the crack of doom, the deep abyss that he had so often (and often so vainly) foretold. The issues seemed appropriately Churchillian in their momentous and noble simplicity: victory or defeat, survival or annihilation, freedom or tyranny, civilization or barbarism. To such an unprecedented national crisis – actually terrible yet potentially heroic – Churchill's magniloquent rhetoric, so often so out of place and so out of date, was for once perfectly attuned. The drama of the time had suddenly become fully equal to the drama of his tone. In 1940 Churchill finally became the hero he had always dreamed of becoming, and his words at last made the historic impact he had always wanted them to make.

During the early stages of his premiership, his oratory served three different purposes with equal success. In the first place, he reported regularly to the Commons about the progress of the war – the formation of the Coalition Government, the fall of France, the Dunkirk evacuation, and so on. Many of his most famous speeches were essentially parliamentary news bulletins, with an additional, uplifting paragraph added on at the end. The second purpose was to rally and reassure the nation as a whole. We shall never know whether Churchill inspired the British people – something he himself always denied – or whether he merely expressed the emotions they all shared but lacked the words to say. Either way, his oratory, so often a monologue with himself, became, for the first and only time, a dialogue with the nation at large. Its third purpose was to convince world – and especially American – opinion, both of the plight of Britain's position and of the strength of Britain's resolve. Here, again, the speeches were perfectly judged, and Roosevelt in particular was deeply impressed. At a time when Britain was on the defensive, when invasion seemed possible at almost any moment, and when victory was virtually unthinkable, Churchill's speeches were themselves the best – and sometimes the only – weaponry available. As Edward R. Murrow once remarked: 'He mobilized the English language, and sent it into battle.'

Inevitably, it proved impossible to maintain this high pitch of emotional and oratorical intensity for the entire duration of the war. The stark and simple issue of surrender or survival was soon replaced by the more intractable and less heroic problems of Allied co-operation and post-war reconstruction. As the conflict dragged on there were signs of discontent at home, and a run of defeats in the Far East led to criticism of Churchill's leadership for being no more than 'a succession of oratorical successes accompanied by a series of military disasters'. He could still produce magnificent panoramic surveys of what was now the global war situation; he repulsed several no-confidence motions with ease; and he delivered great set-piece eulogies of Lloyd George and Roosevelt. But it was no longer so easy for him to simplify and dramatize complex military and political problems, and he was increasingly obliged to defend and to justify allied policies of which he himself disapproved. When Germany surrendered, he delivered an appropriately moving and majestic victory broadcast, but even in his moment of supreme triumph he could not resist a jibe at de Valera for maintaining Irish neutrality throughout the duration of hostilities.

As soon as victory was achieved in Europe, the binding spell of Churchill's oratory was broken. His party political broadcasts during the general election of 1945 were 'confused, woolly, unconstructive, and so wordy that it is impossible to pick out any concrete impression from them'. As leader of the Opposition, his slashing attacks on the Government – predicting, in familiar apocalyptic mode, the direst consequences of the nationalization of industry and the independence of India – were not always convincing. His speeches remained great parliamentary occasions, and he could still sometimes rise to unrivalled heights of feeling and expression. But his greatest successes in these years were achieved outside Parliament and outside Britain. At Fulton and at Zurich his words were those of a private citizen who had recently been dismissed by his country's electorate from all further conduct of their affairs, and they were the familiar Churchillian amalgam of gloom and uplift in equal proportions. But the stature of the speaker, the novelty of the occasions and the timing and content of his speeches meant that they made an immense impact, not only in the Western world, but behind the Iron Curtain as well.

In 1951 Churchill returned to power for the last time. Inevitably, the mood was very different from what it had been fourteen years earlier, and of necessity his rhetoric was less inspirational and more emollient: 'what was magic in 1940 would have been melodrama in 1955'. Furthermore, Churchill himself was by now a very weary Titan indeed. The composition of his speeches became more of a burden to him, and he sometimes used drafts which had been prepared for him by other hands. As an old man the fears and footfalls of his youth returned to haunt him. He constantly worried that he might again break down in

Introduction

Parliament, and he made one speech, in April 1954, so ill judged yet so unalterable that he was virtually howled down in the Commons. Nevertheless, with appropriate medical stimulants, he could still rise to great occasions with unrivalled eloquence; his eulogy of George VI and his own eightieth birthday address were masterly performances; and his final speeches on foreign affairs and the threat of nuclear war were as expressive as any he had ever made. There was some truth in Aneurin Bevan's criticism that in these last years Churchill's deeds no longer matched his words. But then, for much of his career, they never actually had.

IV

In making a selection of Churchill's speeches, the overriding problem has been how to choose from the incomparable and intimidating mountain of words which he left behind. Between 1900 and 1955, Churchill delivered on average one address virtually every week. Even though many of them relate to matters no longer of interest, except to professional historians, there remains much fascinating material that it has not been possible to include here. Of course, the most famous speeches – against appeasement, during the Second World War, and in the years of opposition and power which followed – effectively chose themselves. I have also sought to include characteristic orations from earlier, and less well-known, stages of his career, to give a representative selection of speeches which were famously unsuccessful or notoriously offensive, and to include electioneering addresses and wireless broadcasts as well as set-piece performances in the Commons. With the exception of that on the Transvaal constitution, where some very detailed passages have been omitted, all of the speeches are reproduced in their entirety. In each case, I have sought to explain the general historical background, and also the particular personal circumstances, which lay behind the speech. Churchill's voice may be silenced; but, as he himself intended, his words still speak.

A Churchill Chronology

1874	Born at Blenheim Palace on 30 November
1888–92	Educated at Harrow School
1893–94	Cadet at Royal Military College, Sandhurst
1895	Commissioned in the Fourth Hussars
1896–98	Military service in India and the Sudan
1898	Publishes *The Story of the Malakand Field Force*
1899	Publishes *The River War* and *Savrola*
1899–1900	War correspondent in South Africa
1900–06	MP for Oldham
1900	Publishes *Ian Hamilton's March*, and *London to Ladysmith*
1904	Leaves the Conservative Party and joins the Liberals
1905–08	Under-Secretary of State for the Colonies
1906–08	MP for North-West Manchester
1906	Publishes *Lord Randolph Churchill*
1908	Publishes *My African Journey*
	Marries Clementine Hozier
1908–10	President of the Board of Trade
1908–22	MP for Dundee
1910–11	Home Secretary
1911–15	First Lord of the Admiralty
1915	Chancellor of the Duchy of Lancaster
1915–16	On active war service in France
1917–18	Minister of Munitions
1919–21	Secretary of State for War and Air
1921–22	Secretary of State for the Colonies
1922–24	Out of Parliament
1923–31	Publishes *The World Crisis*
1924–29	Chancellor of the Exchequer
1924–45	MP for Epping
1925	Rejoins Conservative Party
1930	Publishes *My Early Life*
1932	Publishes *Thoughts and Adventures*
1933–38	Publishes *Marlborough: His Life and Times*
1937	Publishes *Great Contemporaries*
1939	Publishes *Step by Step*

A Churchill Chronology

1939–40	First Lord of the Admiralty
1940–45	Prime Minister and Minister of Defence
1945–51	Leader of the Opposition
1945–64	MP for Woodford
1946	Receives the Order of Merit
1948–54	Publishes *The Second World War*
1951–55	Prime Minister
1953	Appointed a Knight of the Garter
	Awarded the Nobel Prize for Literature
1956–58	Publishes *A History of the English-Speaking Peoples*
1963	Proclaimed the first Honorary Citizen of the United States
1964	Celebrates his ninetieth birthday
1965	Dies on 24 January, and is accorded a state funeral in St Paul's Cathedral

PART ONE
Mastering His Voice

1900–1917

I

The Maiden Speech
'A Certain Splendid Memory'

House of Commons, 18 February 1901

CHURCHILL MADE HIS FIRST POLITICAL SPEECH at Claverton Manor, Bath, in July 1897. Two years later, he unsuccessfully contested Oldham at a by-election as a Conservative, but in the 'khaki' election of November 1900 he was returned for the same constituency by a narrow margin. He then departed for a lucrative lecture tour of the United States, and came back to take his seat in the Commons on 14 February 1901. He was just 26 years old.

His maiden speech was delivered only four days later. Partly because he spoke directly after Lloyd George, and partly because of his own already extensive reputation, the Commons was crowded to hear him. He began by making some extempore remarks on Lloyd George's inflammatory address, but the majority of his speech was devoted to a carefully prepared survey of the problems and prospects of South Africa in the aftermath of the Boer War. His final sentence was a direct and deliberate allusion to the memory of his father, Lord Randolph.

He received congratulations from both sides of the House, and the words of Asquith and Joseph Chamberlain were more than perfunctorily polite. The Conservative *Morning Post* felt he had 'fully justified the expectations which had been formed.' But the Liberal *Daily News* noted that 'address, accent, appearance do not help him.' They were right, but they were soon proved wrong.

House of Commons, 18 February 1901

I UNDERSTAND THAT THE HON. MEMBER to whose speech the House has just listened, had intended to move an Amendment to the Address. The text of the Amendment, which had appeared in the papers, was singularly mild and moderate in tone; but mild and moderate as it was, neither the hon. Member nor his political friends had cared to expose it to criticism or to challenge a division upon it, and, indeed, when we compare the moderation of the Amendment with the very bitter speech which the hon. Member has just delivered, it is difficult to avoid the conclusion that the moderation of the Amendment was the moderation of the hon. Member's political friends and leaders, and that the bitterness of his speech is all his own. It has been suggested to me that it might perhaps have been better, upon the whole, if the hon. Member, instead of making the speech without moving his Amendment, had moved his Amendment without making his speech. I would not complain of any remarks of the hon. Member were I called upon to do so. In my opinion, based upon the experience of the most famous men whose names have adorned the records of the House, no national emergency short, let us say, of the actual invasion of this country itself ought in any way to restrict or prevent the entire freedom of Parliamentary discussion. Moreover, I do not believe that the Boers would attach particular importance to the utterances of the hon. Member. No people in the world received so much verbal sympathy and so little practical support as the Boers. If I were a Boer fighting in the field – and if I were a Boer I hope I should be fighting in the field – I would not allow myself to be taken in by any message of sympathy, not even if it were signed by a hundred hon. Members. The hon. Member dwelt at great length upon the question of farm burning. I do not propose to discuss the ethics of farm burning now; but hon. Members should, I think, cast their eyes back to the fact that no considerations of humanity prevented the German army from throwing its shells into dwelling houses in Paris, and starving the inhabitants of that great city to the extent that they had to live upon rats and like atrocious foods in order to compel the garrison to surrender. I venture to think His Majesty's Government would not have been justified in restricting their commanders in the field from any methods of warfare which are justified by precedents set by European and American generals during the last fifty or sixty years. I do not agree very fully with the charges of treachery on the one side and barbarity on the other. From what I saw of the war – and I sometimes saw something of it – I believe that as compared with other wars, especially those in which a civil population took part, this war in South Africa has been on the whole carried on with unusual humanity and generosity. The hon. Member for Carnarvon Boroughs has drawn attention to the case of one general officer, and although I deprecate debates upon the characters of individual general officers who are serving the country at this moment, because I know personally General Bruce Hamilton, whom the hon. Member with admirable feeling described as General Brute Hamilton, I feel unable to address the House without offering my humble testimony to the fact that in all His Majesty's Army there are few men with better feeling, more kindness of heart, or with higher courage than General Bruce Hamilton.

There is a point of difference which has been raised by the right hon. Gentleman the Leader of the Opposition upon the question of the policy to be pursued in South Africa after this war has been brought to a conclusion. So far as I have been able to make out the difference between the Government and the Opposition on this question is that whereas His Majesty's Government propose that when hostilities are brought to a conclusion there shall be an interval of civil government before full representative rights are extended to the peoples of these countries, on the other hand the right hon. Gentleman the Leader of the Opposition believes that these representative institutions will be more quickly obtained if the military government be prolonged as a temporary measure and no interval of civil government be interposed. I hope I am not misinterpreting the right hon. Gentleman in any way. If I am, I trust he will not hesitate to correct me, because I should be very sorry in any way to mistate his views. If that is the situation, I will respectfully ask the House to allow me to examine these alternative propositions. I do not wish myself to lay down the law, or thrust my views upon hon. Members. I have travelled a good deal about South Africa during the last ten months under varying circumstances, and I should like to lay before the House some of the considerations which have been very forcibly borne in upon me during that period.

In the first place I would like to look back to the original cause for which we went to war. We went to war – I mean of course we were gone to war with – in connection with the extension of the franchise. We began negotiations with the Boers in order to extend the franchise to the people of the Transvaal. When I say the people of the Transvaal, I mean the whole people of the Transvaal, and not necessarily those who arrived there first. At that time there were nearly two and a half times as many British and non-Dutch as there were Boers, but during the few weeks before the outbreak of the war every train was crowded with British subjects who were endeavouring to escape from the approaching conflict, and so it was that the Uitlanders were scattered all over the world. It seems to me that when the war is over we ought not to forget the original object with which we undertook the negotiations which led to the war. If I may lay down anything I would ask the House to establish the principle that they ought not to extend any representative institutions to the people of the Transvaal until such time as the population has regained its ordinary level. What could be more dangerous, ridiculous or futile, than to throw the responsible government of a ruined country on that remnant of the population, that particular section of the population, which is actively hostile to the fundamental institutions of the State? I think there ought to be no doubt and no difference of opinion on the point that between the firing of the last shot and the casting of the first vote there must be an appreciable interval that must be filled by a government of some kind or another.

I invite the House to consider which form of government – civil government or military government – is most likely to be conducive to the restoration or the banished prosperity of the country and most likely to encourage the return of the population now scattered far and wide. I understand that there are hon. Members who are in hopes that representative institutions may directly follow military government, but I think they cannot realize thoroughly how very irksome such military government is. I have the greatest respect for British officers, and when I hear them attacked, as some hon. Members have done in their speeches, it makes me very sorry, and very angry too. Although I regard British officers in the field of war, and in dealing with native races, as the best officers in the world, I do not believe that either their training or their habits of thought qualify them to exercise arbitrary authority over civil populations of European race. I have often myself been very much ashamed to see respectable old Boer farmers – the Boer is a curious combination of the squire and the peasant, and under the rough coat of the farmer there are very often to be found the instincts of the squire – I have been ashamed to see such men ordered about peremptorily by young subaltern officers, as if they were private soldiers. I do not hesitate to say that as long as you have anything like direct military government there will be no revival of trade, no return of the Uitlander population, no influx of immigrants from other parts of the world – nothing but despair and discontent on the part of the Boer population, and growing resentment on the part of our own British settlers. If there was a system of civil government on the other hand, which I think we have an absolute moral right to establish if only from the fact that this country through the Imperial Exchequer will have to provide the money – if you had a civil government under such an administrator as Sir Alfred Milner [*cries of 'Hear, hear,' and 'Oh'*] – it is not for me to eulogize that distinguished administrator, I am sure he enjoys the confidence of the whole of the Conservative party, and there are a great many Members on the other side of the House who do not find it convenient in their own minds to disregard Sir Alfred Milner's deliberate opinion on South African affairs. As soon as it is known that there is in the Transvaal a government under which property and liberty are secure, so soon as it is known that in these countries one can live freely and safely, there would be a rush of immigrants from all parts of the world to develop the country and to profit by the great revival of trade which usually follows war of all kinds. If I may judge by my own experience there are many Members of this House who have received letters from their constituents asking whether it was advisable to go out to South Africa. When this policy of immigration is well advanced we shall again have the great majority of the people of the Transvaal firmly attached and devoted to the Imperial connection, and when you can extend representative institutions to them you will find them reposing securely upon the broad basis of the consent of the governed, while the rights of the minority will be effectively protected and preserved by the tactful and judicious intervention of the Imperial authority. May I say that it was this prospect of a loyal and Anglicized Transvaal turning of the scale in our favour in South Africa, which must have been the original 'good hope' from which the Cape has taken its name.

It is not for me to criticize the proposals which come from such a distinguished authority as the Leader of the Opposition, but I find it impossible not to say that in comparing these two alternative plans one with the other I must proclaim my strong preference for the course His Majesty's Government propose to adopt. I pass now from the question of the ultimate settlement of the two late Republics to the immediate necessities of the situation. What ought to be the present policy of the Government? I take it that there is a pretty general consensus of opinion in this House that it ought to be to make it easy and honourable for the Boers to surrender, and painful and perilous for them to continue in the field. Let the Government proceed on both those lines concurrently and at full speed. I sympathize very heartily with my hon. Friend the senior Member for Oldham, who, in a speech delivered last year, showed great anxiety that everything should be done to make the Boers understand exactly what terms were offered to them, and I earnestly hope that the right hon. Gentleman the Colonial Secretary will leave nothing undone to bring home to those brave and unhappy men who are fighting in the field that whenever they are prepared to recognize that their small independence must be merged in the larger liberties of the British Empire, there will be a full guarantee for the security of their property and religion, an assurance of equal rights, a promise of representative institutions, and last of all, but not least of all, what the British Army would most readily accord to a brave and enduring foe – all the honours of war. I hope the right hon. Gentleman will not allow himself to be discouraged by any rebuffs which his envoys may meet with, but will persevere in endeavouring to bring before these people the conditions on which at any moment they may obtain peace and the friendship of Great Britain. Of course, we can only promise, and it rests with the Boers whether they will accept our conditions. They may refuse the generous terms offered them, and stand or fall by their old cry, 'Death or independence!' [*Nationalist cheers*]. I do not see anything to rejoice at in that prospect, because if it be so, the war will enter upon a very sad and gloomy phase. If the Boers remain deaf to the voice of reason, and blind to the hand of friendship, if they refuse all overtures and disdain all terms, then, while we cannot help admiring their determination and endurance, we can only hope that our own race, in the pursuit of what they feel to be a righteous cause, will show determination as strong and endurance as lasting. It is wonderful that hon. Members who form the Irish party should find it in their hearts to speak and act as they do in regard to a war in which so much has been accomplished by the courage, the sacrifices, and, above all, by the military capacity of Irishmen. There is a practical reason, which I trust hon. Members will not think it presumptuous in me to bring to their notice, in that they would be well advised cordially to co-operate with His Majesty's Government in bringing the war to a speedy conclusion, because they must know that no Irish question or agitation can possibly take any hold on the imagination of the people of Great Britain so long as all our thoughts are with the soldiers who are fighting in South Africa.

What are the military measures we ought to take? I have no doubt that other opportunities will be presented to the House to discuss them, but so far as I have been able to understand the whispers I have heard in the air there are, on the whole, considerable signs of possible improvement in the South African situation. There are appearances that the Boers are weakening, and that the desperate and feverish efforts they have made so long cannot be indefinitely sustained. If that be so, now is the time for the Government and the Army to redouble their efforts. It is incumbent on Members like myself, who represent large working-class constituencies, to bring home to the Government the fact that the country does not want to count the cost of the war until it is won. I think we all rejoiced to see the announcement in the papers that 30,000 more mounted men were being dispatched to South Africa. I cannot help noticing with intense satisfaction that, not content with sending large numbers of men, the Secretary of State for War has found some excellent Indian officers, prominent among whom is Sir Bindon Blood, who will go out to South Africa and bring their knowledge of guerrilla warfare on the Indian frontier to bear on the peculiar kind of warfare – I will not call it guerrilla warfare – now going on in South Africa. I shall always indulge the hope that, great as these preparations are, they will not be all, and that some fine afternoon the Secretary of State for War will come down to the House with a brand-new scheme, not only for sending all the reinforcements necessary for keeping the Army up to a fixed standard of 250,000 men, in spite of the losses by battle and disease, but also for increasing it by a regular monthly quota of 2,000 or 3,000 men, so that the Boers will be compelled, with ever-diminishing resources, to make head against ever-increasing difficulties, and will not only be exposed to the beating of the waves, but to the force of the rising tide.

Some hon. Members have seen fit, either in this place or elsewhere, to stigmatize this war as a war of greed. I regret that I feel bound to repudiate that pleasant suggestion. If there were persons who rejoiced in this war, and went out with hopes of excitement or the lust of conflict, they have had enough and more than enough today. If, as the hon. Member for Northampton has several times suggested, certain capitalists spent money in bringing on this war in the hope that it would increase the value of their mining properties, they know now that they made an uncommonly bad bargain. With the mass of the nation, with the whole people of the country, this war from beginning to end has only been a war of duty. They believe, and they have shown in the most remarkable manner that they believe, that His Majesty's Government and the Colonial Secretary have throughout been actuated by the same high and patriotic motives. They know that no other inspiration could sustain and animate the Regulars and Volunteers, who through all these hard months have had to bear the brunt of the public contention. They may indeed have to regret, as I myself have, the loss of a great many good friends in the war. We cannot help feeling sorry for many of the incidents of the war, but for all that I do not find it possible on reflection to accuse the general policy which led to the war, we have no cause to be ashamed of anything that has passed during the war, nor have we any right to be doleful or lugubrious. I think if any hon. Members are feeling unhappy about the state of affairs in South Africa I would recommend them a receipt from which I myself derived much exhilaration. Let them look to the other great dependencies and colonies of the British Empire and see what the effect of the war has been there. Whatever we may have lost in doubtful friends in Cape Colony we have gained ten times, or perhaps twenty times, over in Canada and Australia, where the people – down to the humblest farmer in the most distant provinces – have by their effective participation in the conflict been able to realize, as they never could realize before, that they belong to the Empire, and that the Empire belongs to them. I cannot sit down without saying how very grateful I am for the kindness and patience with which the House has heard me, and which have been extended to me, I well know, not on my own account, but because of a certain splendid memory which many hon. Members still preserve.

2

The Transvaal Constitution

'The Gift of England'

House of Commons, 31 July 1906

As the Conservative Government's commitment to free trade weakened, Churchill found himself increasingly out of sympathy with his own party, and in May 1904 he crossed the floor of the House of Commons and took his seat on the Opposition benches. On the formation of the Liberal Government in December 1905, he was appointed Parliamentary Under-Secretary at the Colonial Office. His senior Minister, Lord Elgin, was a dull and dour Scottish peer, which meant Churchill was effectively – and very happily – responsible for handling imperial business in the Commons.

In the 1906 session, the overriding colonial issue was the future of the Transvaal and the Orange Free State in the aftermath of Britain's hard-won victory in the Boer War. Churchill's first major performance as a junior minister was a notable parliamentary disaster. But this later speech, announcing the proposals for a new constitution for the Transvaal, did much to restore his position. Its final appeal, for a generous, visionary, non-partisan approach, was to become a familiar theme of many of Churchill's subsequent and more famous perorations.

'There were', Asquith's daughter later recalled, 'no flights of rhetoric, there was no party challenge or provocation. There was measured weight and gravitas. He was persuasive, temperate and restrained throughout, showing a perfect sense of the occasion.'

28

House of Commons, 31 July 1906

IT IS MY DUTY THIS AFTERNOON, on behalf of the Government, to lay before the Committee the outline and character of the constitutional settlement which we have in contemplation in regard to the lately annexed Colonies in South Africa. This is, I suppose, upon the whole, the most considerable business with which this new Parliament has had to deal. But although no one will deny its importance, or undervalue the keen emotions and anxieties which it excites on both sides of the House, and the solemn memories which it revives, yet I am persuaded that there is no reason why we should be hotly, sharply, or bitterly divided on the subject; on the contrary, I think its very importance makes it incumbent on all who participate in the discussion – and I will certainly be bound by my own precept – to cultivate and observe a studious avoidance of anything likely to excite the ordinary recriminations and rejoinders of Party politics and partisanship.

After all, there is no real difference of principle between the two great historic Parties on this question. The late Government have repeatedly declared that it was their intention at the earliest possible moment – laying great stress upon that phrase – to extend representative and responsible institutions to the new Colonies; and before His Majesty's present advisers took office the only question in dispute was, When? On the debate on the Address, the right hon. Member for West Birmingham – whose absence today and its cause I am quite sure are equally regretted in all parts of the House – spoke on this question with his customary breadth of view and courage of thought. He said: 'The responsibility for this decision lies with the Government now in power. They have more knowledge than we have; and if they consider it safe to give this large grant, and if they turn out to be right, no one will be better pleased than we. I do not think that, although important, this change should be described as a change in colonial policy, but as continuity of colonial policy.'

If, then, we agreed upon the principle, I do not think that serious or vital differences can arise upon the method. Because, after all, no one can contend that it is right to extend responsible government, but not right to extend it fairly. No one can contend that it is right to grant the forms of free institutions, and yet to preserve by some device the means of control. And so I should hope that we may proceed in this debate without any acute divergences becoming revealed.

I am in a position today only to announce the decision to which the Government have come with respect to the Transvaal. The case of the Transvaal is urgent. It is the nerve-centre of South Africa. It is the arena in which all questions of South African politics – social, moral, racial, and economic – are fought out; and this new country, so lately reclaimed from the wilderness, with a white population of less than 300,000 souls, already reproduces in perfect miniature all those dark, tangled, and conflicting problems usually to be found in populous and old-established European States. The case of the Transvaal differs fundamentally from the case of the Orange River Colony. The latter has been in the past, and will be again in the future, a tranquil agricultural State, pursuing under a wise and tolerant Government a happy destiny of its own. All I have to say about the Orange River Colony this afternoon is this – that there will be no unnecessary delay in the granting of a Constitution; and that in the granting of that Constitution we shall be animated only by a desire to secure a fair representation of all classes of inhabitants in the country, and to give effective expression to the will of the majority.

. When we came into office, we found a Constitution already prepared for the Transvaal by the right hon. Member for St George's, Hanover Square. That Constitution is no more. I hope the right hon. Gentleman will not suspect me of any malevolence towards his offspring. I would have nourished and fostered it with a tender care; but life was already extinct. It had ceased to breathe even before it was born; but I trust the right hon.

Gentleman will console himself by remembering that there are many possibilities of constitutional settlements lying before him in the future. After all, the Abbé Sieyès, when the Constitution of 1791 was broken into pieces, was very little younger than the right hon. Gentleman, and he had time to make and survive two new Constitutions.

Frankly, what I may, for brevity's sake, call the Lyttelton Constitution was utterly unworkable. It surrendered the machinery of power; it preserved the whole burden of responsibility and administration. Nine official gentlemen, nearly all without Parliamentary experience, and I daresay without Parliamentary aptitudes, without the support of that nominated majority which I am quite convinced that the right hon. Member for West Birmingham had always contemplated in any scheme of representative government, and without the support of an organized party, were to be placed in a Chamber of thirty-five elected members who possessed the power of the purse. The Boers would either have abstained altogether from participating in that Constitution, or they would have gone in only for the purpose of wrecking it. The British party was split into two sections, and one section, the Responsibles, made public declarations of their intention to bring about a constitutional deadlock by obstruction and refusing supplies, and all the other apparatus of Parliamentary discontent. In fact, the Constitution of the right hon. Gentleman seemed bound inevitably to conjure up that nightmare of all modern politicians, government resting on consent, and consent not forthcoming.

As I told the House in May, His Majesty's Government thought it their duty to review the whole question. We thought it our duty and our right to start fair, free, and untrammelled, and we have treated the Lyttelton Constitution as if it had never been. One guiding principle has animated His Majesty's Government in their policy – to make no difference in this grant of responsible government between Boer and Briton in South Africa. We propose to extend to both races the fullest privileges and rights of British citizenship; and we intend to make no discrimination in the grant of that great boon, between the men who have fought most loyally for us and those who have resisted the British arms with the most desperate courage. By the Treaty of Vereeniging, in which the peace between the Dutch and British races was declared for ever, by Article 1 of that treaty the flower of the Boer nation and its most renowned leaders recognized the lawful authority of His Majesty King Edward VII, and henceforth, from that moment, British supremacy in South Africa stood on the sure foundations of military honour and warlike achievement.

This decision in favour of even-handed dealing arises from no ingratitude on our part towards those who have nobly sustained the British cause in years gone by. It involves no injustice to the British population of the Transvaal. We have been careful at each point of this constitutional settlement to secure for the British every advantage that they may justly claim. But the future of South Africa, and, I will add, its permanent inclusion in the British Empire, demand that the King should be equally Sovereign of both races, and that both races should learn to look upon this country as their friend....

When I last spoke in this House on the question of the South African Constitution, I took occasion to affirm the excellence of the general principle, one vote one value. I pointed out that it was a logical and unimpeachable principle to act upon; that the only safe rule for doing justice electorally between man and man was to assume – a large assumption in some cases – that all men are equal and that all discriminations between them are unhealthy and undemocratic. Now the principle of one vote one value can be applied and realized in this country, either upon the basis of population, or upon the basis of voters. It makes no difference which is selected; for there is no part of this country which is more married, or more prolific than another, and exactly the same distribution and exactly the same number of members would result whether the voters or the population basis were taken in a Redistribution Bill. But in South Africa the disparity of conditions between the new population and the old makes a very great difference between the urban and the rural populations, and it is undoubtedly true that if it be desired to preserve the principle of one vote one value, it is the voters' basis and not the population basis that must be taken in the Transvaal – and that is the basis which His Majesty's Government have determined to adopt.

The right hon. Gentleman the Member for St George's, Hanover Square, had proposed to establish a franchise qualification of £100 annual value. That is not nearly such a high property-qualification as it would be in this country. I do not quarrel with the right hon. Gentleman's Constitution on the ground that his franchise was not perfectly fair, or not a perfectly *bona fide* and generous measure of representation. But it is undoubtedly true that a property-qualification of £100 annual value told more severely against the Boers than against the British, because living in the towns is so expensive that almost everybody who lives in the towns, and who is not utterly destitute, has a property-qualification of £100 annual value. But in the country districts there are numbers of men, very poor but perfectly respectable and worthy citizens – day labourers, farmers' sons, and others – who would not have that qualification, and who consequently would have been excluded by the property-qualification, low as it is having regard to the conditions in South Africa. Quite apart from South African questions and affairs, His Majesty's Government profess a strong preference for the principle of manhood suffrage as against any property-qualification, and we have therefore determined that manhood suffrage shall be the basis on which votes are distributed.

It is true that in the prolonged negotiations and discussions which have taken place upon this question manhood suffrage has been demanded by one party and the voters' basis by the other, and there has been a tacit, though quite informal agreement that the one principle should balance the other. But that is not the position of His Majesty's Government in regard to either of these propositions. We defend both on their merits. We defend 'one vote, one value', and we defend manhood suffrage, strictly on their merits as just and equitable principles between man and man throughout the Transvaal. We have therefore decided that all adult males of twenty-one years of age, who have resided in

33

the Transvaal for six months, who do not belong to the British garrison – should be permitted to vote under the secrecy of the ballot for the election of Members of Parliament.

Now there is one subject to which I must refer incidentally. The question of female suffrage has been brought to the notice of various members of the Government on various occasions and in various ways. We have very carefully considered that matter, and we have come to the conclusion that it would not be right for us to subject a young Colony, unable to speak for itself, to the hazards of an experiment which we have not had the gallantry to undergo ourselves; and we shall leave that question to the new Legislature to determine.

I come now to the question of electoral divisions. There are two alternatives before us on this branch of the subject – equal electoral areas or the old magisterial districts. When I say 'old', I mean old in the sense that they are existing magisterial districts. There are arguments for both of these courses. Equal electoral areas have the advantage of being symmetrical and are capable of more strict and mathematical distribution. But the Boers have expressed a very strong desire to have the old magisterial districts preserved. I think it is rather a sentimental view on their part, because upon the whole I think the wastage of Boer votes will, owing to excessive plurality in certain divisions, be slightly greater in the old magisterial districts than in equal electoral areas. The Boers have, however, been very anxious that the old areas of their former Constitution, of their local life, should be interfered with as little as possible, and that is a matter of serious concern to His Majesty's Government. Further, there is a great saving of precious time and expense in avoiding the extra work of new delimitation which would be necessary if the country were to be cut up into equal mathematical electoral areas.

The decision to adopt the old magisterial areas, which divide the Transvaal into sixteen electoral divisions, of which the Witwatersrand is only one, involves another question. How are you to subdivide these magisterial districts for the purpose of allocating members? Some will have two, some three, some a number of members; and on what system will you allocate the members to these divisions? We have considered the question of proportional representation. It is the only perfect way in which minorities of every shade and view and interest can receive effective representation. And Lord Elgin was careful to instruct the Committee as a special point to inquire into the possibility of adopting the system of proportional representation. The Committee examined many witnesses, and went most thoroughly into this question. They, however, advise us that there is absolutely no support for such a proposal in the Transvaal, and that its adoption – I will not say its imposition – would be unpopular and incomprehensible throughout the country. If a scientific or proportional representation cannot be adopted, then I say unhesitatingly that the next best way of protecting minorities is to go straight for single-member seats. Some of us have experience of double-barrelled seats in this country; there used to be several three-barrelled seats. But I am convinced that if either of those two systems had been applied to the electoral divisions of the Transvaal, it would only have led to the swamping of one of two local minorities which with single-member divisions would have returned just that very class of moderate, independent, Dutch or British Members whom we particularly desire to see represented in the new Assembly. Therefore, with the desire of not extinguishing these local minorities, His Majesty's Government have decided that single-member constituencies, or man against man, shall be the rule in the Transvaal. But I should add that the subdivision of these electoral districts into their respective constituencies will not proceed upon hard mathematical lines, but that they will be grouped together in accordance with the existing field cornetcies of which they are composed, as that will involve as little change as possible in the ideas of the rural population, and in the existing boundaries.

The Committee will realize that this is a question with an elusive climax. It is like going up a mountain. Each successive peak appears in turn the summit, and yet there is always another pinnacle beyond. We have now settled that the Members are to be allotted to single-member constituencies based on the old magisterial districts according to the adult male residents there.

But how are we to apply that principle? How are we to find out how many adult males there are in each of the districts of the country, and so to find the quota of electors or proper number of Members for each division? The proverbial three alternatives present themselves. We might take the Lyttelton voters' list revised and supplemented. We might make a new voters' list, or we might take the census of 1904. . . .

Lord Selborne has pointed out to us that it might take just as long a time to revise the Lyttelton voters' list as to make a new voters' list, which would occupy seven months. So that, with the necessary interval for the arrangements for election, ten months would elapse before the Transvaal would be able to possess responsible institutions. I think we shall have the assent of all South African parties in our desire to avoid that delay. I am sorry that so much delay has already taken place. It was necessary that the Cabinet should secure complete information. But to keep a country seething on the verge of an exciting general election is very prejudicial to trade. It increases agitation and impedes the healthy process of development. We are bound to terminate the uncertainty at the earliest possible moment; and we have therefore determined to adopt the census of 1904.

Let me ask the Committee now to examine the sixteen magisterial districts. I think it is necessary to do so before allocating the Members amongst them. In all the discussions in South Africa these have been divided into three areas – the Witwatersrand, Pretoria, and the 'Rest of the Transvaal.' Pretoria is the metropolis of the Transvaal. It has a very independent public opinion of its own; it is strongly British, and it is rapidly increasing. It is believed that Pretoria will return three, four, or five Members of the Responsible Party, which is the moderate British Party, and is independent of and detached from the Progressive Association. The 'Rest of the Transvaal' consists of the old constituencies who sent Boer Members to the old Legislature. There will, however, be one or two seats which may be won by Progressive or Responsible British candidates, but in general 'The rest of the country' will return a compact body of members of Het Volk.

Having said that, I now come to the Rand. We must consider the Rand without any bias or prejudice whatever. The Rand is not a town or city, but a mining district covering 1,600 square miles, whose population of adult males practically balances the whole of the rest of the country. The Rand population is not, as some people imagine, a foreign population. The great majority of it is British, and a very large portion of it consists of as good, honest, hard-working men as are to be found in any constituency in this country. But there are also on the Rand a considerable proportion of Dutch. Krugersdorp Rural is Dutch, and has always been excluded from the Rand in the discussions that have taken place in South Africa, and included in the 'Rest of the Transvaal.' But in addition to that there are the towns of Fordsburgh, which is half Dutch, and two other suburbs which also have a Dutch population; and it is believed that these will afford seats for members of the Responsible British Party with the support of Het Volk. I must say further that the British community upon the Rand is divided into four main political parties. There is the Transvaal Progressive Association, a great and powerful association which arises out of the mining interest. There is the Responsible Government Association; there is the Transvaal Political Association – a moderate body standing between the Responsibles and the Progressives – and there are the labour associations, which are numerous. There are three main labour associations, or really four – the Independent Labour Party, the Transvaal Labour League, the Trade and Labour Council of the Witwatersrand, and the Trade and Labour Council of Pretoria. Why do I bring these facts before the Committee? I do so because I feel it necessary to show how impossible it is to try to dismiss the problems of this complicated community with a gesture or to solve their difficulties with a phrase, and how unfair it would be to deprive such a community, in which there are at work all the counter-checks and rival forces that we see here in our own political life, of its proper share of representation.

37

Applying the adult male list in the census of 1904 to the three areas I have spoken of, I should allot thirty-two Members to the Rand, six to Pretoria, and thirty to the rest of the country; or, if you include Krugersdorp Rural in the Rand, it would read thirty-three to the Rand, six to Pretoria, and twenty-nine to the rest of the country. Arrived at that point, the Committee in South Africa had good hopes, not merely of arriving at a just settlement, but of arriving at an agreement between all the parties. I am not going to afflict the House with a chronicle of the negotiations which took place. They were fruitless. It is enough to say that there were good hopes that if the Progressive complaint, that the adoption of the census of 1904 did not allow for the increase in the population which has taken place since the census was taken, could be met, a general agreement could be reached. The Boers, whose belief that we were going to treat them fairly and justly has been a pleasant feature in the whole of these negotiations, and will, believe me, be an inestimable factor of value in the future history of South Africa – the Boers with reluctance and under pressure, but guided by the Committee, with whom they were on friendly terms, were willing to agree to a distribution which allotted one more seat to meet this increase of the population in the Witwatersrand area, and the proposal then became thirty-three, six, and thirty, or, including Krugersdorp Rural, thirty-four, six, and twenty-nine. The Responsible Party agreed to that. The Progressives hesitated. The great majority of them certainly wished to come in and come to a general agreement on those terms. Certain leaders, however, stood out for one or two or three seats more, and although Lord Selborne expressed the opinion that the arrangement proposed, namely thirty-three, six, and thirty, excluding Krugersdorp Rural, was a perfectly fair one to the British vote in the Transvaal, those leaders still remained unconvinced and obdurate, and all hopes of a definite agreement fell through.

The Committee returned to this country, bringing with them the recommendation that the Government on their own responsibility should fix the allocation of seats at that very point where the agreement of one Party was still preserved and where the agreement of the other was so very nearly won. And that is what we have decided to do. We have decided to allocate thirty-four seats, including Krugersdorp Rural, to the Rand, six to Pretoria, and twenty-nine to the rest of the country. Lord Selborne wishes it to be known that he concurs in this arrangement. Now I am quite ready to admit that every Constitution ought to rest either upon symmetry or upon acceptance. Our Transvaal Constitution does not rest upon either symmetry or acceptance, but it is very near symmetry and very near acceptance, and in so far as it has departed from symmetry it has moved towards acceptance, and is furthermore sustained throughout by fair dealing, for I am honestly convinced that the addition of an extra member to the Witwatersrand areas which has been made is justified by the increase of the population which has taken place since the census.

On such a basis as this the Transvaal Assembly will be created. It will consist of sixty-nine members, who will receive for their services adequate payment. They will be elected for five years. The Speaker will vacate his seat after being elected. The reason for that provision is that the majority in this Parliament, as in the Cape Parliament, with which the Government is carried on, is likely to be very small, and it would be a great hardship if the Party in power were to deprive itself of one of the two or three votes which, when Parties are evenly balanced, are necessary for carrying on the government. It would be a great disaster if we had in the Transvaal a succession of weak Ministries going out upon a single vote, one way or the other. And it is found that when Parties have a very small majority and are forced to part with one of their Members for the purpose of filling the chair, they do not always select the Member who is best suited to that high office, but the Member who can best be spared.

Now let me come to the question of language. Under the Constitution of the right hon. Gentleman the Member for St George's, Hanover Square, the Members of the Assembly would have been permitted to speak Dutch if they asked permission and obtained permission from the Speaker. We are not able to lend ourselves to that condition. We are of opinion that such a discrimination would be invidious. The recognition of their language is precious to a small people. I have never been able to work myself into a passion because there are in parts of South Africa Dutch people who wish to have Dutch teachers to teach Dutch children Dutch. I have not so poor an opinion of the English language, with its priceless literary treasures and its world-wide business connections, as not to believe that it can safely be exposed to the open competition of a dialect like the *taal*. We believe that the only sure way to preserve in the years that are to come such a language as the *taal* would be to make it a proscribed language, which would be spoken by the people with deliberation and with malice, as a protest against what they regarded, and would rightly regard, as an act of intolerance. Therefore we have decided to follow the Cape practice and allow the members of the Transvaal Parliament to address that Assembly indifferently in Dutch or English.

I shall be asked what will be the result of the arrangement that we have made. I decline to speculate or prophesy on that point. It would be indecent and improper. I cannot even tell in this country at the next election how large the Liberal majority will be. Still less would I recommend hon. Gentlemen here to forecast the results of contests in which they will not be candidates. I cannot tell how the British in the Transvaal will vote. There are a great many new questions, social and economic, which are beginning to apply a salutary counter-irritant to old racial sores. The division between the two races, thank God, is not quite so clear-cut as it used to be. But this I know – that as there are undoubtedly more British voters in the Transvaal than there are Dutch, and as these British voters have not at any point in the Constitutional Settlement been treated unfairly, it will be easily within their power to obtain a British majority, if they all combined to obtain it. I nourish the hope that the Government that will be called into life by these elections will be a coalition Government with some moderate leader acceptable to both parties, and a Government which embraces in its Party members of both races. Such a solution would be a godsend to South Africa. But whatever may be the outcome, His Majesty's Government are confident that the Ministers who may be summoned, from whatever Party they may be drawn, to whatever race they may belong, will in no circumstances fail in their duty to the Crown.

I should like to say also that this Parliament will be of a high representative authority, and it will be the duty of whoever may be called upon to represent Colonial business in this House to stand between the Parliament and all unjustifiable interference from whatever quarters of the House it may come.

I now approach the question of the Second Chamber. That is not a very attractive subject. We on this side of the House are not particularly enamoured of Second Chambers, and I do not know that our love for these institutions will grow sweeter as the years pass by. But we have to be governed by colonial practice; and there is no colony in the Empire that has not a Second Chamber. The greater number of these Second Chambers are nominated; and I think that the quality of nominated Second Chambers, and their use in practice, have not been found to be inferior to those of the elective bodies. His Majesty's Government desire to secure, if they can, some special protection for native interests which is not likely to be afforded by any electoral arrangement, I am sorry to say. We are unable, however, to countenance the creation in a permanent form of a nominated Second Chamber. But in view of the position of native affairs, in view of the disadvantage of complicating the elections, to which all classes in the Transvaal have been so long looking forward, and most particularly because of the extra delays that would be involved in the creation of a new elective body, the Cabinet have resolved for this Parliament only, and as a purely provisional arrangement, to institute a nominated Legislative Council of fifteen members. They will be nominated by the Crown, that is to say at home, and vacancies, if any, by death or resignation, will be filled by the High Commissioner, on the advice of the responsible Ministers. During the course of the first Parliament in the Transvaal arrangements will be completed for the establishment of an elective Second Chamber, and if necessary further Letters Patent will be issued to constitute it.

Under the Treaty of Vereeniging we undertook that no franchise should be extended to natives before the grant of self-government. I am not going to plunge into the argument as to what word the 'native' means, in its legal or technical character, because in regard to such a treaty, upon which we are relying for such grave isues, we must be bound very largely by the interpretation which the other party places upon it; and it is undoubted that the Boers would regard it as a breach of that treaty, if the franchise were in the first instance extended to any persons who are not white men. We may regret that decision. We may regret that there is no willingness in the Transvaal and Orange River Colony to make arrangements which have been found not altogether harmful in Cape Colony. But we are bound by this treaty. Meanwhile, we make certain reservations. Any legislation which imposes disabilities on natives which are not imposed on Europeans will be reserved to the Secretary of State, and the Governor will not give his assent before receiving the Secretary of State's decision. Legislation that will effect the alienation of native lands will also be reserved. It is customary to make some provision in money for native interests, such as education, by reserving a certain sum for administration by the High Commissioner or some other political or Imperial official. We propose to reserve Swaziland to the direct administration of the High Commissioner, with the limiting provision that no settlement he may make is to be less advantageous to the natives than the existing arrangement.

On November 30 1906, the arrangement for recruiting Chinese in China will cease and determine. Our consuls will withdraw the powers they have delegated to the mining agents, and I earnestly trust that no British Government will ever renew them. A clause in the Constitution will provide for the abrogation of the existing Chinese Labour Ordinance after a reasonable interval. I am not yet in a position to say what will be a reasonable interval, but time must be given to the new Assembly to take stock of the position and to consider the labour question as a whole. I said just now there would be a clause with regard to differential legislation as between white persons and others, and to this clause will be added the words: 'No law will be assented to which sanctions any condition of service or residence of a servile character.' We have been invited to use the word 'slavery' or the words 'semblance of slavery', but such expressions would be needlessly wounding, and the words we have chosen are much more effective, because much more precise and much more restrained, and they point an accurate forefinger at the very evil we desire to prevent.

I have now finished laying before the House the constitutional settlement, and I should like to say that our proposals are interdependent. They must be considered as a whole; they must be accepted or rejected as a whole. I say this in no spirit of disrespect to the Committee, because evidently it is a matter which the Executive Government should decide on its own responsibility; and if the policy which we declare were changed, new men would have to be found to carry out another plan. We are prepared to make this settlement in the name of the Liberal Party. That is sufficient authority for us; but there is a higher authority which we should earnestly desire to obtain. I make no appeal, but I address myself particularly to the right hon. Gentlemen who sit opposite, who are long versed in public affairs, and who will not be able all their lives to escape from a heavy South African responsibility. They are the accepted guides of a Party which, though in a minority in this House, nevertheless embodies nearly half the nation. I will ask them seriously whether they will not pause before they commit themselves to violent or rash denunciations of this great arrangement. I will ask them, further, whether they cannot join with us to invest the grant of a free Constitution to the Transvaal with something of a national sanction. With all our majority we can only make it the gift of a Party; they can make it the gift of England. And if that were so, I am quite sure that all those inestimable blessings which we confidently hope will flow from this decision, will be gained more surely and much more speedily; and the first real step will have been taken to withdraw South African affairs from the arena of British party politics, in which they have inflicted injury on both political parties and in which they have suffered

43

grievous injury themselves. I ask that that may be considered; but in any case we are prepared to go forward alone, and Letters Patent will be issued in strict conformity with the settlement I have explained this afternoon if we should continue to enjoy the support of a Parliamentary majority.

3

Haranguing the Hustings

'A Gust of Public-House Passion'

Victoria Opera House, Burnley, 17 December 1909

IN 1908, WHEN ASQUITH SUCCEEDED CAMPBELL-BANNERMAN as Liberal Prime Minister, Churchill was promoted to be President of the Board of Trade with a seat in the Cabinet. Two years later, he advanced still further, to become Home Secretary. He was not yet 40, and his rise had been truly meteoric: indeed, it was quite without parallel in recent political history.

Throughout this period, he was deeply involved in domestic affairs and social reform, in collaboration with (and much under the influence of) Lloyd George. The Government's legislative programme was heavy, and Churchill spoke frequently and powerfully in support of trade boards, labour exchanges, unemployment and sickness insurance. When the House of Lords imprudently rejected the 'People's Budget' in 1909, his attacks on the second chamber were second only to those of Lloyd George himself in savagery, ridicule, humour and wit.

On 16 December 1909, during the first of two general elections fought on the subject, Lord Curzon made an impassioned defence of aristocracy at Oldham. The following day, Churchill gave this memorable reply in a nearby constituency. It is an outstanding example of his early platform style, and shows how resourcefully and successfully he learned to adapt his formal and ornate House of Commons manner to the more robust demands of the hustings.

45

Victoria Opera House, Burnley, 17 December 1909

THE CHAIRMAN HAS TOLD YOU in homely but pithy fashion the three great issues on which you have to pronounce in the next few weeks. Burnley must give a clear and decided answer, and, above all, must not run any risk of an answer being given which would totally misrepresent the opinions of the great majority of the constituents [*cheers*].

The first of the three issues, the Chairman told you, is the defence of our Free Trade system [*cheers*]. I have been much struck by the character of the Tariff 'Reform' posters which we see placarded on the walls in Lancashire. It is very easy to draw a picture of a harrowing scene and to write 'Free Trade' over it. It would be just as easy, and I am not sure it would not be a little more accurate, to print over the same picture the words 'A victim of the drink traffic', or 'A victim of the land monopoly' [*cheers*]. After all, it is one thing to discern an evil; it is another to discern the cause, and nothing could be worse than to try to remedy an evil without truly discovering its actual cause. There is unemployment in our country. If that unemployment is due to Free Trade, then I presume it would be fair to argue that unemployment in Germany and in the United States is due to the fiscal system which they pursue. As the system they pursue is not Free Trade but Protection, our Tariff 'Reform' friends will find themselves in the position of arguing that unemployment in this country is produced by Free Trade and unemployment in Germany and the United States is produced by Protection [*cheers*].

I want to ask you this question, and I would like our Tariff 'Reform' friends in Lancashire to endeavour to answer it. It is this: How will Tariff 'Reform' kill short time? I see that a Conservative newspaper, criticizing some speeches which I have been making in Lancashire lately, used words to the effect that

Lancashire would desert the cause of Free Trade because it was suffering from a period of short time. But how would deserting the cause of Free Trade affect short time? The causes which make for prosperity in the cotton trade are very complex, and all who have studied them all their lives and know about them, as you do, are the least inclined to dogmatize upon them and say that there is a simple explanation. The supply of the raw material, the price at which cotton can be obtained is an important factor in the prosperity of the cotton trade, and it is more than ever an important factor after a period such as that which we have just gone through, when there has been a great expansion in the trade, when there have been a great many mills put up – perhaps too rapidly – and when the development and expansion of the mills of Lancashire seem to have gone forward in a bound and rather more quickly than the increasing growth of the cotton fields of the world could accommodate. That is a very serious matter for us, and when I was at the Colonial Office I exerted myself a great deal to develop as far as possible other areas of cotton-growing supply [*cheers*]. The safety of our cotton supply will only be achieved when we can buy from a great many different countries, instead of only from one. That is what we are doing now in regard to corn. We are able to buy from every country which has corn to sell. Of course you cannot develop great cotton areas in a moment. It will take years – ten or fifteen years – before these regions begin to take effect upon the home market.

Alone of all the great trades of this country it can be said that the cotton trade would receive no compensation whatever from a tariff system [*cheers*]. This system is vaunted to you as a sure remedy for all the ills that flesh is heir to, and we are told it will remedy every trouble that vexes the heart of man, and will secure to everyone good wages and constant employment. I am quite certain that these are lies [*cheers*]. They are cruel and misleading in all parts of England and Scotland, but they are specially cruel and misleading here in Lancashire [*cheers*]. Lancashire would suffer in all the vital elements of its economic and commercial strength if, in a moment of weakening or of delirium her shrewd

47

and capable citizens were to allow themselves to be seduced by such unsubstantial and dangerous arguments [*cheers*].

I saw the other day when I was speaking in Liverpool that as a result of criticisms of the Tariff 'Reform' proposals the Liverpool Chamber of Shipping passed a very curious resolution, to the effect that if Tariff 'Reform' came, Liverpool would have to be a free port [*laughter*]. I can quite understand their motive. Nothing is clearer than that a policy the object of which is to reduce the amount of goods carried to and fro across the sea, and the effect of which would be to require every parcel of goods landed in this country to go through all sorts of laboured formalities and pay all sorts of duty, would be very injurious to the prosperity of Liverpool, and therefore the citizens of Liverpool are bound in common sense to resist such a policy. But some of our Tariff 'Reform' friends in Liverpool want to have it both ways. They want to vote for Tariff 'Reform' and yet keep Liverpool a free port [*laughter*]. Why should we stop at Liverpool? What about Manchester, which by unheard of exertions has created itself a seaport forty miles inland [*cheers*]? And what about Dundee [*laughter and cheers*] and what about the port of London, and of Hull, of Newcastle and the great ports of the Tyne. All of these would have as good a claim to be free ports as Liverpool, and my suggestion is that we should follow out the principle to its logical conclusion and make all England a free port, the great free port of the world, as it is at present [*cheers*]. That is a policy which will not take as much trouble to carry out, because it is the policy on which the greatness of Britain has been built up [*cheers*].

The second of the issues before us is the Budget [*loud cheers*]. The Budget is to pay the bill. Liabilities have been incurred, the expenditure is in progress, the pensioners are coming forward every week for their pensions [*cheers*]. Dreadnoughts are being built [*laughter*]. We don't hear so much about them nowadays. The Conservative party have had to turn off the navy panic, because the paying panic [*laughter*] has proved much more powerful among their supporters. We hold that Parliament in imposing the inevitable taxes is entitled not only to lay a heavier proportionate burden on the rich than on the poor, but to see that that burden should be proportionately greater, should be on a graduated scale in order to ensure equality of sacrifice [*cheers*]. In addition to this, we hold that we are entitled to lay special burdens upon certain forms of wealth which are clearly social in their origin. But it may be said, 'Your plan includes other expenditure besides that on the navy and old-age pensions. What about national insurance, what about insurance against unemployment, what about labour exchanges, and what about economic and agricultural development?' These objects, our opponents say, are at any rate not indispensable.

It is quite true that the taxation we impose this year, and which is sufficient for the needs of this year, will yield a more abundant revenue in future years; and if, at the same time, a reduction in the expenditure on armaments became possible – that is a very important matter [*cheers*] – then we should have large revenues at our disposal. But is that a reason for objecting to the Budget? How do we propose to spend these growing revenues which the Budget will yield in future years. Why, the object of every single constructive proposal to which the revenues raised by the Budget will be devoted, not less than the method by which the taxes have been distributed, is to buttress and to fortify the homes of the people [*cheers*].

When I began my campaign in Lancashire I challenged any Conservative speaker to come down and say why the House of Lords, composed as the present House of Lords is, should have the right to rule over us, and why the children of that House of Lords should have the right to rule over our children [*cheers*]. My challenge has been taken up with great courage [*laughter*] by Lord Curzon [*groans*]. No, the House of Lords could not have found any more able and, I will add, any more arrogant defender, and at Oldham on Wednesday – you have heard of Oldham [*laughter*] – so have I [*laughter*]. Well, at Oldham Lord Curzon treated a great public meeting to what I can only call a prize essay on the Middle Ages [*laughter*]. I do not say it was not a very eloquent speech. It was a beautiful speech. I read it with the most intense pleasure, with feelings of artistic pleasure, and also a sense of satisfaction, because I would like Lord Curzon to make that speech in every town and city throughout our country. I would ask nothing better than that he should have an opportunity of putting these views forward with all his ability and address to great audiences throughout the country. I am sure it would save some of us a lot of trouble [*laughter*].

Let us look at one or two of the arguments on which Lord Curzon relied. He began with a defence of hereditary legislators. That is a very plucky thing to do [*laughter*]. He said, 'Look at the Monarchy!' But the Sovereign is not a hereditary legislator. In this country the Sovereign reigns but he does not govern. The King acts on the advice of Ministers. The Crown in England has not had for hundreds of years the power of making laws, and for two or three centuries has not had the power of stopping laws when they have been passed. It is a very wise thing in every State that the supreme office should be removed beyond the reach of private ambition and should be above the shock and change of party warfare. It is as a constitutional Monarchy that we reverence and honour the British Crown. I do not think the people of England would be prepared for one moment to agree to the Sovereign of these realms exercising the power which the Tsar of Russia exercises [*'hear, hear'*]. Lord Curzon could scarcely have chosen a more inaccurate 'fact' upon which to rely.

Then he told us that Mr Pitt, Mr Fox, and Grenville in days gone by exercised great dominance in the House of Commons, and that forty years after all their sons were also in great offices and playing a very important part. He went on to say that something like that had reproduced itself today, though on a smaller scale. Whereas some years ago you had Mr Gladstone, Mr Chamberlain, and Lord Robert Cecil (afterwards Lord Salisbury) in the House of Commons, so now you saw their sons distinguished. Then he turned to me [*laughter*]. Did I owe anything to my father? Why, of course, I owe everything to my father [*laughter and cheers*]. But what defence is all this of a House of hereditary legislators? Because my father was member for Woodstock, I do not suggest that I should be permanently member for Woodstock, irrespective of what the people of Woodstock may think of me. It is quite true that some instances can be cited of men who have succeeded distinguished fathers and have attained equal and even greater distinction themselves. But how many cases can be shown of the contrary? [*Laughter, and a voice: 'Rub it in.'*]. You can almost count the hereditary instances on your fingers. In fact Lord Curzon did not cite as many instances as there are fingers on his hands. But only consider the enormous number of contrary instances which have been veiled in a decent and merciful obscurity [*laughter*]. If the electors of a particular constituency like to let old associations count – if they choose to say, 'We will vote for this young man because we knew his father' – what derogation is it from their free right of choice; in what way is their full power to choose their own representative affected in any degree? If that argument of Lord Curzon proves anything, it proves that if there is anything in the doctrine of heredity that doctrine will receive consideration under the representative system wherever it deserves.

But the claim of the House of Lords is not that if the electors, like the sons of distinguished men may have legislative functions entrusted to them; it is that, whether they like it or not, the sons and the grandsons and the great-grandsons, and so on till the end of time, of distinguished men shall have legislative functions entrusted to them. That claim resolves itself into this, that we should maintain in our country a superior class, with law-giving functions inherent in their blood, transmissible by them to their remotest posterity, and that these functions should be exercised irrespective of the character, the intelligence, or the experience of the tenant for the time being [*laughter*] and utterly independent of the public need and the public will. That is a proposition which only needs to be stated before any average British jury to be rejected with instantaneous contempt [*cheers*]. Why has it never been rejected before? In my opinion it has never been rejected, because the House of Lords has never before been taken seriously by the democratic electorate, which has been in existence since 1885. They have never been taken seriously because they were believed to be in a comatose and declining condition, upon which death would gradually supervene. Now we see the House of Lords stepping into the front rank of politics; not merely using

51

their veto over any legislation sent up by any majority, however large, from any House of Commons, however newly elected, but also claiming new powers over the whole of the finances – powers which would make them the main governing centre in the State [*cheers*]. That is why we are forced to examine their pretensions very closely; and when we have examined them, I venture to think there will not be much left of them [*cheers*].

'Oh, but,' says Lord Curzon, going on with the defence of this hereditary Chamber, 'we don't have to trim our sails to catch passing gusts of popular passion.' Well, what are they doing now. Their whole contention is that they consider the Budget is a bad Budget, that it is wrong and vicious, and that it will do all manner of evil to the country. But they say if at the election the nation, the electors, upon a gust of popular passion, return a majority favourable to the Budget they will immediately pass the Budget [*laughter and cheers*]. That may be very prudent of them, and it may be very proper of them, but it certainly is not standing against the gusts of popular passion [*laughter and cheers*]. And what about the Trades Disputes Act? Why, I don't hesitate to say that the House of Lords, or a great majority of that House, regarded that as a thoroughly wicked bill. Lord Halsbury, the ex-Lord Chancellor, described it as pernicious and wicked, as a bill which contained a section more disgraceful than had appeared in any other statute. But it had what the House of Lords thought was 'a gust of popular passion' behind it; they stepped aside, and it passed [*laughter and cheers*].

Then there were the old-age pensions, which were denounced by Lord Lansdowne and by many others in the House of Lords in unmeasured terms as being a system calculated to destroy thrift and to weaken the self-respect of the working classes, which, in the opinion of the House of Lords, can only be maintained by a liberal application of the workhouse [*laughter and cheers*]. So great was the dislike of the Peers to the measure that they actually carried an amendment saying that after five or six years the whole system should come up again for review and would lapse if it were not renewed. But that is where 'a gust of popular passion' came in [*great laughter and cheers*]. The bill was passed though they believed it was going to ruin the country [*laughter*]. I am very glad it was passed. But it is no use for the House of Lords, when the only thing it does is to step out of the way when a measure which it regards as wrong has what it thinks is a popular backing behind it, to come forward and pose as stern independent arbiters of our destiny who resist any passing movement in the minds of the electorate [*cheers*]. Indeed the gravamen of the charge that I make against the House of Lords is that they are developing a studied habit of caucus electioneering [*cheers*]. I say that so far from standing against gusts of popular passion, they are always endeavouring to play the party game of the Tory party [*cheers*].

When you come to a question like the Licensing Bill, which I am quite ready to admit was not what is called good electioneering, but which was an earnest effort to grapple with one of the most awful social evils [*loud cheers*] – when you come to a question like that, when the House of Lords think they can score a petty, cheap point of party popularity with certain sections by rejecting it, then whatever appeals are made to them by the best men in the House of Lords, whatever compromises are offered by the Government, whatever appeals are addressed to them by the churches – by the Archbishop, by their own Church of England Temperance Society – and however earnest is the desire that an attempt should be made to grapple with the evil, they brush it out of the way in one moment because they are hoping to get, not a gust of public passion, but a gust of public-house passion [*loud and prolonged cheers*].

Now I come to the third great argument of Lord Curzon. 'All civilization,' he said – he was quoting a great French writer, an Agnostic, Renan – 'All civilization has been the work of aristocracies' [*laughter*]. They liked that in Oldham [*laughter*]. There was not a duke, not an earl, not a marquis, not a viscount in Oldham who did not feel that a compliment had been paid to him [*loud laughter*]. What does Lord Curzon mean by aristocracy? It is quite clear from the argument of his speech that he did not mean Nature's aristocracy, by which I mean the best and most gifted beings in each generation in each country, the wisest, the bravest, the most generous, the most skilful, the most beautiful, the strongest and the most active. If he had meant that I think we should probably agree with him. Democracy properly understood means the association of all through the leadership of the best, but the context of Lord Curzon's quotation and the argument of his speech, which was designed entirely to prove that the House of Lords was a very desirable institution for us to maintain in its present form, clearly shows that by aristocracy he meant the hereditary legislator, the barons, earls, dukes, etc. – I do not mean anything disrespectful by the etc. [*laughter*] – and their equivalents in other countries. That is what he meant by aristocracy in the argument he employed at Oldham. Well, again I say this has only to be dismissed as absurd [*cheers*].

'All civilization has been the work of aristocracies.' Why, it would be much more true to say the upkeep of the aristocracy has been the hard work of all civilizations [*loud cheers and 'Say it again'*]. Nearly all great ideas and the energy by which all the great services by which mankind has been benefited have come from the mass of the people. Take the great agent of civilization – religion. The religions of the world have come from the people, the religions of the world have come from the poor, and most of all is that true of Christianity. Christianity was preached by poor men, humble men in the smallest employments, and preached to the poor, the outcast, the despised and rejected of those hard times – Christianity which today rules the world, and has contributed to civilization all those precious ideas which keep our modern life clean and healthy. What great picture was ever painted by a duke? [*laughter*]. I have heard of a lord who wrote good poetry – Lord Byron – but he did not write the sort of poetry that the House of Lords liked. In science all the great discoveries have been made by men outside this charmed circle which Lord Curzon conceives to embrace all the talents. And in mechanical invention – another great agent of civilization – there again you come right down to the working people of Lancashire, in many cases, for some of the most notable inventions upon which the prosperity of our civilized life has been erected [*cheers*]. Even when you come to war – though you can hardly call war

54

one of the causes of civilization; it certainly has been a very potent agent in the destinies and development of humanity – well, there have been many great generals who have become peers, but there have been much fewer peers who have become great generals. Lord Curzon reminded us that many Lords have filled high offices in the State. He described how they had forty-one Prime Ministers in the House of Lords and only sixteen in the poor, miserable House of Commons; what Secretaries of State, First Lords of the Admiralty, and a long succession of offices they had had in the House of Lords, whilst so very few had been held in the House of Commons. I can quite believe that. It only shows the undue political authority which has been engrossed all these years by a small, limited and unrepresentative class [*cheers*]. Lord Curzon proceeds to tell us that many distinguished men were proud to join the House of Lords in former times. I think it was only natural that they were eager to put their feet upon such an easy and at times absolutely indispensable road to almost any great employment in the services of the country. 'All civilization', Lord Curzon tells us, 'is the work of aristocracies.' He had his quotation: I will have mine. Mine is not nearly such an elegant or recondite extract as his. You have all heard mine before. Let us say, in the words of Robbie Burns, 'A man's a man for a' that.' [*cheers*]. I back my horse against his over any course in Lancashire. I will back it over any course in Scotland [*laughter*].

All these questions might have been allowed to slumber. But they have been raised by the action of the House of Lords; and, as they are raised, you are bound to give your answer to them. Mr Chamberlain, I notice, in his letter to the papers, sorrowfully laments that Tariff 'Reform' is not going to be the only issue at the election. No, it is not going to be the only issue. I think the Conservative party would have been beaten on either of the issues, but on the two together they will be overwhelmed [*loud cheers*].

4

The Navy's Task

'We Have Got to Keep It Strong'

The Guildhall, London, 9 November 1911

AS ONE OF THE TWO MINISTERS PRIMARILY RESPONSIBLE for the growing government spending on the domestic front, Churchill had been opposed to increased naval expenditure in 1908, and had publicly discounted the possibility of war with Germany. But the emphatic evidence of the expansion of the German fleet, the Agadir Crisis of July 1911, the clear signs of incompetence and inefficiency at the Admiralty, and Churchill's abiding interest in military matters meant that he eagerly accepted the challenge to modernize and reform the British Navy.

In October 1911, he replaced Reginald McKenna as First Lord of the Admiralty, and McKenna took the Home Office instead. Until May 1915, the welfare of the navy was Churchill's constant preoccupation. He established a naval staff, improved the conditions of the lower deck, converted the fleet from coal to oil power, supported innovations in gunnery and improvements in ship design, and greatly increased the size of the navy.

Most of his speeches to Parliament were extremely lengthy and complex and do not deserve reprinting here. But at the very outset of his period of office, within days of his appointment, he spoke on naval defence at the Lord Mayor's Banquet. He alluded tactfully to his predecessor, and affirmed his confidence in Britain's invincible naval might, while making it perfectly plain that urgent reforms and improvements were also necessary.

The Guildhall, London, 9 November 1911

THIS IS THE FIRST TIME THAT I HAVE ENJOYED the great honour of replying on such an occasion as this to the toast so happily and so kindly proposed, and I am very glad to be associated in that duty with my old friend and former commander Sir William Nicholson, whom I first knew and served under when he was Chief of the Staff on the North-west Frontier, and when I was Sir William Lockhart's orderly officer. I can assure you that I have assumed the duties of the office to which I have been called with a deep sense of reverence for the great traditions of the navy and with a simple and sincere desire to discharge without failure what must ever be regarded as a national trust [*cheers*]. I begin under circumstances which are unusually favourable. I would like to express my obligation to men of all parties, and particularly to my political opponents, for the fairness and good feeling with which I have been treated at this juncture. I succeed also to a situation of great advantage. The navy is strong. It is strong actually, it is strong relatively, it is highly efficient [*cheers*]. The officers and men whom you have complimented tonight are the best that our manhood can produce [*cheers*]. The more closely the ships of every type are scrutinized, the more accurately they are compared with the corresponding vessels in other fleets, the more certain and unmistakable will the superiority and preponderance of the British Navy become. I owe much to the courage and foresight of my predecessor, Mr McKenna [*cheers*]. I recognize, and ask you here to recognize, the liberal provision which Parliament in recent years has made for the maintenance of its first line of defence. The services and the country owe besides a deep and lasting debt to Lord Fisher [*cheers*], the ablest naval administrator which this country has known [*cheers*]. And now that the controversies which real reforms and the animosities which a forcible personality often creates are passing away, we

57

are beginning to enjoy the results of his great work without the friction which perhaps inevitably was attendant upon this question; and I can tonight reply to the toast on behalf of a service united in sentiment, free within the proper limits of professional opinion, and animated in all ranks by a single-hearted desire to serve the State ['*Hear, hear*']. My voyage, therefore, begins in bright and favourable weather, if I may be allowed thus early to adopt metaphors which are proper to the office I hold.

The navy is strong – we have got to keep it strong [*loud and prolonged cheers*], – strong enough, that is, to use for all that it may have to do. And not only strong but ready, instantly ready, to put forth its greatest strength to the best possible advantage [*cheers*]. I speak, of course, with the reserves which are necessary to a Minister who has newly entered upon his duties; but, as far as I know, there is no reason at present why this double task of maintaining its immediate readiness for service should not be achieved without a failure to fulfil the expectations of my right hon. Friend who is now Home Secretary when he said that the Estimates for the coming year will show some reduction from the abnormal level on which they now stand ['*Hear, hear*']. On every ground, provided that national security is not in the slightest degree compromised, such a reduction is to be desired ['*Hear, hear*'].

But here let me say a few words of the utmost plainness. Our naval preparations are necessarily based upon the naval preparations of other Powers. It would be affection – and quite a futile kind of affection – to pretend that the sudden and rapid growth of the German Navy is not the main factor in our determination whether in regard to expenditure or new construction. To disguise this would be to do less than justice to the extraordinary and prodigious developments which have resulted from German energy and German science in recent years. It would further be foolish to deny the plain truth that naval competition between these two mighty Empires – who all the time have such enormous common interests, who all the time have no natural cause for quarrel – it would be foolish to deny that naval competition between them lies at the root and in the background of almost every difficulty which has baffled the earnest efforts which are repeatedly made – and in which the city of London has taken a noble part – to arrive at really friendly feelings between the two countries. While that competition continues every element of distrust and unrest is warm and active, and one evil leads to another in a long and ugly concatenation. We are not so arrogant as to suppose that the blame and the error which follows so often on human footsteps lies wholly on one side. But the maintenance of naval supremacy is our whole foundation. Upon it stands not the Empire only, not merely the great commercial prosperity of our people, not merely a fine place in the world's affairs. Upon our naval supremacy stands our lives and the freedom we have guarded for nearly a thousand years.

Next year the Navy Law – which when completed will give Germany a magnificent and formidable fleet, second only to our own – next year the law prescribes that the limit of expansion has been reached and that the annual quota of new ships added to the German Navy will fall to a half the quota of recent years. Hitherto that law, as fixed by Parliament, has not been in any way exceeded, and I gladly bear witness to the fact that the statements of the German Ministers about it have been strictly borne out by events. Such is the state of affairs in the world that the mere observance of that law without an increase would come to Europe as a great and sensible relief. We should feel that heavy as naval expenditure will undoubtedly be, the high-water mark at any rate has been reached, and all over the world men would breathe more freely and the nations would enter upon a more trustful and more genial climate of opinion. In this we should readily associate ourselves; and if, on the other hand, my Lord Mayor, the already vast programmes of other Powers for war upon the sea should be swollen by the new and added expansions, that would be a matter of extreme regret to us and other States. But I am bound to say on behalf of His Majesty's Government that of all the states and nations of the world Britain will be found the best able to bear the strain and the last to fail at the call of duty [*cheers*].

5

The Dardanelles Scapegoat

'I Have Done My Best'

Dundee, 5 June 1915

THANKS TO CHURCHILL'S REFORMING ZEAL, the navy was much better equipped to face the challenges of war in 1914 than it had been when he took office at the Admiralty. In October of that year, Churchill recalled the aged but indomitable Lord Fisher from retirement to be First Sea Lord. It began as a brilliant partnership, but, by early May 1915, predictable differences of temperament and strategic outlook led to Fisher's resignation.

Very shortly after, Churchill himself was forced to leave his post. He was personally blamed by many people for the disasters at the Dardanelles, and the Conservative Opposition would only join a Coalition Government under Asquith if Churchill was removed from the Admiralty. He struggled hard to survive, but in the end was forced to accept the sinecure appointment of Chancellor of the Duchy of Lancaster. Meanwhile, A. J. Balfour took his place at the Admiralty.

On 5 June 1915, Churchill went to Dundee to defend his work as First Lord before his constituents. He spoke with pride of the navy's achievements, rebuked the press for its continuing attacks upon the Government and upon himself, and ended with a ringing appeal to the nation which clearly foreshadows his great speeches of 1940. 'Mr Churchill', *The Star* noted, 'has spoken the words the nation wanted to hear.' But it would be some time before he was to do so again.

Dundee, 5 June 1915

I THOUGHT IT RIGHT TO TAKE AN OPPORTUNITY of coming here to my constituency in view of all the events which have recently taken place, and also of the fact that considerably more than a year has passed since I have had the opportunity of speaking in Dundee. I have not come here to trouble you with personal matters, or to embark on explanations or to indulge in reproaches or recriminations. In wartime a man must do his duty as he sees it, and take his luck as it comes or goes. I will not say a word here or in Parliament which I cannot truly feel will have a useful bearing upon the only thing that matters – upon the only thing I care about – namely, the waging of victorious war upon the enemy [*cheers*].

I was sent to the Admiralty in 1911, after the Agadir crisis had nearly brought us into war, and I was sent with the express duty laid upon me by the Prime Minister, to put the Fleet in a state of instant and constant readiness for war in case we were attacked by Germany [*cheers*]. Since then, for nearly four years, I have borne the heavy burden of being, according to the time-honoured language of my patent, 'responsible to Crown and Parliament for all the business of the Admiralty' and, when I say responsible, I have been responsible in its real sense, that I have had the blame for everything that has gone wrong [*laughter and cheers*]. Those years have comprised the most important period in our naval history – a period of preparation for war, a period of vigilance and mobilization, and a period of actual war under conditions of which no man had any experience. I have done my best [*cheers*], and the archives of the Admiralty will show in the utmost detail the part I have played in all the great transactions that have taken place. It is to them I look for my defence.

I look also to the general naval situation. The terrible dangers of the beginning of the war are over, the seas have been swept clear; the submarine menace has been fixed within definite limits; the personal ascendancy of our men, the superior quality of our ships on the high seas, have been established beyond doubt or question [*cheers*]; our strength has greatly increased, actually and relatively from what it was in the beginning of the war, and it grows continually every day by leaps and bounds in all the classes of vessels needed for the special purpose of the war. Between now and the end of the year, the British Navy will receive reinforcements which would be incredible if they were not actual facts. Everything is in perfect order. Nearly everything has been foreseen, all our supplies, stores, ammunition, and appliances of every kind, our supplies and drafts of officers and men – all are there. Nowhere will you be hindered. You have taken the measure of your foe, you have only to go forward with confidence [*cheers*]. On the whole surface of the seas of the world no hostile flag is flown [*loud cheers*].

In that achievement I shall always be proud to have had a share. My charge now passes to another hand, and it is my duty to do everything in my power to give to my successor loyal support in act, in word, and in thought [*cheers*]. I am very glad indeed that Mr Balfour [*cheers*] has been able to undertake this great task [*cheers*]. The operations which are now proceeding at the Dardanelles will give him the opportunity of using that quality of cool, calm courage and inflexibility which fifteen years ago prevented Ladysmith from being left to its fate and surrendered to the enemy.

I have two things to say to you about the Dardanelles. First, you must expect losses both by land and sea; but the Fleet you are employing there is your surplus Fleet, after all other needs have been provided for. Had it not been used in this great enterprise it would have been lying idle in your southern ports. A large number of the old vessels of which it is composed have to be laid up, in any case before the end of the year, because their crews are wanted for the enormous reinforcements of new ships which the industry of your workshops is hurrying into the water. Losses of ships therefore as long as the precious lives of the officers and men are saved, as in nearly every case they have been – losses of that kind, I say, may easily be exaggerated in the minds both of friend and foe.

And military operations will also be costly, but those who suppose that Lord Kitchener [*loud cheers*] has embarked upon them without narrowly and carefully considering their requirements in relation to all other needs and in relation to the paramount needs of our army in France and Flanders – such people are mistaken and, not only mistaken, they are presumptuous.

My second point is this – in looking at your losses squarely and soberly, you must not forget, at the same time, the prize for which you are contending. The Army of Sir Ian Hamilton, the Fleet of Admiral de Robeck, are separated only by a few miles from a victory such as this war has not yet seen. When I speak of victory, I am not referring to those victories which crowd the daily placards of any newspapers. I am speaking of victory in the sense of a brilliant and formidable fact, shaping the destinies of nations and shortening the duration of the war. Beyond those few miles of ridge and scrub on which our soldiers, our French comrades, our gallant Australians, and our New Zealand fellow subjects are now battling, lies the downfall of a hostile empire, the destruction of an enemy's fleet and army, the fall of a world-famous capital, and probably the accession of powerful Allies. The struggle will be heavy, the risks numerous, the losses cruel; but victory when it comes will make amends for all. There never was a great subsidiary operation of war in which a more complete harmony of strategic, political and economic advantages has combined, or which stood in truer relation to the main decision which is in the central theatre. Through the narrows of the Dardanelles and across the ridges of the Gallipoli Peninsula lie some of the shortest paths to a triumphant peace. That is all I say upon that subject this afternoon, but later on, perhaps, when the concluding chapters in this famous story have been written, I may be allowed to return again to the subject.

I am not with the croakers [*cheers*]. I see some of our newspaper friends are reproaching themselves, and reproaching others, for having been too optimistic. Let them lay their consciences to rest. It is the general duty of the Press, for the most part faithfully discharged, to sustain the public confidence and spirit in time of war. All the great commanders of the past, the rulers of States in times of crises, have always laboured to discourage pessimism by every means in their power [*cheers*]. Our Allies the French have a recent saying that pessimism in the civilian is the counterpart of cowardice in the soldier. That does not mean you must not face facts. You should face facts, but surely from the facts of our situation you will find the means of deriving much encouragement. Why, when we look back and remember that we entered this conflict of military nations, of great States prepared mainly for war, that we entered this conflict ten months ago a peaceful civilian nation, that no part of our national life, excepting always the Navy [*cheers*] – the British Navy was as ready as the German Army [*loud cheers*] and has proved itself more equal to its task [*cheers*] — but when we remember that no part of our national life, except the Navy, was adapted to war on a great scale, have we not in all that has happened since much to be proud of and much to be thankful for [*cheers*]? Is it not wonderful for instance that after so many years of peace we should have found ready to hand a Kitchener to recruit and organize our armies [*cheers*], a dauntless leader like Sir John French to command them [*cheers*], skilful generals like Sir Douglas Haig, Sir Ian Hamilton, a naval Commander-in-Chief like Sir John Jellicoe, admirals like Beatty and Sturdee and de Robeck, and the gallant commodore who flies his broad pennant in the saucy *Arethusa*? And depend upon it behind them there are many more only waiting for the golden gleam of opportunity to perform surpassing deeds of merit in our cause. It is the duty of all in times like these to give loyalty and confidence to their leaders, be they the soldiers in the active sphere or the statesmen who sit in anxious council here at home, to give them loyalty and confidence, not only when all goes smoothly, for that is easy, but to make them feel that they will not be blamed for necessary losses incurred in valiant enterprise or rounded on in reproach at the first check or twist of fortune. Then you will get from your leaders, be they military or civilian, you will get from them the courage, the energy, the audacity, and readiness to run

64

all risks and shoulder the responsibilities without which no great result in war can ever be achieved [*cheers*].

Now I would like to say something which will get me into trouble [*laughter*]. I do not think that the newspapers ought to be allowed to attack the responsible leaders of the nation [*loud cheers*], whether in the field or at home, or to write in a manner which is calculated to spread doubts and want of confidence in them or in particular operations, or to write anything which is calculated to make bad blood between them. I apply this not only to the admirals and generals, but to the principal Ministers at home, and especially the heads of the great fighting department. No other nation now at war would allow the newspapers such a licence in the present time, and if there is to be criticism, if there must be criticism, first, it should be the only loyal criticism of earnest intention. But if there is to be criticism, let it be in Parliament. If the speeches are such that we cannot allow the enemy to be a party to our discussions, then let Parliament, as is its right, sit for the time being with closed doors, but it seems imperative, in the interests of the country for the future, and for the safety and success of our arms, that irresponsible or malicious carping should not continue.

We in this country are the firm supporters of a free Press. A free Press is a natural and healthy feature in national life, so long as you have also a free Parliament and a free platform; but when, owing to war conditions, Parliament observes a voluntary, but severe restraint, and when many of the subjects cannot be freely discussed without giving information to the enemy, then the balance of society is no longer true and grave injury results from the unrestrained action of the newspapers.

I have very much regretted that the Liberal Government which is now no more had no opportunity of stating its case in Parliament. It would, I think, have been found that Lord Kitchener had a very strong case to unfold on behalf of the War Office, and even I might have had something to say on behalf of the Admiralty; but the Government has perished, its long career, so memorable in our home affairs, is ended, its work whether in South Africa or Ireland has passed for good or for ill into history.

I know that there are gathered here this afternoon many of those who were its opponents, and that we are going to work together on a different basis now; but before I come to the new Government and its prospects, I must ask your leave and your courtesy to say a few words in justice to the old [*cheers*]. There was a Government which sought peace long and faithfully and to the end, but which, nevertheless, maintained our naval defence so that all the needs and dangers were provided against; there was a Government who placed in the field six times as many divisions of soldiers as had ever been contemplated by any party in the State at any time in our history; there was a Government which fulfilled in your name, in the name of the nation, every obligation of duty and of honour to France and Belgium [*cheers*]; there was a Government which brought us into the war a united people and with such a record that in future times, when the wounded world looks back with its searching scrutiny upon all the events which have lead up to this great catastrophe – will leave us such a record as will show to all time that Britain was absolutely guiltless of the slightest stain [*cheers*]. I thought you would permit me to say these few words about the Liberal Administration, of which I have had the honour to remain for so many years a member, and that I might say them in justice to those who compose it and to the Chief who led it, and to the great party which so faithfully sustained it.

And before I leave it I would ask your leave to say a word about a great friend of mine, well known to you in Scotland and passed now out of public life – Lord Haldane [*cheers*]. I deeply regret that he has ceased to fill the great office which he adorned. No more sincere patriot served the Crown. There never has been an occasion in the Cabinets of the last seven years in which I have sat, that, as the need arose, Lord Haldane has not, from his great knowledge of the German governmental system, warned us to be on our guard against the dangerous side of their nature [*cheers*]. There never has been a time when he has not supported every provision for the defence of this country, military or naval. He it was who entered into those intricate arrangements with France which enabled our Army to be so swiftly brought to the

66

scene of action, just in the nick of time. He it was who prepared that Expeditionary Army in the face of much opposition and in days when every penny was hard to get. He it was who organized the Territorial Force [*cheers*], which has so splendidly vindicated itself and its founder, and upon whose gallantry, discipline and numbers, the weight and even the success of our military operations hitherto have notably, if not mainly, depended [*cheers*]. Till a few months ago all the land forces which we employed in this war, which we put in the field, were the products of Lord Haldane's organization, and in the fateful and convulsive days before Great Britain drew the sword of honour, when the chill of doubt struck into many hearts, whether we should act as we were bound – in those days no man stood closer to Sir Edward Grey and no man saw more clearly where our duty led us [*cheers*].

With that I leave the past. A new Government has been formed, old opponents have laid aside their differences, personal interests and party interests have been adjusted or suppressed, and the Administration may now claim to represent the political energies and abilities and to command the loyalties of a united nation [*cheers*]. To support that Government, to make it a success, to make it an efficient instrument for waging war, to be loyal to it, to treat it fairly, and judge it with consideration and respect, is not a matter of likes and dislikes, not a matter of ordinary political choice of option. It is for all of us a matter of self-preservation [*cheers*]. For nearly three weeks the country has had its attention diverted from the war by the business of Cabinet-making and the dividing of offices and honours, and all those commonplace but necessary details of our political system which are so entertaining in time of peace [*laughter*].

Now that is all over. It has taken long enough, but it is over, and I ask myself this question: What does the nation expect of the new National Government? I can answer my question. I am going to answer it in one word – action [*loud cheers*]. That is the need, that is the only justification, that there should be a stronger national sentiment, a more powerful driving force, a greater measure of consent in the people, a greater element of leadership and design in the rulers – that is what all parties expect and require in return for the many sacrifices which all parties have after due consideration made from their particular interests and ideals. Action – action, not hesitation; action, not words; action, not agitation. The nation waits its orders. The duty lies upon the Government to declare what should be done, to propose to Parliament, and to stand or fall by the result. That is the message which you wish me to take back to London – act; act now; act with faith and courage. Trust the people. They have never failed you yet.

Long speeches are not suited to the times in which we live, and, therefore, I shall detain you only a very few minutes more, as to the rights of the State in the hour of supreme need over all its subjects there can be no dispute. They are absolute. Nothing matters but that the nation lives and preserves that freedom without which life would be odious. The only question which arises is as to the degree to which it is necessary to exercise these indisputable rights. Now, I say frankly to you that if it were not possible to win this war without taking men by compulsion and sending them into the field, I should support such a measure, but I do not believe that it will be found necessary [*cheers*], and I am sure it is not necessary now. On the contrary, such is the character of our people that the only places which will never lack volunteers are the bloody trenches of France and Flanders [*cheers*].

No nation has ever at any time in history found such a spirit of daring and sacrifice widespread, almost universal, in the masses of its people. The French Revolution could not defend the soil of France without compulsion. The American commonwealth could not maintain the integrity of its State without compulsion, but modern Britain has found millions of citizens who all of their own free will have eagerly or soberly resolved to fight and die for the principles at stake and to fight and die in the hardest, the cruellest, and the least rewarded of all the wars that men have fought. Why, that is one of the most wonderful and inspiring facts in the whole history of this wonderful island, and in afterdays depend upon it, it will be taken as a splendid signal of the manhood of our race and of the soundness of our institutions [*cheers*]. And having got so far, being now on the high road to three millions of men in the service of the Crown as Volunteers – having gone so far, to cast away this great moral advantage which adds to the honour of our Armies and to the dignity of our State, simply for the purpose of hustling into the firing line a comparatively small proportion of persons, themselves not, perhaps, the best suited to the job, who, even when taken, could not be for many months equipped – to do that after all that has happened, would, it seems to me, be unwise in the extreme [*cheers*].

But service at home, service for home defence and to keep our fighting men abroad properly supplied and maintained, that seems to me to stand on a different footing, remember, we are confronted with a foe who would without the slightest scruple extirpate us, man, woman and child, by any method open to him if he had the opportunity. We are fighting a foe who would not hesitate one moment to obliterate every single soul in this great country this afternoon if it could be done by pressing a button. We are fighting a foe who would think as little of that as a gardener would think of smoking out a wasps' nest. Let us recognize that this is a new fact in the history of the world [*cheers*] – or, rather, it is an old fact, sprung up out of the horrible abysses of the past. We are fighting with a foe of that kind, and we are locked in a mortal struggle. To fail is to be enslaved, or, at the very best, to be destroyed. Not to win decisively is to have all this misery over again after an uneasy truce, and to fight it over again, probably under less favourable circumstances and, perhaps, alone. Why, after what has happened there could never be peace in Europe until the German military system has been so shattered and torn and trampled that it is unable to resist by any means the will and decision of the conquering Power [*loud cheers*]. For this purpose our whole nation must be organized [*cheers*] – must be socialized, if you like the word – must be organized and mobilized, and I think there must be asserted in some form or other – I do not attempt to prejudge that – but I think there must be asserted in some form or other by the Government, a reserve power to give the necessary control and organizing authority and to make sure that every one of every rank and condition, men and women as well, do, in their own way, their fair share [*cheers*]. Democratic principles enjoin it, social justice requires, national safety demands it, and I shall take back to London, with your authority, the message, 'Let the Government act according to its faith' [*cheers*].

Above all, let us be of good cheer [*cheers, and a voice 'Shame the Devil and to hell with the Huns'*]. Let us be of good cheer. I have told you how the Navy's business has been discharged. You see for yourselves how your economic life and energy have been maintained without the slightest check, so that it is certain you can realize the full strength of this vast community. The valour of our soldiers has won general respect in all the Armies of Europe [*cheers*]. The word of Britain is now taken as the symbol and the hallmark of international good faith. The loyalty of our Dominions and Colonies vindicates our civilization, and the hate of our enemies proves the effectiveness of our warfare [*cheers*]. Yet I would advise you from time to time, when you are anxious or depressed, to dwell a little on the colour and light of the terrible war pictures now presented to the eye. See Australia and New Zealand smiting down in the last and finest crusade the combined barbarism of Prussia and of Turkey [*cheers*]. General Louis Botha holding South Africa for the King [*cheers*]. See Canada defending to the death the last few miles of shattered Belgium. Look further, and, across the smoke and carnage of the immense battlefield, look forward to the vision of a united British Empire on the calm background of a liberated Europe.

Then turn again to your task. Look forward, do not look backward. Gather afresh in heart and spirit all the energies of your being, bend anew together for a supreme effort. The times are harsh, need is dire, the agony of Europe is infinite, but the might of Britain hurled united into the conflict will be irresistible. We are the grand reserve of the Allied cause, and that grand reserve must now march forward as one man [*loud and prolonged cheers*].

6

A Disastrous Proposal

'Recalling Lord Fisher'

House of Commons, 7 March 1916

IN NOVEMBER 1915, CHURCHILL RESIGNED from the Government, took up active service in France, and was eventually given command of a battalion of Royal Scots Fuseliers. The courage he displayed during his six months' service in the trenches won him new admirers, but it took him away from the scene of political action. He yearned to return to political office, and he rightly feared that Balfour's tenure of the Admiralty was too languid and lethargic for the demands of the times.

This extraordinary speech, which Churchill delivered while on leave from the trenches, showed him at his best and at his worst as a parliamentary orator. It began as a careful and well-documented indictment of the Government's conduct of the war, and especially of Balfour's performance at the Admiralty, which held the attention of the House. But the effect was totally ruined when Churchill concluded by proposing the reinstatement of his late antagonist, Admiral Fisher, as First Sea Lord.

He did not remain in the Commons to learn of the reaction, which was one of widespread derision and incredulity. Even his closest friends thought his final proposal was an act of suicidal folly. The cogency of his criticisms was forgotten and, on the following day, Balfour made a devastating retort which left Churchill helpless and humiliated. It was widely believed that his political career was ended for good.

House of Commons, 7 March 1916

THE HOUSE IS INDEBTED TO MY RIGHT HON. FRIEND the First Lord of the Admiralty for the calm broad survey he has taken of the vast activities of his Department in all quarters of the sea, and for the felicitous language in which he has referred to the various branches of the naval and semi-naval personnel. I am myself much indebted to him for the courtesy and consideration of his references to the work of the previous Board, but I am the more sorry from that cause that here and there in my remarks this afternoon, which shall be as brief as they can possibly be made, I shall have to strike a jarring note, a note not of reproach, not of censure nor of panic, but a note in some respects of warning. There is one part of my right hon. Friend's speech which above all other parts, certainly first among all other parts, carried with it the enthusiastic support of the House. In Sir John Jellicoe we have a naval leader of the first qualities. The command of a battle fleet is far more intimate and personal than any function discharged by generals on land. The Commander-in-Chief leads or guides his squadrons into action and disposes of their array almost by his personal gesture. For this not only the highest qualities, exceptional qualities and special aptitudes of mind and body are required and also immense practice, and of all the naval chiefs in the world there is none whose practice and habit of handling and manoeuvring large fleets of armoured ships at sea can for one moment be compared with the opportunities which Sir John Jellicoe has so fully and so long enjoyed. As long as his flag is flying and he has his brilliant lieutenants, Sir Doveton Sturdee and Sir David Beatty, both of whom have naval actions of memorable character associated with their name, we may be absolutely sure that all our ships at sea will be manoeuvred and handled in the presence of the enemy or in the difficult and dangerous waters through which they have to pass with the utmost professional skill and with unflinching resolution. It is, however, the forces at their disposal at any given period and the relation of those forces to the forces of the enemy that must of course to a very large extent govern the course of affairs at sea.

Every First Lord and every Board of Admiralty are the heirs of their predecessors. I have, I think, reminded the House that, although I had been for three years at the Admiralty, when War broke out not a single one of the battleships I had obtained from Parliament had yet taken its place in the line of battle. Just as I was the heir of the present Chancellor of the Exchequer and his admirable provision, so my right hon. Friend is my heir, but it is an inheritance not entirely of blessing. A great programme of new construction in time of peace imposes upon the heir the need to fight Parliament for his money during many years, and in time of war casts a burden and strain upon all connected with the Department, and particularly upon the head, which can scarcely be measured by those who are not acquainted with him. I think my right hon. Friend has recognized that he has succeeded to a large estate, both in respect of labours and of property. Whether you look at battleships or cruisers or light cruisers or submarines or destroyers, or all the types which are now coming into view, he certainly succeeded to an immense provision bound to tax to the utmost the energies of his Department. If those programmes have been executed fully, punctually, there is no reason whatever for even the remotest forms of anxiety. On the contrary, I entirely agree with my right hon. Friend that our position, which was sufficient to be assured at the outbreak of war, has improved and will improve actually and relatively. I am, of course, thoroughly acquainted with the details of this programme, for which, with Prince Louis and Lord Fisher, I was responsible, but the point about them of substance that we must keep in our mind today is, How are they being executed? Are they being executed at full blast – are they being executed punctually? I rather wish that the First Lord had found it possible to give an assurance to the House that the dates to which Lord Fisher and I were working would be substantially and with inconsiderable exceptions maintained throughout the great new field of new construction. I am certain that under those circumstances we could have felt that the situation was thoroughly sound.

I sympathize, of course, very much with the right hon. Gentleman when he finds the ridiculous statement made to the effect that new construction had been stopped and that there was a great reversal of the previous policy, and which appeared to indicate that the Board of Admiralty were not carrying out an immense gigantic programme of new construction. But that does not quite dispose of the point that I am going to make with some iteration during my remarks. The right hon. Gentleman admitted that he and his advisers were not wholly satisfied with the progress that was being made.

[*Mr Balfour: 'I said I should like to have more ships'*].

I am bound to say that since I returned to this country I have received from sources, on which I must to some extent rely, impressions of a less completely satisfactory and reassuring kind than would naturally be derived from the annual statement of the Minister responsible. These matters touch the life of the State, they must be spoken of with the utmost restraint, and I entirely agree with the right hon. Gentleman that detail must necessarily be avoided. The right hon. Gentleman spoke of the period at the beginning of the War, our position then, our anxieties then, and, as he considered, the much less anxious period in which we are at present. That is not a line of argument which I think should be pursued too far. We have now reached a period in the War when new naval developments are possible. First of all we can be sure that every capital ship which had been begun before the declaration of War, by us or by Germany, can, if it has been so desired, be ready for battle. Any ship that is not ready can only be delayed through accident or through some decision of policy. I admit that this is a wide field, because there are many good reasons which might lead to the delay or postponement of vessels. For instance, when war begins the first thing to do would probably be to concentrate on the ships you would have the use of soonest: or, again, improvements or new developments may be suggested by the progress of the War which imposed delay; but it was within the power of both Admiralties to complete all their vessels if in their good judgement they had thought it necessary to do so.

We do not know what Germany has done, an impenetrable veil, as the right hon. Gentleman knows, has fallen for eighteen months over the German dockyards, naval and commercial. The right hon. Gentleman says he does not know what progress is being made there. That is a serious statement – not one in connection with which I make any reproach, but it is a grave fact which we must bear in mind that we do not know what is going on there. But let us be sure of this: something is in progress there. The great German Navy has been built up under the special care of the Emperor through many years of vast expense, effort, toil, and scheming. Can we conceive that the German Government, as we know it to our cost, would be content to allow that Navy to lie impotent and derided in the Kiel Canal without any hope of action? If there were any possibility within the range of their extraordinary military intelligences by which it could be rendered a really effective factor in the course of the struggle, is it likely that they would have acquiesced in the total loss of utility and of all the efforts, organization, and resources which have made them the second naval Power? We should be most impudent if we were to act on such an assumption. We are bound to assume that Germany has completed every vessel begun before the War. It may not be so – I dare say it is not so – but we must assume it. We ought to assume it. If, therefore, the German ships have been completed and ours have not been so completed, then I say that serious and solid reasons must be required in the case of each vessel to justify and explain its postponement or delay. I do not say that those reasons are not forthcoming, but certainly the utmost energies must be employed to complete the ships at the earliest moment.

I must ask the House to remember that these latest vessels are the ones upon which we relied to meet and overmatch any new developments in German heavy guns. I am only discussing ships whose dimensions figure in the naval annuals and almanacks which are now published; I am not touching on any matter which is not known or published to the world: I am very careful to avoid doing that. These are the ships armed with 15-inch guns. We secured that gun for the 'Queen Elizabeth' class by running a risk and taking a responsibility in time of peace rarely taken by a Board of Admiralty. We actually constructed the whole of a class and ordered the whole of the guns for a class of five great ships without ever making a trial gun. We thus saved a whole year, and armed a whole batch of ships with that very powerful weapon, which has turned out to be as good a gun as the 13.5 – which was the best we had ever had – and, of course, far more powerful. Such an event is like winning a victory, and its fruits must be fully reaped. Naval opinion was very divided at the time on the question of this advance to a higher calibre, but there is no division in opinion now. We obtained the sanction of Parliament for fourteen ships armed with 15-inch guns, of which, if I remember rightly, eleven or twelve had been actually begun before the outbreak of war. If those ships are completed as arranged, the margin will be sufficient for all contingencies which are foreseeable. But there is another fact to be borne in mind, which should lead us to approach all these matters with caution. We have not only reached a period in the War when all the capital ships begun before the War can certainly be completed, but we are just entering upon a period when new capital ships begun since the War may be ready on either side. Here again, I know of course what we have done, and that secret is jealously guarded; but we cannot tell what Germany has done. We have left the region of the known, of the declared or defined; we have left the region of naval annuals and almanacks; and we have entered the sphere of the uncertain. We have entered a sphere which is within certain limits not merely uncertain but incalculable. For this reason we cannot afford to allow any delay to creep into the execution of our programme, because we must from now on provide, not only against the known and against the declared ships, but against what will be a continually increasing element of the unknown. I must also just point out another argument which shows that, great as were the anxieties with which we were faced in the first four months of the War, they have not by any means been removed, or, indeed, sensibly diminished by the course of events. The House will remember the old argument I used to feed them with, that of the average moment and the selected moment.

[*Mr G. Faber: 'What about "digging them out"?'*]

I agree with the hon. Member. It was a very foolish phrase, and I regret that it slipped out.

[*Mr Faber: 'I am sorry I said it'.*]

On the outbreak of War we were fortunate in being able to place every single ship ready in its proper war station, so it was not our average moment at all. For a certain time that position held. Then came the need for refits, making a steady reduction from every squadron and every flotilla. But by that time new ships purchased, and others, had come in, and so the general progress was maintained. The principle of the average moment as against the selected moment still operates, because when the German fleet comes to sea, if comes it ever does, it will come with its maximum strength, and it will be faced by a cruising Fleet always at sea, which will always have a portion deducted from it. The War is full of surprises to all of us; but so far the Admiralty has kept ahead. But that has not been done – I am very anxious to couch my argument in language which will not be offensive or vexing to my right hon. Friend, whose courtesy I have always experienced, but I must say that it has not been done by easy methods. It was done by rough and harsh and even violent methods, and by a tireless daily struggle. Remember, everything else is in movement too. We see our own great expansion, but remember, everything else around us is expanding and developing at the same time. You cannot afford to indulge even for the shortest period of time in resting on your oars. You must continually drive the vast machine forward at its utmost speed. To lose momentum is not merely to stop, but to fall. We have survived, and we are recovering from a shortage of munitions for the Army. At a hideous cost in life and treasure we have regained control, and ascendancy lies before us at no great distance. A shortage in naval material, if it were to occur from any cause, would give no chance of future recovery. Blood and money, however lavishly poured out, would never repair the consequences of what might be even an unconscious relaxation of effort.

I have come down here this afternoon to say these things with the deepest sense of responsibility. I say them because I am sure there is time to avoid all these dangers, because I am sure that it is not too late. If it were too late, silence would be vital. It is not; there is time; and I am anxious that the words of warning and exhortation which I am going to use, and am using, which may possibly excite resentment, but which must, nevertheless, be said, should be spoken while it is quite certain they may produce a useful effect. But I say advisedly that, though there is time, the Admiralty must not think the battle over. They must forthwith hurl themselves with renewed energy into their task, and press it forward without the loss of a day. What I have said of the great vessels applies with undiminished force to the flotillas of every description, but most especially to destroyers. Before the War we had slightly reduced the number of destroyers in the 1913–14 programme, in order to build bigger and more powerful destroyers for the same money, and also in order to develop our light cruiser programme of the 'Arethusa' class. The War showed immediately that light cruisers, although necessary and admirable, were no substitute for destroyers, and a large number of destroyers, in dealing with submarines. Hence, in the days of Prince Louis we set to work on a new programme. Then came Lord Fisher with his new impulse, and during the autumn of 1914, when we worked together, things were not only planned, but done on a scale beyond anything ever thought possible. If the programmes of small craft of all kinds on which we then embarked have been and are being carried through with punctuality, they will suffice for all immediate eventualities.

[*Mr Balfour: 'They are largely increased'.*]

No doubt others are coming on behind them, but other dangers are coming on as well. I am dealing only with this limited aspect. If, however, they have been allowed to fall into arrears, if their delivery has been allowed to slide back from month to month, then I say the Navy and the Grand Fleet might find themselves deprived of securities and advantages which we had prepared for them, and which we deemed it indispensable they should receive. I am very sorry I have to trouble the House after they have listened to a most comprehensive statement from the responsible Minister, but the matter is of supreme importance. It is no use saying, 'We are doing our best'. You have got to succeed in doing what is necessary. The right hon. Gentleman spoke about the limit of labour. There is no limit of labour where the British Navy is concerned. The vital units of the Fleet and the flotillas which are being constructed must be a first charge on all our naval resources. There are no competing needs with paramount needs. I do not think the House thought it was satisfactory that the right hon. Gentleman should at this late stage tell us that he has not, in regard to Admiralty labour, approached or dealt with the question of dilution ...

[*The Prime Minister, Mr Asquith: 'He did not say so'.*]

I understood him to say so. At any rate, he has not yet adopted it.

[*An Hon. Member: 'Too late again!'*]

If he did not say so, I misunderstood him. The right hon. Gentleman spoke both of the dilution of labour and of bringing men back from the front as if that would be a remedy, and I understood a remedy which has not yet been adopted. I do not think that that leaves the subject in an absolutely satisfactory condition. I know my right hon. Friend's difficulties, and the toils and burdens upon him, but he must overcome them. The resources of British shipyards are incomparable, and fully equal, if used at the highest possible speed and power ...

[*Mr Balfour made an observation which was inaudible in the Reporters' Gallery.*]

How do you suppose that, for instance, the 'Monitor' Fleet, with all its details, which have been so improvidently scattered to the world – this great fleet of vessels, some of them carrying the largest guns in the world – was brought into existence in the course of six months? No one can form any conception of the achievements which can be produced from the British yards if they are really driven to their fullest capacity.

I pass from the programmes of material for which the Board

were responsible, to the possibility of novel dangers, requiring novel expedients. In a naval war particularly, you must always be asking about the enemy – what now, what next? You must always be seeking to penetrate, and your measures must always be governed and framed on the basis that he would do what you would least like him to do. My right hon. Friend [*Mr Balfour*] showed that the late Board had surmounted some of the very serious and difficult dangers at the beginning of the War, but one he did not mention, the menace of the submarine attack on merchantmen was overcome by measures taken this time last year of an extraodinary scale and complexity. But although the German submarine campaign has up to date been a great failure, and although it will probably continue to be a failure – here again you cannot afford to assume that it will not present itself in new and more difficult forms, and that new exertions and new inventions will not be demanded, and you must be ready with your new devices before the enemy is ready with his, and your resourcefulness and developments must continually proceed upon a scale which exceeds the maximum you expect from him. I find it necessary to utter this word of warning, which for obvious reasons I should not proceed to elaborate.

There is another matter which I cannot avoid mentioning, though I shall do so in language of the utmost precaution. A strategic policy for the Navy, purely negative in character, by no means necessarily implies that the path of greatest prudence is being followed. I wish to place on record that the late Board would certainly not have been content with an attitude of pure passivity during the whole of the year 1916. That is all I say upon a matter of that kind. But there is one smaller matter which illustrates what I mean. We hear a great deal about air raids. A great remedy against Zeppelin raids is to destroy the Zeppelins in their sheds. I cannot understand myself why all these many months, with resources far greater than those which Lord Fisher and I ever possessed, it has not been found possible to carry on the policy of raiding which, in the early days even, carried a handful of naval pilots to Cologne, Dusseldorf and Friedrich-shafen, and even to Cuxhaven itself. But I have not spoken today without intending to lead up to a conclusion. I have not used words of warning without being sure first that they are spoken in time to be fruitful, and secondly, without having a definite and practical proposal to make. When, in November 1914, Prince Louis of Battenberg told me he felt it his duty to retire and lay down the charge he had executed so faithfully, I was certain that there was only one man who could succeed him. I knew personally all the high officers of the Navy, and I was sure that there was no one who possessed the power, the insight and energy of Lord Fisher. I therefore made it plain that I would work with no other Sea Lord. In this way the oppositions, naval and otherwise, which have always, perhaps not unnaturally, obstructed Lord Fisher's faithful footsteps, were overcome. He returned to his old place, and the six months of war administration which followed will, I believe, rank as one of the remarkable periods in the history of the Royal Navy.

I did not believe it possible that our very cordial and intimate association would be ruptured, but the stress and shocks of this War are tremendous, and the situations into which men are plunged expose them to strain beyond any that this generation has had experience of. We parted on a great enterprise upon which the Government had decided and to which they were committed and in which the fortunes of a struggling and ill-supported Army were already involved; it stood between us as a barrier. I therefore should have resisted, on public grounds, the return of Lord Fisher to the Admiralty – and I have on several occasions expressed this opinion in the strongest terms to the Prime Minister and the First Lord of the Admiralty. We have now reached an entirely different situation, and I have no doubt whatever what it is my duty to say now. There was a time when I did not think that I could have brought myself to say it, but I have been away for some months, and my mind is now clear. The times are crucial. The issues are momentous. The great War deepens and widens and expands around us. The existence of our country and of our cause depend upon the Fleet. We cannot afford to deprive ourselves or the Navy of the strongest and most vigorous forces that are available. No personal consideration must stand between the country and those who can serve her best. I feel that there is in the present Admiralty administration, for all their competence, loyalty and zeal, a lack of driving force and mental energy which cannot be allowed to continue, which must be rectified while time remains and before evil results, and can only be rectified in one way. I am sure the nation and the Navy expect that the necessary step will be taken. I agree with my right hon. Friend here [Mr G. Lambert] in the proposals which he made to the Navy when he last spoke, and I urge the First Lord of the Admiralty without delay to fortify himself, to vitalize and animate his Board of Admiralty by recalling Lord Fisher to his post as First Sea Lord.

PART TWO

Scorning and Warning

1917–1939

7

The Bolshevik Menace

'An Aggressive and Predatory Form'

Connaught Rooms, London, 11 April 1919

VERY SOON AFTERWARDS, CHURCHILL ENDED his active war service, returned to London and spent the next twelve months trying to justify his conduct at the Admiralty, to earn a living and to force his way back into office. Eventually, his political fortunes began to recover when Lloyd George brought him back into his Coalition Government in June 1917 as Minister of Munitions. After the General Election of December 1918, he became Secretary of State for War and Air.

During his tenure of these offices, Churchill became much preoccupied with what he saw as the menace of Bolshevism. He feared that the Russian Revolution would develop as the French Revolution had done, and strongly supported British and Allied intervention in support of the White Russian armies during the civil war. In fact, Churchill greatly misjudged the strength of the anti-Bolshevik forces, and by the spring of 1920 it was clear that his policy was doomed to failure.

This speech was delivered at a time when the outcome seemed much less certain. It is a very early example of Churchill's apocalyptic mode, which was to become so familiar during the inter-war years. The language seems both extravagantly violent and excessively pessimistic. But it must be remembered that in the aftermath of victory the prospects did, indeed, seem uncertain, for the victors no less than for the vanquished.

Connaught Rooms, London, 11 April 1919

WE ARE ALL ANXIOUSLY AWAITING THE RESULTS of the deliberations of the Peace Conference. We are in what is called the hush before a storm. Within a few weeks, or possibly less, we shall know what are the terms the Allies have agreed to impose on the enemy. Then after an interval we shall know whether the enemy will accept those terms or whether further measures are necessary on our part. In the meantime, I do not think we ought to concern ourselves with particular points. Any agreement which is reached by the very experienced and able heads of Governments now gathered together in Paris must be a comprehensive and general agreement. It must be judged as a whole, and no part of it must be judged except in relation to the general settlement. Fragmentary disclosures and fragmentary discussions would be mischievous and futile. We have chosen our ablest men. They are thinking of nothing else. They can have no other interests but our own to study. They are working on their task night and day. They are entitled to present their case as a whole and to receive the fullest measure of public sympathy and confidence meanwhile. The difficulties and perplexities of their task are unexampled, nor can the problem which has to be solved be solved to universal satisfaction. Nobody is going to get all they want. I would go so far as to say nobody ought to get all they want. Everybody must expect to have something to grumble about [laughter].

It is not a game of grab we are playing, but the quest of a just peace and a lasting peace. If that is achieved individual disappointments will be forgotten in the general joy. If it is not achieved no paper triumph of any individual country, gained by any nation or any Minister or representative, would be any use at all to that nation or to the world in general. Therefore, the work on which the Peace Conference is engaged must be judged as a whole, and not on this point or on that.

The course of events in the United Kingdom since the Armistice gives us good reason to be satisfied. When I think of the difficulties as I envisaged them on November 11 last year, and see how we have got over them, or how many of them we have got over in that period, I think we have good reason to be satisfied and grateful. Nearly two and a half million men have been demobilized from the Army and brought home to their families and peaceful industry. More than one million munition workers engaged in special war industry have found other tasks to do, and have been discharged from State employment. The labour troubles which must necessarily be expected at a time like this, and which on occasion appeared so menacing, have been tided over by the great skill and patience shown on the part of the Prime Minister and Mr Bonar Law, and also by the representatives of the responsible trade unions in this country [*'hear, hear'*]. The Army, which was so much unsettled by the working of the pivotal system of demobilization a few months ago, has now regained its old attitude of sober, solid, contented discipline. All these are important and vital matters, and although it is quite true that the trade revival is still hampered by restrictions from which in some cases it cannot immediately be free, if the world as a whole were as well off as Britain is, all the world would be very thankful this afternoon [*cheers*].

I have been informed since I arrived here that the city of Hull has not been so appreciative of our labours as one could wish [*laughter*], but I do not attach undue importance to by-elections which follow in the wake of a General Election where undoubtedly the swing was more than anyone expected or even desired [*laughter*]. It is natural that there should be reaction, and it is even healthy that there should be reaction. But nothing in these reactions should be taken by the Government as in any way deflecting them from their clear and definite course of reviving the prosperity of this country, of increasing the democratization of its institutions, of broadening the basis of social welfare in our land, and abroad of securing by the strong arm of Britain the legitimate fruits which our soldiers have gained in the great war from which we have emerged.

87

Scorning and Warning

I only wish that the march of events on the Continent had been as favourable as in our own island. On the contrary, the process of degeneration has been steady and even rapid over large parts of Europe. The British Government has issued a White-book giving a vivid picture, based on authentic evidence, of Bolshevist atrocities. Tyranny presents itself in many forms. The British nation is the foe of tyranny in every form. That is why we fought Kaiserism and that is why we would fight it again. That is why we are opposing Bolshevism. Of all tyrannies in history the Bolshevist tyranny is the worst, the most destructive, and the most degrading. It is sheer humbug to pretend that it is not far worse than German militarism. The miseries of the Russian people under the Bolshevists far surpass anything they suffered even under the Tsar. The atrocities by Lenin and Trotsky are incomparably more hideous, on a larger scale, and more numerous than any for which the Kaiser himself is responsible. There is this also to be remembered – whatever crimes the Germans have committed, and we have not spared them in framing our indictment, at any rate they stuck to their Allies. They misled them, they exploited them, but they did not desert, or betray them. It may have been honour among thieves, but that is better than dishonour among murderers.

Lenin and Trotsky had no sooner seized on power than they dragged the noble Russian nation out of the path of honour and let loose on us and our Allies a whole deluge of German reinforcements, which burst on us in March and April of last year. Every British and French soldier killed last year was really done to death by Lenin and Trotsky, not in fair war, but by the treacherous desertion of an ally without parallel in the history of the world. There are still Russian Armies in the field, under Admiral Koltchak and General Deniken, who have never wavered in their faith and loyalty to the Allied cause, and who are fighting valiantly and by no means unsuccessfully against that foul combination of criminality and animalism which constitutes the Bolshevist regime. We are helping these men, within the limits which are assigned to us, to the very best of our ability. We are helping them with arms and munitions, with

88

instructions and technical experts, who volunteered for service. It would not be right for us to send our armies raised on a compulsory basis to Russia. If Russia is to be saved it must be by Russian manhood. But all our hearts are with these men who are true to the Allied cause in their splendid struggle to restore the honour of united Russia, and to rebuild on a modern and democratic basis the freedom, prosperity and happiness of its trustful and good-hearted people.

There is a class of misguided or degenerate people in this country and some others, who profess to take so lofty a view that they cannot see any difference between what they call rival Russian factions. They would have you believe that it is 'six of one and half-a-dozen of the other.' Their idea of a League of Nations is something which would be impartial as between Bolshevism on the one hand, and civilization on the other. We are still forced to distinguish between right and wrong, loyalty and treachery, health and disease, progress and anarchy. There is one part of the world in which these distinctions which we are bound to draw can translate itself into action. In the north of Russia the Bolshevists are continually attacking the British troops we sent there during the course of the war against Germany in order to draw off the pressure from the West, and who are now cut off by the ice from the resources of their fellow countrymen. Here we are in actual warfare with the representatives of a Bolshevist Government and with its Army, and, whatever views may be held by any section in the country on Russian affairs, we must all agree that our men who were sent there by the Government have to be properly supported and relieved from their dangerous situation [cheers]. We have no intention whatever of deserting our lads and of leaving them on this icy shore to the mercy of a cruel foe. The Prime Minister has given me the fullest authority to take whatever measures the General Staff of the Army think necessary to see that our men are relieved, and brought safely through the perils with which they are confronted, and so far as is physically possible we shall take whatever measures are required [cheers].

A second White-book issued by the Government deals with

the interior situation in Germany. When the Aldwych Club last entertained me, I remember saying to you that in war there are no substitutes for victory. You must either win or lose. And in victory there are no substitutes for peace [*cheers*]. I am in favour of making peace with Germany. After the war is over, after the enemy is beaten, after he has sued for mercy, I am in favour of making peace with him. Just as in August 1914, our duty was to make war on Germany, so now our duty is to make peace with Germany.

Making peace with Germany does not mean making friends with Germany [*cheers*]. Peace means – I do not say forgiveness, for after all that has happened this generation can never forgive – but peace, put at its very lowest, means a state of affairs where certain common interests are recognized, where the beaten side, having taken their beating and having paid their forfeit – that is a matter which must be attended to, and will be attended to [*cheers*] – may have still a chance of life, and have a chance for the future and some means of atonement. I do not think we can afford to carry on this quarrel, with all its apparatus of hatred, indefinitely. I do not think the structure of the civilized world is strong enough to stand the strain. With Russian on our hands in a state of utter ruin, with a greater part of Europe on the brink of famine, with bankruptcy, anarchy and revolution threatening the victorious as well as the vanquished, we cannot afford to drive over to the Bolshevist camp the orderly and stable forces which now exist in the German democracy. All the information I receive from military sources indicates that Germany is very near collapse. All my military advisers, without exception, have warned me that the most vital step we ought to take immediately to secure victory is to feed Germany, to supply Germany with food and the raw materials necessary for them to resume their economic life.

But the situation in Germany is grave. The Socialist Government of Scheidemann and Ebert and Noske is tottering, and if it falls no one knows what will take its place. If Germany sinks into Bolshevist anarchy she will no doubt be skinned alive, and not only will there be no indemnity, but we shall ourselves be impoverished, and our trade revival will be paralysed by the increasing disorder and ruin of the world. I ask you not to let your eyes be blinded with false counsel. The policy which the Prime Minister has consistently pursued in Paris amid all the difficulties and turmoil of that tower of Babel had been clear and simple – to disarm Germany, to feed Germany, and to make peace with Germany. A way of atonement is open to Germany. By combating Bolshevism, by being the bulwark against it, Germany may take the first step toward ultimate reunion with the civilized world. I am sure the advice you would receive from those gifted soldiers who have conducted our Armies to victory would be to feed Germany, to make Germany do her share in clearing up the mess and ruin her Imperialistic Government has caused, and to stand by meanwhile, with a strong British and Allied Army on the Rhine, to guard against foul play or any failure to comply with our just and reasonable demands.

Very great perils still menace us in the world. Two mighty branches of the human race, the Slavs and the Teutons, are both plunged at the present time in the deepest misery. The Great Power which was our foe, and the Great Power which was our friend, are both in the pit of ruin and despair. It is extremely undesirable that they should come together. Germany is struggling against breaking down into Bolshevism. But if that were to happen it would produce reaction which it is no exaggeration to say would reach as far as China.

The Russian Bolshevist revolution is changing in its character. It has completed the Anarchist destruction of the social order in Russia itself. The political, economic, social, and moral life of the people of Russia has for the time being been utterly smashed. Famine and terror are the order of the day. Only the military structure is growing out of the ruin. That is still weak, but it is growing steadily stronger, and it is assuming an aggressive and predatory form, which French Jacobinism assumed after the fall of Robespierre, and before the rise of Napoleon. Bolshevist armies are marching on towards food and plunder, and in their path stand only the little weak States, exhausted and shattered by the war.

If Germany succumbs either from internal weakness, or from actual invasion, to this Bolshevist pestilence, Germany no doubt will be torn to pieces, but where shall we be? Where will be that peace for which we are all longing; where will be that revival of prosperity without which our domestic contentment is impossible. Where will be that League of Nations on which so many hopes are founded? If that should come to pass there will be two Leagues, not one. There will be the League of defeated nations and the League of victorious nations, and the League of defeated nations may easily be rearming while the League of victorious nations is laying aside the sword and shield. Once again there will have been created that terrible balance of antagonism which was the prelude to the explosion of the Great War five years ago [*cheers*].

We must not allow our attention to be diverted from the truth by our wishes or our inclinations. Those present have great influence on the formation of public opinion and I say to you, keep a strong Army loyal, compact, contented, adequate for the work which it has to do; make peace with the German people; resist by every means at your disposal the advances of Bolshevist tyranny in every country in the world.

8

A Budget Broadcast

'Let Us Go Forward Together'

BBC, London, 25 April 1928

CHURCHILL'S PUBLICLY TRUMPETED DETESTATION of Communist Russia signalled that he was on his way back to the Conservative Party, which he formally rejoined in 1925. Between 1922 and 1924, however, he was both out of office and out of Parliament, and after he was re-elected as a 'Constitutionalist' candidate for Epping, he was amazed – as were many others – when he was appointed Chancellor of the Exchequer in Stanley Baldwin's second Conservative Administration.

Churchill's record as Chancellor remains a subject of historical controversy; but there can be no denying the brilliance of his five Budget presentations. Like his speeches introducing the Naval Estimates, when he was First Lord of the Admiralty, they were lengthy and lucid expositions of highly technical and complex subjects. His speech of 1928, for instance, ran to three and a half hours, and included very extensive proposals for rating reform in an effort to help ailing industry and depressed agriculture.

Immediately after, Churchill delivered this, one of his earliest broadcasts. It was supposed to be a non-controversial statement. But despite Churchill's carefully judged opening remarks, Sir John Reith, the Director-General of the BBC, thought it too partisan. Beatrice Webb agreed, describing it as a 'vividly rhetorical representation of his own case.'

SCORNING AND WARNING

BBC, London, 25 April 1928

I HAVE A SET OF MY OWN AND I KNOW how it feels to get into touch through this marvellous invention with the actual events and the men who are shaping them. So I was very glad when I was invited to talk tonight. I shall not say anything that is partisan or in the nature of party politics; and really I do not need to do so because this Budget is aimed sincerely at national objects in which men of all parties, and even those of no party at all, have an equal interest.

In my position and with all the information I have about income tax, I can see, probably more clearly than anyone else, what trades are prospering and what industries are suffering most. I have come to the conclusion that we must make a special effort to help the basic and heavy industries. The basic and heavy industries of our country, iron and coal and cotton, steel and shipbuilding, all these are flagging. Great numbers of men are unemployed and numbers of firms making no profit, or indeed an actual loss. I am therefore trying to give them a helping hand, and practically every one is agreed that the first and most useful way of doing this is to relieve them of their burden of rates. I have, therefore, proclaimed a fundamental proposition that the tools and plants of production – the properties, the buildings, the land, the machinery used for actual creative production – should not be taxed.

Let us tax profits, but not the tools. The present system of rating dates from the days of Queen Elizabeth and is quite unfitted for modern life. Rates for each district are dependent on the politics of the district. The rates press more heavily on unsuccessful businesses than on successful ones. Where business is bad the rates press more heavily upon it. Now all this is wrong, there is no sense in it at all. We depend for our existence upon export trades and millions of people get their wages from these basic industries. Railway freights are another burden. These are

94

oppressively high in those industries which depend upon the use of vast masses of heavy material.

The agricultural produce on which we live, the coal on which all industry lives, the mining timber, iron ore, steel, all rating relief going to railways will help these. Now observe the cumulative effects of relief, how they pile up. First, let us take the vicious circle, coal rated, coke rated, iron ore rated, pig iron rated again, and other rated products used to make steel, rated again, and, moreover, all these commodities have to be transported by rail which is rated. In these circumstances you get many districts suffering which, but for this invidious and ill-applied rate burden, might support a happy and healthful industrial population, and which in many cases are well fitted to do so. Let us take the other side of the picture.

Coal, coke and limestone, relieved of rates, arriving at steel works with all these new advantages to find the steel works relieved of rates. Out of the steel works comes the material for construction of bridges and railways; from these same steel works will come material for cheaper ships, cheaper not by cutting down wages, but by cutting down burdens. Rates or freights by themselves, however reduced, will not be enough to solve the problem. Something more has to be added, something that may arise out of psychological impulse. We are seeking good will and co-operation in industry. This is the chance for employers and workers to take hands and purge out inefficiency in industry. This is the time; relief itself is not sufficient, but, used properly and used to full advantage, the relief may well mean the opening of a new era. The opportunity is here. Do not let us miss an opportunity that may not easily or soon recur.

Such is the problem with which we are grappling, and such is the remedy we are seeking to apply. And how are we going to get the money to pay the local authorities? You cannot take rates away from them without giving them something back. Here, again, there is another very big story which I can do no more than outline. In the nineteenth century the glory of Great Britain was her coal; on that we built our great industrial system, on that millions of British people came into the world, on that our mighty power was founded. Without that we cannot live.

In the twentieth century we have entered the oil age. In the nineteenth century we were far ahead of our competitors, but in the twentieth century we have hardly any oil in the British Empire. It is absolutely necessary for us to obtain this oil at the present time, and to get it we have to buy or import it from foreign lands. Whereas we used to sell great quantities of coal, last year we paid as much for the oil we imported as the value of the coal we exported. We used to be a source of fuel. We are becoming a sink. We need it; we must have it. Can't we make it ourselves? Scientists tell us they can already turn British coal into oil. Germans are doing it in their country. I agree it must be gradual, but it took a long time to build the British Constitution and to found the British Empire; it is a long way to Tipperary!

Our ancestors were not afraid of time. Now I am sure the motoring community, who are not by any means the least fortunate or the least patriotic or the least far-sighted of our fellow-citizens, will take a broad and a long view about this tax on foreign imported liquid fuel. I expect them to look at this tax of fourpence a gallon on imported fuel, not as if they were doing a penny-wise sum of what it actually costs them, but as if they were trustees for the future of Great Britain.

I want to make you understand that we are on the move, and that we are marching to the aid of British productive industry in town and country, with every shilling, and every man and every gun we can get together. I must explain that a large policy like this can only be unfolded step by step and stage by stage. If we have relieved three-quarters of the rates of productive industry and relieved agriculture of all its rates, we have got to pay the local authorities back, otherwise how could they carry on? But in this process of paying them back we are going to have a more modernized and better system of local government. Months of labour have been spent on it. All the difficulties which occur to the mind of any intelligent person who examines this subject have been weighed and balanced.

The policy begun in the Budget yesterday deals with two

equally great objects: First, the relief of productive industry, and secondly, the modernization of our local government system. The first part is what we are doing now, and the second part will occupy Parliament all the winter. Do not let us mix them up together; one step at a time, and each step made good. Let us go forward together, let us not be afraid of taking trouble or risks. Britain is not going to be done in this new age. She is going to hold her own and keep her place in this new gigantic world that is going up around us. But she will survive only if her people are more intelligent, her policy is more far-sighted, and her economic system more highly organized, her social standards more just, her people more united, and more consciously self-governed. Let us make sure none of us fail in our zeal and in our duty at this critical time.

9

The Indian Threat

'A Seditious Middle Temple Lawyer'

Winchester House, Epping, 23 February 1931

AFTER THE CONSERVATIVES WERE DEFEATED in the General Election of June 1929, Churchill naturally joined the party's Business Committee (Shadow Cabinet) in opposition. In October of the same year, the Viceroy of India published the 'Irwin Declaration', reaffirming the goal of dominion status, and proposing a Round Table Conference in London to discuss constitutional reform. Soon after, he sought to placate nationalist opinion in India by meeting with Gandhi himself.

As Leader of the Opposition, Baldwin enthusiastically supported this policy. But Churchill, who was busy writing *My Early Life*, and reliving his days as a soldier in India at the turn of the century, was vehemently opposed to any concessions on the part of the British Government. He foresaw nothing but doom and disaster ahead, both for Britain and for India, and in January 1931 he resigned from the Conservative Business Committee and began his campaign against what became the Government of India Act of 1935.

Inevitably, he was obliged to justify his conduct to his own constituency association, and he did so in this speech. It was the most violent he had delivered on the subject thus far, and his constituents responded favourably to his appeal for support. For obvious reasons, the vituperative description of Gandhi has never been forgiven or forgotten in India.

Winchester House, Epping, 23 February 1931

YOU HAVE BEEN CALLED TOGETHER at my desire in order that I may lay before you the reasons why I have felt it my duty to take an independent line about India and to withdraw from the Business Committee of the Conservative party of which I had the honour to be a member. The Business Committee is a very sensible name for the small group of those members of both Houses with whom Mr Baldwin is accustomed to consult on the general policy of the party and its conduct in Parliament. I valued highly the privilege of being included in it, and also it gave an opportunity of continuing in close, confidential touch with several of my principal colleagues and personal friends in the last Conservative Government. I was therefore very sorry to have to cut myself off from this interesting and agreeable work, and I can assure you I should not have done so without due cause. I still propose, if that is desired, to remain Chairman of the Conservative Finance Committee and to conduct the criticism of the Budget and other financial measures of the Socialist Government. I need scarcely say that I intend to do my utmost to assist our leader in the opposition to the Government in the House of Commons. I shall do my utmost to turn them out at the earliest opportunity, and procure their condign punishment and defeat at the general election, and to bring about by every means in my power a decisive victory for a united Conservative party. I found, however, that while I remained a member of this small inner circle I could not give full effect to my convictions about India. Naturally when men sit round a table and discuss political matters in intimate confidence they are largely bound by the decisions which are taken, and although there is more latitude out of office than in a Cabinet, nevertheless it is most undesirable that differences should appear among those who are thus associated.

Now let us see what these differences are. I agreed to our

Conservative delegates taking part in the Round Table Conference, as I thought they would keep the Socialist Government from committing us to any dangerous or unwise departure. This our delegates tell us they have done, and I agree with them that they may justly claim that we are not committed by any action of theirs to the scheme of a new constitution for India which emerged from the Round Table Conference. I was, however, surprised and alarmed at the sudden landslide of opinion which took place upon that Conference and at the impression which was created throughout this country and in India that all the three parties were in agreement in principle to set up a federal constitution under Indian ministers responsible to an all-India Assembly. Still more was I alarmed when this enormous departure was itself presented as only a temporary and transitory arrangement soon to give place to what is called 'full Dominion status' for India carrying with it the control not only of law and order and of finance, but of the Army, and the right to secede from the British Empire. I do not think it is wise to hold out any hopes of any such position being reached for many generations to come. At any rate, I hold it of the utmost importance that we should make it clear that there is no chance of such a goal being reached in our lifetime, or in any period which it is profitable for us to consider. Secondly, I much regret to have to state that I disapprove altogether of the policy pursued by the present Viceroy of India, which as I shall show you presently has been attended by results already disastrous and threatening greater evils in the future.

These difficulties came to a head when Mr Baldwin expressed his complete disagreement with the speech I made in the House of Commons at the end of last month, and when he said that it would be the duty of the Conservative party if returned to power to try to 'implement' the scheme put forward by the Round Table Conference. It was quite evident to everyone after that speech that the differences between us upon India were not merely matters of emphasis or procedure, but that they were profound and practical differences covering the whole field of Indian Policy and affecting the whole mood and spirit in which we discharge our duty to India. In the words which Lord Hartington, afterwards Duke of Devonshire, used to Mr Gladstone in 1886 about Ireland, I can only say that upon India Mr Baldwin and I 'do not mean the same thing'. I am sure you will agree that in these circumstances I had no choice but to separate myself upon this single question in the most friendly manner from a leader for whom I entertain both high respect and regard.

Having taken up this position in public about India I must inform you that it is my intention to go through with it. I shall endeavour to marshal British opinion against a course of action which would bring in my judgement the greatest evils upon the people of India, upon the people of Great Britain, and upon the structure of the British Empire itself. It follows, therefore, of course, that I should not be able to serve in any Administration about whose Indian policy I was not reassured. I would far rather be a loyal private member of the Conservative party than bear official responsibility for actions and events which might well involve a mortal injury to the greatness and cohesion of our Empire. I invite you to endorse this attitude upon my part, and I hope you will find yourselves able to give me your full approval and even encouragement in acting in this matter in accordance with my convictions.

The Indian problem at the present time divides itself into two parts. There is the question of a new constitution for India, and there is the question of the day-to-day administration of that country and the proper maintenance of British authority. If you will permit me, I will say a few words on both these matters. In dealing with Oriental races for whose well-being you are responsible it is a mistake to try to gloss over grave differences, to try to dress up proposals in an unwarrantably favourable guise, to ignore or conceal or put in the background rugged but unpleasant facts. The right course on the contrary is to state soberly and firmly what the British position is, and not be afraid to say 'this would not suit us', 'that would not be good for you', 'there is no chance of this coming to pass', 'we shall not agree to that being done'. All these firm negatives ought to be stated frankly and plainly so that false hopes are not excited unduly and lead to disappointment and reproaches. We should always try to be better than our word and let any concessions we make be real and true. The Socialist Government on the other hand has been trying to deal with the Indian Nationalist politicians by the same sort of blarney and palaver which sometimes passes muster in Parliament or on British political platforms. I do not want to see the Conservative party, which is the main instrument by which the British Empire can be defended, dragged any further in their wake. I do not want to see the Indian politicians misled as to what our real intentions are.

Now you will observe that statements have been made within the last few days upon Mr Baldwin's authority that we are not committed to anything except to give fair consideration to any proposals that may be made. I was very glad to hear those statements. After all, it is everybody's duty to give fair consideration to any proposals on any subject which are sincerely advanced. But that is very different from the impression which the country has sustained, and it is very different from the impression conveyed to the Indian politicians. Our leader's phrase about 'implementing' the constitution prepared by the Round Table Conference and the whole purport of this speech were cabled to the Indian delegates on the ship by which they were returning to India. We are told that they were overjoyed at what they read, and naturally they assumed that the great Conservative party was in agreement with the Socialist and Liberal parties and was prepared to implement a federal constitution with responsible government at the centre. On the strength of this they proceeded to draft a manifesto to the Indian Congress, and have ever since been labouring to persuade the more extreme elements to come to join them in a further conference to be held in India. They ought to be told, as we are told, that the Conservative party is wholly uncommitted, and that they have been unintentionally misled. But Mr Ramsay MacDonald, the Prime Minister, is also evidently under a misapprehension; because he said in answer to a question which I put him in the House of Commons last week that on the subject of India the Government considered that they 'had got their marching orders from the House': meaning thereby that all parties were agreed. It seems to me important that these misapprehensions, if such they be, about the official attitude of the Conservative party, should be corrected both here and in India on the highest authority and with the least delay.

The proper constitutional course for Parliament to adopt is to proceed to consider the Simon Report which was signed by the representatives of all parties. There are no doubt many things in that report which would have to be very carefully examined, some of which are no longer applicable; nevertheless it forms the only proper constitutional basis upon which discussion of the reform of Indian government should proceed by the joint action of all parties. The Round Table Conference may have thrown some new and interesting light upon Indian affairs of which of course full notice should be taken. But the whole foundation for the joint treatment of the Indian problem by the three British parties is the Simon Report, and once that report has been put on one side, as it has been almost contemptuously by the Socialist Government, it is imperative that the Conservative party should recover the fullest possible liberty of judgement. So much for the constitutional aspect.

Now I come to the administration of India. In my opinion we ought to dissociate ourselves in the most public and formal manner from any complicity in the weak, wrong-headed and most unfortunate administration of India by the Socialists and by the Viceroy acting upon their responsibility. It is alarming and also nauseating to see Mr Gandhi, a seditious Middle Temple lawyer, now posing as a fakir of a type well known in the East, striding half-naked up the steps of the Viceregal palace, while he is still organizing and conducting a defiant campaign of civil disobedience, to parley on equal terms with the representative of the King-Emperor. Such a spectacle can only increase the unrest in India and the danger to which white people there are exposed. It can only encourage all the forces which are hostile to British authority. What good can possibly come of such extraordinary negotiations? Gandhi has said within the last few weeks that he demands the substance of independence, though he

103

kindly adds that the British may keep the shadow. He declares that the boycott of foreign cloth must be continued until either prohibition or a prohibitive tariff can be put up against it by an Indian national Parliament. This, if accepted, would entail the final ruin of Lancashire. He has also pressed for the repudiation of the Indian loans, and has laid claim to the control of the Army and foreign affairs. These are his well-known aims. Surely they form a strange basis for heart-to-heart discussions – 'sweet' we are told they were – between this malignant, subversive fanatic and the Viceroy of India.

All this is intended by the Socialists to be the preliminary to another Round Table Conference in India to which it is hoped to persuade the extremists to come. At this new gathering the far-reaching and half-baked recommendations of the Round Table Conference will be taken only as a starting-point. From this starting-point will begin the attack upon the safeguards which have hitherto been kept apologetically in the background. I think it vital that the Conservative party should without delay get itself into a strong position of resistance, and should begin to arouse public opinion throughout the country against these most unwise and dangerous proceedings. I intend at any rate to do my best, and I shall be much strengthened if you put your whole weight behind me. India is no ordinary question of party politics. It is one of those supreme issues which come upon us from time to time. When they arise the men and women who faithfully guard the life of Britain and her Empire in every rank and employment, in every part of the country, feel the same vibration. They felt it on August 4 1914. They felt it in the General Strike. They feel it now.

Our responsibility in India has grown up over the last 150 years. It is a responsibility for giving the best possible chance for peaceful existence and progress to about three hundred and fifty millions of helpless primitive people who are separated by an almost measureless gulf from the ideas and institutions of the Western world. We now look after them by means of British Officials on fixed salaries who have no axe to grind, who make no profit out of their duties, who are incorruptible, who are impartial between races, creeds and classes, and who are directed by a central Government which in turn is controlled by the British Parliament based on twenty-nine million electors. It is now proposed to transfer these British responsibilities to an electorate comparatively small and almost entirely illiterate. The Indian Congress and other elements in this agitation represent neither the numbers, the strength nor the virtue of the Indian people. They merely represent those Indians who have acquired a veneer of Western civilization, and have read all those books about democracy which Europe is now beginning increasingly to discard. There are among them many estimable and clever people, and it has always been and always must be our policy to associate them as much as we possibly can with the machinery of Indian Government. But it would be altogether wrong to entrust the welfare of the great masses to the Indian political classes. That would not be 'India for the Indians'; that would only be India for some Indians, that would only be India for a very few Indians. Undoubtedly any such abrogation on our part of our duty would mean that the Indian peoples would be exploited, oppressed and cast down in the scale of the world's affairs as the proletariat of China is cast down in misery today. At present the Government of India is responsible to the British Parliament, which is the oldest, the least unwise and the most democratic parliament in the world. To transfer that responsibility to this highly artificial and restricted oligarchy of Indian politicians would be a retrograde act. It would be a shameful act. It would be an act of cowardice, desertion and dishonour. It would bring grave material evils, both upon India and Great Britain; but it would bring upon Great Britain a moral shame which would challenge for ever the reputation of the British Empire as a valiant and benignant force in the history of mankind.

The faithful discharge of our duty in India is not only a cause, but a symbol. It is the touchstone of our fortunes in the present difficult time. If we cannot do our duty in India, be sure we shall have shown ourselves unworthy to preserve the vast Empire which still centres upon this small island. The same spirit of unimaginative incompetence and weak compromise and supine drift will paralyse trade and business and prevent either financial reorganization or economic resurgence. What we require to do now is to stand erect and look the world in the face, and do our duty without fear or favour. A decisive opportunity may soon be at hand. Victory may once again reward the Conservative party. Let it be a victory with a real meaning behind it. Let it be a victory which proclaims to all the world that the heart of the Empire is true and that its hand is just – and strong.

IO

Britain's Air Defences
'We Are Vulnerable'

House of Commons, 7 February 1934

THE CLOSING STAGES OF CHURCHILL'S ill-fated opposition to the Government of India Act coincided with the opening salvoes in his campaign against German rearmament and territorial expansion. Following a visit to Austria in connection with his work on his biography of Marlborough, he made his first major speech in the Commons on German ambitions in November 1932, and less than a year later, he first warned that Germany was actively rearming.

It was only with this speech that he began to dwell on the related theme of Britain's own military unpreparedness, especially in the realm of air power. The Government White Paper on Disarmament, published at the end of January, reiterated the commitment of MacDonald and Baldwin to continuing European arms limitation. But as Churchill cogently argued, this effectively meant more pressure on France to disarm, while German rearmament would continue unabated.

In a dramatic (and not strictly accurate) phrase, he warned that 'we are vulnerable as we have never been vulnerable before'. In reply, Baldwin spoke of Churchill's 'eloquent' and 'picturesque' language, and described his speech as 'of great interest, of excellent temper, and full of sound sense.' Sir Herbert Samuel was far less complimentary, telling the Commons that Churchill's policy effectively meant 'Long live anarchy, and let us all go rattling down to ruin together.'

House of Commons, 7 February 1934

I REMEMBER IN THE DAYS of the late Conservative Administration, when I had the honour of serving under the Lord President, who is going to reply tonight, that we thought it right to take as a rule that there would be no major war within ten years in which we should be engaged. Of course, such a rule can only be a very crude guidance to the military and naval chiefs who have to make their plans, and it had to be reconsidered prospectively at the beginning of each year. I believe that it was right in all the circumstances. With Locarno and the more mellow light which shone on the world at that time, with the hopes that were then very high, it was probably right to take that principle as a guide from day to day, and from year to year. No one could take that principle as a guide today. No Cabinet, however pacific and peace-loving, could base their naval and military organization upon such an assumption as that. A new situation has been created, mainly in the last three or four years, by rubbing this sore of the Disarmament Conference until it has become a cancer, and also by the sudden uprush of Nazi-ism in Germany, with the tremendous covert armaments which are proceeding there today. Everyone sitting on the Government Bench knows how seriously the position has been changed. Only yesterday we defined once again our commitments to other countries. They are very serious commitments. The White Paper which we discussed yesterday contains a grave sentence:

His Majesty's Government ... have a right to expect that, if these provisions and pledges were solemnly entered into, they would not be lightly violated, and that any violation of them would be met in the most practical and effective way by immediately assembling Governments and States in support of international peace and agreement against the disturber and the violator.

I think that those are serious words to use in such a document, and it would be most unwise for us to proceed with our diplomacy in one direction, and not make our necessary preparation in the other sphere. At Birmingham this year the Lord President went out of his way with great solemnity to issue a warning about the European situation, and he pointed out how strictly we should adhere to all the engagements into which we have entered. We must consider our military, naval and aviation defence in relation to facts of this character.

We are engaged in imposing equality of armies as far as we can upon the nations of the Continent – France, Germany, Poland and Italy. Suppose it is asked in a few years that there should be equality of navies too? When the Government are asked about this, they say, 'Oh, no, that would not apply; we should not agree to that.' Suppose we are asked some time in the future to restore colonies for which we hold a mandate; the Government would say, 'Certainly not; we should not open that question in any way.' What do we back our opinions with; what armaments and what force have we behind these serious issues of opinion on which we declare our will and right? What happens, for instance, if, after we have equalized and reduced the army of France to the level of that of Germany, with all the reaction which will have followed in the sentiment of Europe upon such a change, and if Germany then proceeds to say, 'How can you keep a great nation of 65,000,000 in the position in which it is not entitled to have a navy equal to the greatest of the fleets upon the seas?'

You will say, 'No; we do not agree. Armies – they belong to other people. Navies – that question affects Britain's interests, and we are bound to say, "No."' But what position shall we be in to say that 'No'?

Wars come very suddenly. I have lived through a period when one looked forward, as we do now, with anxiety and uncertainty to what would happen in the future. Suddenly something did happen – tremendous, swift, overpowering, irresistible. Let me remind the House of the sort of thing that happened in 1914. There was absolutely no quarrel between Germany and France.

One July afternoon the German Ambassador drove down to the Quai d'Orsay and said to M. Viviani, the French Prime Minister, 'We have been forced to mobilize against Russia, and war will be declared. What is to be the position of France?' The French Prime Minister made the answer, which his Cabinet had agreed upon, that France would act in accordance with what she considered to be her own interests. The Ambassador said, 'You have an alliance with Russia, have you not?'

'Quite so,' said the French Prime Minister.

And that was the process by which, in a few minutes, the area of the struggle, already serious in the east, was enormously widened and multiplied by the throwing in of the two great nations of the west. But sometimes even a declaration of neutrality does not suffice. On this very occasion, as we now know, the German Ambassador was authorized by his Government, in case the French did not do their duty by their Russian ally, in case they showed any disposition to back out of the conflict which had been resolved on by the German nation, to demand that the fortress of Toul and Verdun should be handed over to German troops as a guarantee that the French, having declared neutrality, would not change their mind at a subsequent moment.

That is how that great thing happened in our own lifetime, and I am bound to say that I cannot see in the present administration of Germany any assurance that they would be more nice-minded in dealing with a vital and supreme situation than was the Imperial Government of Germany, which was responsible for this procedure being adopted towards France. No, Sir, and we may, within a measurable period of time, in the lifetime of those who are here, if we are not in a proper state of security, be confronted on some occasion with a visit from an ambassador, and may have to give an answer in a very few hours; and if that answer is not satisfactory, within the next few hours the crash of bombs exploding in London and cataracts of masonry and fire and smoke will apprise us of any inadequacy which has been permitted in our aerial defences. We are vulnerable as we have never been before. I have often heard criticisms of the Liberal Government before the War. All I can say is that a far graver complaint rests upon those who now hold power if, by any chance, against our wishes and against our hopes, trouble should come.

Not one of the lessons of the past has been learned, not one of them has been applied, and the situation is incomparably more dangerous. Then we had the Navy, and no air menace worth considering. Then the Navy was the 'sure shield' of Britain. As long as it was ready in time and at its stations we could say to any foreign Government, 'Well, what are you going to do about it? We will not declare ourselves. We will take our own time, we will work out our own course. We have no desire to hurt anyone, but we shall not be pressed or forced into any hasty action unless we think fit and well.' We cannot say that now. This cursed, hellish invention and development of war from the air has revolutionized our position. We are not the same kind of country we used to be when we were an island, only twenty-five years ago. That is borne in upon me more than anything else. It is not merely a question of what we like and what we do not like, of ambitions and desires, of rights and interests, but it is a question of safety and independence. That is involved now as never before.

It seems to me that there are three definite decisions which we should now take at once, and without any delay. The first affects the Army. We ought to begin the reorganization of our civil factories so that they can be turned over rapidly to war purposes. All over Europe that is being done, and to an amazing extent. This process is incomparably more efficient than anything that existed in the days of Prussian Imperialism before the War. Every factory in those countries is prepared to turn over to the production of some material for the deplorable and melancholy business of slaughter. What have we done? There is not an hour to lose. Those things cannot be done in a moment. The process should be started, and the very maximum of money that can be usefully spent will be spent from today on – if we act with wisdom.

Then there is the question of the Navy. For the Navy, at any rate, we should regain freedom of design. We should get rid of this London Treaty which has crippled us in building the kind of ships we want, and has stopped the United States from building a great battleship which she probably needed and to which we should have not had the slightest reason to object. It has forced us to spend some of our hard-earned money – the little there is for these purposes – unwisely. It has forced us to take great ships which would have been of enormous utility in convoying vessels bearing food to these islands and to sink them in the ocean, when they had ten to fifteen years of useful life in them. We must regain our freedom at the earliest possible moment, and we shall be helped in doing so by the fact that another of the parties to that Treaty [Japan] is resolved to regain her freedom too.

Then there is the air. I cannot conceive how, in the present state of Europe and of our position in Europe, we can delay in establishing the principle of having an Air Force at least as strong as that of any Power that can get at us. I think that is a perfectly reasonable thing to do. It would only begin to put us back to the position in which we were brought up. We have lived under the shield of the Navy. To have an Air Force as strong as the air force of France or Germany, whichever is the stronger, ought to be the decision which Parliament should take, and which the National Government should proclaim.

There is only one other point which I will mention, and that is the co-ordination of the three Services. I doubt very much whether, at this stage, there is room for economy in any of them, but at any rate it would be advantageous, in my opinion, if the problem were studied from a central point of view, because things are changing very much. The emphasis should be thrown here or there, according to the needs of modern conditions, and there should be much more effective co-ordination than now exists. I ask that some time in this Session we can have a discussion on the three Services combined. It would be a valuable discussion – one such as has frequently been allowed in previous years, and was never more necessary than at the present time.

The responsibility of His Majesty's Government is grave indeed, and there is this which makes it all the graver: it is a responsibility which they have no difficulty in discharging if they choose. We are told they have to wait for public opinion, that they must bring that along and must be able to assure the good people here that everything is being done with the most pacific intentions – they must make a case. But nothing like that can stand between them and their responsibility to the Crown and Parliament for the safety and security of the country. The Government command overwhelming majorities in both branches of the Legislature. Nothing that they ask will be denied to them. They have only to make their proposals, and they will be supported in them. Let them not suppose that if they make proposals, with confidence and conviction, for the safety of the country, their countrymen will not support them. Why take so poor a view of the patriotic support which this nation gives to those who it feels are doing their duty by it? I cannot feel that at the present time the Government are doing their duty in these matters of defence, and particularly in respect of the air. It seems to me that while we are becoming ever more entangled in the European situation, and while we are constantly endeavouring to weaken, relatively, our friends upon the continent of Europe, we nevertheless are left exposed to a mortal thrust, and are deprived of that old sense of security and independence upon which the civilization of our island has been built.

11

The Failure to Re-arm
'The Locust Years'

House of Commons, 12 November 1936

BY THE AUTUMN OF 1936, CHURCHILL had become convinced that Germany was now stronger in air power than Britain and France combined, and in early November he urged the Prime Minister to allow a full-scale, two-day debate on defence. During that debate, Churchill delivered this speech, which was undoubtedly one of the very greatest of his career, and which made a real impact on the Commons – albeit only in the short run.

Even by Churchill's standards, the documentation was remarkably full, the rhetoric unusually powerful, and the argument brilliantly sustained. 'His style', Harold Nicolson recorded, 'is more considered and slower than usual, but he drives his points home with a sledge-hammer.' The sentence beginning 'So they go on in strange paradox, decided only to be undecided', must certainly rank as one of Churchill's finest. Even *The Times*, so often so hostile to him during this period, described the speech as 'brilliant'.

Baldwin's limp and lame reply – his famous 'appalling frankness' speech – only served to increase the sense of unease which MPs felt in the light of Churchill's remarks. The Prime Minister's reputation appeared to be in serious decline. But the sudden eruption of the Abdication Crisis in the following month dramatically restored his prestige, while once more casting grave doubt on Churchill's judgement and reliability.

House of Commons, 12 November 1936

I HAVE, WITH SOME FRIENDS, put an Amendment on the Paper. It is the same as the Amendment which I submitted two years ago, and I have put it in exactly the same terms because I thought it would be a good thing to remind the House of what has happened in these two years. Our Amendment in November 1934 was the culmination of a long series of efforts by private Members and by the Conservative party in the country to warn His Majesty's Government of the dangers to Europe and to this country which were coming upon us through the vast process of German rearmament then already in full swing. The speech which I made on that occasion was much censured as being alarmist by leading Conservative newspapers, and I remember that Mr Lloyd George congratulated the Prime Minister, who was then Lord President, on having so satisfactorily demolished my extravagant fears.

What would have been said, I wonder, if I could two years ago have forecast to the House the actual course of events? Suppose we had then been told that Germany would spend for two years £800,000,000 a year upon warlike preparations; that her industries would be organized for war, as the industries of no country have ever been; that by breaking all Treaty engagements she would create a gigantic air force and an army based on universal compulsory service, which by the present time, in 1936, amounts to upwards of thirty-nine divisions of highly equipped troops, including mechanized divisions of almost unmeasured strength, and that behind all this there lay millions of armed and trained men, for whom the formations and equipment are rapidly being prepared to form another eighty divisions in addition to those already perfected. Suppose we had then known that by now two years of compulsory military service would be the rule, with a preliminary year of training in labour camps; that the Rhineland would be occupied by powerful forces and fortified with great skill, and that Germany would be building with our approval, signified by treaty, a large submarine fleet.

Suppose we had also been able to foresee the degeneration of the foreign situation, our quarrel with Italy, the Italo-German association, the Belgian declaration about neutrality – which, if the worst interpretation of it proves to be true, so greatly affects the security of this country – and the disarray of the smaller Powers of Central Europe. Suppose all that had been forecast – why, no one would have believed in the truth of such a nightmare tale. Yet just two years have gone by and we see it all in broad daylight. Where shall we be this time two years? I hesitate now to predict.

Let me say, however, that I will not accept the mood of panic or of despair. There is another side – a side which deserves our study, and can be studied without derogating in any way from the urgency which ought to animate our military preparations. The British Navy is, and will continue to be, incomparably the strongest in Europe. The French Army will certainly be, for a good many months to come, at least equal in numbers and superior in maturity to the German Army. The British and French Air Forces together are a very different proposition from either of those forces considered separately. While no one can prophesy, it seems to me that the Western democracies, provided they are knit closely together, would be tolerably safe for a considerable number of months ahead. No one can say to a month or two, or even a quarter or two, how long this period of comparative equipoise will last. But it seems certain that during the year 1937 the German Army will become more numerous than the French Army, and very much more efficient than it is now. It seems certain that the German Air Force will continue to improve upon the long lead which it already has over us, particularly in respect of long-distance bombing machines. The year 1937 will certainly be marked by a great increase in the adverse factors which only intense efforts on our part can, to any effective extent, countervail.

The efforts at rearmament which France and Britain are making will not by themselves be sufficient. It will be necessary for the Western democracies, even at some extension of their risks, to gather round them all the elements of collective security or of combined defensive strength against aggression – if you prefer, as I do myself, to call it so – which can be assembled on the basis of the Covenant of the League of Nations. Thus I hope we may succeed in again achieving a position of superior force, and then will be the time, not to repeat the folly which we committed when we were all-powerful and supreme, but to invite Germany to make common cause with us in assuaging the griefs of Europe and opening a new door to peace and disarmament.

I now turn more directly to the issues of this Debate. Let us examine our own position. No one can refuse his sympathy to the Minister for the Co-ordination of Defence. From time to time my right hon. Friend lets fall phrases or facts which show that he realizes, more than anyone else on that bench it seems to me, the danger in which we stand. One such phrase came from his lips the other night. He spoke of 'the years that the locust hath eaten'. Let us see which are these 'years that the locust hath eaten' even if we do not pry too closely in search of the locusts who have eaten these precious years. For this purpose we must look into the past. From the year 1932, certainly from the beginning of 1933, when Herr Hitler came into power, it was general public knowledge in this country that serious rearmament had begun in Germany. There was a change in the situation. Three years ago, at the Conservative Conference at Birmingham, that vigorous and faithful servant of this country, Lord Lloyd, moved the following resolution:

> That this Conference desires to record its grave anxiety in regard to the inadequacy of the provisions made for Imperial Defence.

That was three years ago, and I see, from *The Times* report of that occasion, that I said:

> During the last four or five years the world had grown gravely darker ... We have steadily disarmed, partly with a sincere desire to give a lead to other countries, and partly through the severe financial pressure of the time. But a change must now be made. We must not

117

continue longer on a course in which we alone are growing weaker while every other nation is growing stronger.

The resolution was passed unanimously, with only a rider informing the Chancellor of the Exchequer that all necessary burdens of taxation would be cheerfully borne. There were no locusts there, at any rate.

I am very glad to see the Prime Minister [Mr Baldwin] restored to his vigour, and to learn that he has been recuperated by his rest and also, as we hear, rejuvenated. It has been my fortune to have ups and downs in my political relations with him, the downs on the whole predominating perhaps, but at any rate we have always preserved agreeable personal relations, which, so far as I am concerned, are greatly valued. I am sure he would not wish in his conduct of public affairs that there should be any shrinking from putting the real issues of criticism which arise, and I shall certainly proceed in that sense. My right hon. Friend has had all the power for a good many years, and therefore there rests upon him inevitably the main responsibility for everything that has been done, or not done, and also the responsibility for what is to be done or not done now. So far as the air is concerned, this responsibility was assumed by him in a very direct personal manner even before he became Prime Minister. I must recall the words which he used in the Debate on 8 March 1934, nearly three years ago. In answer to an appeal which I made to him, both publicly and privately, he said:

> Any Government of this country – a National Government more than any, and this Government – will see to it that in air strength and air power this country shall no longer be in a position inferior to any country within striking distance of our shores.

Well, Sir, I accepted that solemn promise, but some of my friends, like Sir Edward Grigg and Captain Guest, wanted what the Minister for the Co-ordination of Defence, in another state of being, would have called 'further and better particulars', and they raised a debate after dinner, when the Prime Minister, then Lord President, came down to the House and really showed less than his usual urbanity in chiding those Members for even venturing to doubt the intention of the Government to make good in every respect the pledge which he had so solemnly given in the afternoon. I do not think that responsibility was ever more directly assumed in a more personal manner. The Prime Minister was not successful in discharging that task, and he admitted with manly candour a year later that he had been led into error upon the important question of the relative strength of the British and German air power.

No doubt as a whole His Majesty's Government were very slow in accepting the unwelcome fact of German rearmament. They still clung to the policy of one-sided disarmament. It was one of those experiments, we are told, which had to be, to use a vulgarism, 'tried out', just as the experiments of non-military sanctions against Italy had to be tried out. Both experiments have now been tried out, and Ministers are accustomed to plume themselves upon the very clear results of those experiments. They are held to prove conclusively that the policies subjected to the experiments were all wrong, utterly foolish, and should never be used again, and the very same men who were foremost in urging those experiments are now foremost in proclaiming and denouncing the fallacies upon which they were based. They have bought their knowledge, they have bought it dear, they have bought it at our expense, but at any rate let us be duly thankful that they now at last possess it.

In July 1935, before the General Election, there was a very strong movement in this House in favour of the appointment of a Minister to concert the action of the three fighting Services. Moreover, at that time the Departments of State were all engaged in drawing up the large schemes of rearmament in all branches which have been laid before us in the White Paper and upon which we are now engaged. One would have thought that that was the time when this new Minister or Co-ordinator was most necessary. He was not, however, in fact appointed until nearly nine months later, in March 1936. No explanation has yet been given to us why these nine months were wasted before the taking of what is now an admittedly necessary measure. The Prime Minister dilated the other night, no doubt very properly, on the great advantages which had flowed from the appointment of the Minister for the Co-ordination of Defence. Every argument used to show how useful has been the work which he has done accuses the failure to appoint him nine months earlier, when inestimable benefits would have accrued to us by the saving of this long period.

When at last, in March, after all the delays, the Prime Minister eventually made the appointment, the arrangement of duties was so ill-conceived that no man could possibly discharge them with efficiency or even make a speech about them without embarrassment. I have repeatedly pointed out the obvious mistake in organization of jumbling together – and practically everyone in the House is agreed upon this – the functions of defence with those of a Minister of Supply. The proper organization, let me repeat, is four Departments – the Navy, the Army, the Air and the Ministry of Supply, with the Minister for the Co-ordination of Defence over the four, exercising a general supervision, concerting their actions, and assigning the high priorities of manufacture in relation to some comprehensive strategic conception. The House is familiar with the many requests and arguments which have been made to the Government to create a Ministry of Supply. These arguments have received powerful reinforcement from another angle in the report of the Royal Commission on Arms Manufacture.

The first work of this new Parliament, and the first work of the Minister for the Co-ordination of Defence if he had known as much about the subject when he was appointed as he does now, would have been to set up a Ministry of Supply which should, step by step, have taken over the whole business of the design and manufacture of all the supplies needed by the Air Force and the Army, and everything needed for the Navy, except warships, heavy ordnance, torpedoes and one or two ancillaries. All the rest of the industries of Britain should have been surveyed from a general integral standpoint, and all existing resources utilized so far as was necessary to execute the programme.

The Minister for the Co-ordination of Defence has argued as usual against a Ministry of Supply. The arguments which he used were weighty, and even ponderous – it would disturb and delay existing programmes; it would do more harm than good; it would upset the life and industry of the country; it would destroy the export trade and demoralize finance at the moment when it was most needed; it would turn this country into one vast munitions camp. Certainly these are massive arguments, if they are true. One would have thought that they would carry conviction to any man who accepted them. But then my right hon. Friend went on somewhat surprisingly to say, 'The decision is not final.' It would be reviewed again in a few weeks. What will you know in a few weeks about this matter that you do not know now, that you ought not to have known a year ago, and have not been told any time in the last six months? What is going to happen in the next few weeks which will invalidate all these magnificent arguments by which you have been overwhelmed, and suddenly make it worth your while to paralyse the export trade, to destroy the finances, and to turn the country into a great munitions camp?

The First Lord of the Admiralty in his speech the other night went even farther. He said, 'We are always reviewing the position.' Everything, he assured us, is entirely fluid. I am sure that that is true. Anyone can see what the position is. The Government simply cannot make up their minds, or they cannot get the Prime Minister to make up his mind. So they go on in strange paradox, decided only to be undecided, resolved to be irresolute, adamant for drift, solid for fluidity, all-powerful to be impotent. So we go on preparing more months and years – precious, perhaps vital to the greatness of Britain – for the locusts to eat. They will say to me, 'A Minister of Supply is not necessary, for all is going well.' I deny it. 'The position is satisfactory.' It is not true. 'All is proceeding according to plan.' We know what that means.

Let me come to the Territorial Army. In March of this year I stigmatized a sentence in the War Office Memorandum about the Territorial Army, in which it was said the equipment of the Territorials could not be undertaken until that of the Regular Army had been completed. What has been done about all that?

It is certain the evils are not yet removed. I agree wholeheartedly with all that was said by Lord Winterton the other day about the Army and the Territorial Force. When I think how these young men who join the Territorials come forward, almost alone in the population, and take on a liability to serve anywhere in any part of the world, not even with a guarantee to serve in their own units; come forward in spite of every conceivable deterrent; come forward – 140,000 of them, although they are still not up to strength – and then find that the Government does not take their effort seriously enough even to equip and arm them properly, I marvel at their patriotism. It is a marvel; it is also a glory, but a glory we have no right to profit by unless we can secure proper and efficient equipment for them.

A friend of mine the other day saw a number of persons engaged in peculiar evolutions, genuflections and gestures in the neighbourhood of London. His curiosity was excited. He wondered whether it was some novel form of gymnastics, or a new religion – there are new religions which are very popular in some countries nowadays – or whether they were a party of lunatics out for an airing. On approaching closer he learned that they were a Searchlight Company of London Territorials who were doing their exercises as well as they could without having the searchlights. Yet we are told there is no need for a Ministry of Supply.

In the manœuvres of the Regular Army many of the most important new weapons have to be represented by flags and discs. When we remember how small our land forces are – altogether only a few hundred thousand men – it seems incredible that the very flexible industry of Britain, if properly handled, could not supply them with their modest requirements. In Italy, whose industry is so much smaller, whose wealth and credit are a small fraction of this country's, a Dictator is able to boast that he has bayonets and equipment for 8,000,000 men. Halve the figure, if you like, and the moral remains equally cogent.

The Army lacks almost every weapon which is required for the latest form of modern war. Where are the anti-tank guns, where are the short-distance wireless sets, where the field anti-aircraft guns against low-flying armoured aeroplanes? We want to know how it is that this country, with its enormous motoring and motor-bicycling public, is not able to have strong mechanized divisions, both Regular and Territorial. Surely, when so much of the interest and the taste of our youth is moving in those mechanical channels, and when the horse is receding with the days of chivalry into the past, it ought to be possible to create an army of the size we want fully up to strength and mechanized to the highest degree.

Look at the Tank Corps. The tank was a British invention. This idea, which has revolutionized the conditions of modern war, was a British idea forced on the War Office by outsiders. Let me say they would have just as hard work today to force a new idea on it. I speak from what I know. During the War we had almost a monopoly, let alone the leadership, in tank warfare, and for several years afterwards we held the foremost place. To England all eyes were turned. All that has gone now. Nothing has been done in 'the years that the locust hath eaten' to equip the Tank Corps with new machines. The medium tank which they possess, which in its day was the best in the world, is now looking obsolete. Not only in numbers – for there we have never tried to compete with other countries – but in quality these British weapons are now surpassed by those of Germany, Russia, Italy and the United States. All the shell plants and gun plants in the Army, apart from the very small piece-time services, are in an elementary stage. A very long period must intervene before any effectual flow of munitions can be expected, even for the small forces of which we dispose. Still we are told there is no necessity for a Ministry of Supply, no emergency which should induce us to impinge on the normal course of trade. If we go on like this, and I do not see what power can prevent us from going on like this, some day there may be a terrible reckoning, and those who take the responsibility so entirely upon themselves are either of a hardy disposition or they are incapable of foreseeing the possibilities which may arise.

Now I come to the greatest matter of all, the air. We received on Tuesday night, from the First Lord of the Admiralty [Sir

Samuel Hoare], the assurance that there is no foundation whatever for the statement that we are 'vastly behindhand' with our Air Force programme. It is clear from his words that we are behindhand. The only question is, what meaning does the First Lord attach to the word 'vastly'? He also used the expression, about the progress of air expansion, that it was 'not unsatisfactory'. One does not know what his standard is. His standards change from time to time. In that speech of the 11th of September about the League of Nations there was one standard, and in the Hoare-Laval Pact there was clearly another.

In August last some of us went in a deputation to the Prime Minister in order to express the anxieties which we felt about national defence, and to make a number of statements which we preferred not to be forced to make in public. I personally made a statement on the state of the Air Force to the preparation of which I had devoted several weeks and which, I am sorry to say, took an hour to read. My right hon. Friend the Prime Minister listened with his customary exemplary patience. I think I told him beforehand that he is a good listener, and perhaps he will retort that he learned to be when I was his colleague. At any rate, he listened with patience, and that is always something. During the three months that have passed since then I have checked those facts again in the light of current events and later knowledge, and were it not that foreign ears listen to all that is said here, or if we were in secret Session, I would repeat my statement here. And even if only one half were true I am sure the House would consider that a very grave state of emergency existed, and also, I regret to say, a state of things from which a certain suspicion of mismanagement cannot be excluded. I am not going into any of those details. I make it a rule, as far as I possibly can, to say nothing in this House upon matters which I am not sure are already known to the General Staffs of foreign countries; but there is one statement of very great importance which the Minister for the Co-ordination of Defence made in his speech on Tuesday. He said:

> The process of building up squadrons and forming new training units and skeleton squadrons is familiar to everybody connected

with the Air Force. The number of squadrons in present circumstances at home today is eighty, and that figure includes sixteen auxiliary squadrons, but excludes the Fleet Air Arm, and, of course, does not include the squadrons abroad.

From that figure, and the reservations by which it was prefaced, it is possible for the House, and also for foreign countries, to deduce pretty accurately the progress of our Air Force expansion. I feel, therefore, at liberty to comment on it.

Parliament was promised a total of seventy-one new squadrons, making a total of 124 squadrons in the home defence force, by 31 March 1937. This was thought to be the minimum compatible with our safety. At the end of the last financial year our strength was fifty-three squadrons, including auxiliary squadrons. Therefore, in the thirty-two weeks which have passed since the financial year began we have added twenty-eight squadrons – that is to say, less than one new squadron each week. In order to make the progress which Parliament was promised, in order to maintain the programme which was put forward as the minimum, we shall have to add forty-three squadrons in the remaining twenty weeks, or over two squadrons a week. The rate at which new squadrons will have to be formed from now till the end of March will have to be nearly three times as fast as hitherto. I do not propose to analyse the composition of the eighty squadrons we now have, but the Minister, in his speech, used a suggestive expression, 'skeleton squadrons' – applying at least to a portion of them – but even if every one of the eighty squadrons had an average strength of twelve aeroplanes, each fitted with war equipment, and the reserves upon which my right hon. Friend dwelt, we should only have a total of 960 first-line home-defence aircraft.

What is the comparable German strength? I am not going to give an estimate and say that the Germans have not got more than a certain number, but I will take it upon myself to say that they most certainly at this moment have not got less than a certain number. Most certainly they have not got less than 1,500 first-line aeroplanes, comprised in not less than 130 or 140 squadrons, including auxiliary squadrons. It must also be remembered that Germany has not got in its squadrons any machine the design and construction of which is more than three years old. It must also be remembered that Germany has specialized in long-distance bombing aeroplanes and that her preponderance in that respect is far greater than any of these figures would suggest.

We were promised most solemnly by the Government that air parity with Germany would be maintained by the home defence forces. At the present time, putting everything at the very best, we are, upon the figures given by the Minister for the Co-ordination of Defence, only about two-thirds as strong as the German Air Force, assuming that I am not very much understating their present strength. How then does the First Lord of the Admiralty [Sir Samuel Hoare] think it right to say:

> On the whole, our forecast of the strength of other Air Forces proves to be accurate; on the other hand, our own estimates have also proved to be accurate.
>
> I am authorized to say that the position is satisfactory.

I simply cannot understand it. Perhaps the Prime Minister will explain the position. I should like to remind the House that I have made no revelation affecting this country and that I have introduced no new fact in our air defence which does not arise from the figures given by the Minister and from the official estimates that have been published.

What ought we to do? I know of only one way in which this matter can be carried further. The House ought to demand a Parliamentary inquiry. It ought to appoint six, seven or eight independent Members, responsible, experienced, discreet Members, who have some acquaintance with these matters and are representative of all parties, to interview Ministers and to find out what are, in fact, the answers to a series of questions; then to make a brief report to the House, whether of reassurance or of suggestion for remedying the shortcomings. That, I think, is what any Parliament worthy of the name would do in these circumstances. Parliaments of the past days in which the greatness of our country was abuilding would never have hesitated. They would have felt they could not discharge their duty to their constituents if they did not satisfy themselves that the safety of the country was being effectively maintained.

The French Parliament, through its committees, has a very wide, deep knowledge of the state of national defence, and I am not aware that their secrets leak out in any exceptional way. There is no reason why our secrets should leak out in any exceptional way. It is because so many members of the French Parliament are associated in one way or another with the progress of the national defence that the French Government were induced to supply, six years ago, upward of £60,000,000 sterling to construct the Maginot Line of fortifications, when our Government was assuring them that wars were over and that France must not lag behind Britain in her disarmament. Even now I hope that Members of the House of Commons will rise above considerations of party discipline, and will insist upon knowing where we stand in a matter which affects our liberties and our lives. I should have thought that the Government, and above all the Prime Minister, whose load is so heavy, would have welcomed such a suggestion.

Owing to past neglect, in the face of the plainest warnings, we have now entered upon a period of danger greater than has befallen Britain since the U-boat campaign was crushed; perhaps, indeed, it is a more grievous period than that, because at that time at least we were possessed of the means of securing ourselves and of defeating that campaign. Now we have no such assurance. The era of procrastination, of half-measures, of soothing and baffling expedients, of delays, is coming to its close. In its place we are entering a period of consequences. We have entered a period in which for more than a year, or a year and a half, the considerable preparations which are now on foot in Britain will not, as the Minister clearly showed, yield results which can be effective in actual fighting strength; while during this very period Germany may well reach the culminating point of her gigantic military preparations, and be forced by financial and economic stringency to contemplate a sharp decline, or perhaps some other exit from her difficulties. It is this lamentable conjunction of events which seems to present the danger of Europe in its most disquieting form. We cannot avoid this period; we are in it now. Surely, if we can abridge it by even a few months, if we can shorten this period when the German Army will begin to be so much larger than the French Army, and before the British Air Force has come to play its complementary part, we may be the architects who build the peace of the world on sure foundations.

Two things, I confess, have staggered me, after a long Parliamentary experience, in these Debates. The first has been the dangers that have so swiftly come upon us in a few years, and have been transforming our position and the whole outlook of the world. Secondly, I have been staggered by the failure of the House of Commons to react effectively against those dangers. That, I am bound to say, I never expected. I never would have believed that we should have been allowed to go on getting into this plight, month by month and year by year, and that even the Government's own confessions of error would have produced no concentration of Parliamentary opinion and force capable of lifting our efforts to the level of emergency. I say that unless the House resolves to find out the truth for itself it will have committed an act of abdication of duty without parallel in its long history.

12

Munich

'A Total and Unmitigated Defeat'

House of Commons, 5 October 1938

ON 30 SEPTEMBER 1938, NEVILLE CHAMBERLAIN returned from Munich bearing what he believed was Hitler's reassurance of 'peace in our time'. For a brief interlude, he was the most popular man in the country, and his parliamentary majority was never in doubt. But during the Commons debate on the settlement, which lasted from 3 to 6 October, some very powerful speeches were made in opposition to the betrayal of Czechoslovakia, especially by Duff Cooper, who had resigned as First Lord of the Admiralty, Archibald Sinclair, Clement Attlee, Anthony Eden and Richard Law.

As so often, it was Churchill, who spoke late in the debate for 49 minutes, who provided, in another superb oration, the most damning indictment of all. *The Daily Telegraph* believed that his warnings, by now increasingly verified by events, 'have entitled him to be heard'. In the final vote, thirty Conservative MPs abstained – the most convincing demonstration yet of the opposition to Chamberlain within the ranks of his own supporters.

By this time, however, feeling against Churchill in the Conservative Party was very stong indeed. *The Times* claimed that he 'treated a crowded House to prophecies which made Jeremiah appear an optimist', and even Beaverbrook's *Daily Express* dismissed it as 'an alarmist oration by a man whose mind is soaked in the conquests of Marlborough'.

129

House of Commons, 5 October 1938

IF I DO NOT BEGIN THIS AFTERNOON by paying the usual, and indeed almost inevitable, tributes to the Prime Minister for his handling of this crisis, it is certainly not from any lack of personal regard. We have always, over a great many years, had very pleasant relations, and I have deeply understood from personal experiences of my own in a similar crisis the stress and strain he has had to bear; but I am sure it is much better to say exactly what we think about public affairs, and this is certainly not the time when it is worth anyone's while to court political popularity. We had a shining example of firmness of character from the late First Lord of the Admiralty two days ago. He showed that firmness of character which is utterly unmoved by currents of opinion, however swift and violent they may be. My hon. Friend the Member for South-West Hull [Mr Law], to whose compulsive speech the House listened on Monday, was quite right in reminding us that the Prime Minister has himself throughout his conduct of these matters shown a robust indifference to cheers or boos and to the alternations of criticism or applause.

If that be so, such qualities and elevation of mind should make it possible for the most severe expressions of honest opinion to be interchanged in this House without rupturing personal relations, and for all points of view to receive the fullest possible expression. Having thus fortified myself by the example of others, I will proceed to emulate them. I will, therefore, begin by saying the most unpopular and most unwelcome thing. I will begin by saying what everybody would like to ignore or forget but which must nevertheless be stated, namely, that we have sustained a total and unmitigated defeat, and that France has suffered even more than we have. The utmost my right hon. Friend the Prime Minister has been able to secure by all his immense exertions, by all the great efforts and mobilization which took place in this country, and by all the anguish and strain through which we have passed in this country, the utmost he has been able to gain for Czechoslovakia in the matters which were in dispute has been that the German dictator, instead of snatching the victuals from the table, has been content to have them served to him course by course.

The Chancellor of the Exchequer [Sir John Simon] said it was the first time Herr Hitler had been made to retract – I think that was the word – in any degree. We really must not waste time after all this long Debate upon the difference between the positions reached at Berchtesgaden, at Godesberg and at Munich. They can be very simply epitomized, if the House will permit me to vary the metaphor. £1 was demanded at the pistol's point. When it was given, £2 were demanded at the pistol's point. Finally, the dictator consented to take £1 17s. 6d. and the rest in promises of goodwill for the future.

Now I come to the point, which was mentioned to me just now from some quarters of the House, about the saving of peace. No one has been a more resolute and uncompromising struggler for peace than the Prime Minister. Everyone knows that. Never has there been such intense and undaunted determination to maintain and secure peace. That is quite true. Nevertheless, I am not quite clear why there was so much danger of Great Britain or France being involved in a war with Germany at this juncture if, in fact, they were ready all along to sacrifice Czechoslovakia. The terms which the Prime Minister brought back with him could easily have been agreed, I believe, through the ordinary diplomatic channels at any time during the summer. And I will say this, that I believe the Czechs, left to themselves and told they were going to get no help from the Western Powers, would have been able to make better terms than they have got after all this tremendous perturbation; they could hardly have had worse.

There never can be any absolute certainty that there will be a fight if one side is determined that it will give way completely. When one reads the Munich terms, when one sees what is happening in Czechoslovakia from hour to hour, when one is sure, I will not say of Parliamentary approval but of Parliamentary acquiescence, when the Chancellor of the Exchequer makes a speech which at any rate tries to put in a very powerful and persuasive manner the fact that, after all, it was inevitable and indeed righteous: when we saw all this – and everyone on this side of the House, including many members of the Conservative Party who are vigilant and careful guardians of the national interest, is quite clear that nothing vitally affecting us was at stake – it seems to me that one must ask, What was all the trouble and fuss about?

The resolve was taken by the British and the French Governments. Let me say that it is very important to realize that it is by no means a question which the British Government only have had to decide. I very much admire the manner in which, in the House, all references of a recriminatory nature have been repressed. But it must be realized that this resolve did not emanate particularly from one or other of the Governments but was a resolve for which both must share in common the responsibility. When this resolve was taken and the course was followed – you may say it was wise or unwise, prudent or short-sighted – once it had been decided not to make the defence of Czechoslovakia a matter of war, then there was really no reason, if the matter had been handled during the summer in the ordinary way, to call into being all this formidable apparatus of crisis. I think that point should be considered.

We are asked to vote for this Motion [That this House approves the policy of His Majesty's Government by which war was averted in the recent crisis and supports their efforts to secure a lasting peace.] which has been put upon the Paper, and it is certainly a Motion couched in very uncontroversial terms, as, indeed, is the Amendment moved from the Opposition side. I cannot myself express my agreement with the steps which have been taken, and as the Chancellor of the Exchequer has put his side to the case with so much ability I will attempt, if I may be permitted, to put the case from a different angle. I have always held the view that the maintenance of peace depends upon the accumulation of deterrents against the aggressor, coupled with a sincere effort to redress grievances. Herr Hitler's victory, like so many of the famous struggles that have governed the fate of the world, was won upon the narrowest of margins. After the seizure of Austria in March we faced this problem in our Debates. I ventured to appeal to the Government to go a little further than the Prime Minister went, and to give a pledge that in conjunction with France and other Powers they would guarantee the security of Czechoslovakia while the Sudeten-Deutsch question was being examined either by a League of Nations Commission or some other impartial body, and I still believe that if that course had been followed events would not have fallen into this disastrous state. I agree very much with my right hon. Friend the Member for Sparkbrook [Mr Amery] when he said on that occasion: 'Do one thing or the other; either say you will disinterest yourself in the matter altogether or take the step of giving a guarantee which will have the greatest chance of securing protection for that country.'

France and Great Britain together, especially if they had maintained a close contact with Russia, which certainly was not done, would have been able in those days in the summer, when they had the prestige, to influence many of the smaller states of Europe; and I believe they could have determined the attitude of Poland. Such a combination, prepared at a time when the German dictator was not deeply and irrevocably committed to his new adventure, would, I believe, have given strength to all those forces in Germany which resisted this departure, this new design. They were varying forces – those of a military character which declared that Germany was not ready to undertake a world war, and all that mass of moderate opinion and popular opinion which dreaded war, and some elements of which still have some influence upon the Government. Such action would have given strength to all that intense desire for peace which the helpless German masses share with their British and French fellow men, and which, as we have been reminded, found a passionate and rarely permitted vent in the joyous manifestations with which the Prime Minister was acclaimed in Munich.

All these forces, added to the other deterrents which combinations of Powers, great and small, ready to stand firm upon the front of law and for the ordered remedy of grievances, would have formed, might well have been effective. Between submission and immediate war there was this third alternative, which gave a hope not only of peace but of justice. It is quite true that such a policy in order to succeed demanded that Britain should declare straight out and a long time beforehand that she would, with others, join to defend Czechoslovakia against an unprovoked aggression. His Majesty's Government refused to give that guarantee when it would have saved the situation, yet in the end they gave it when it was too late, and now, for the future, they renew it when they have not the slightest power to make it good.

All is over. Silent, mournful, abandoned, broken, Czechoslovakia recedes into the darkness. She has suffered in every respect by her association with the Western democracies and with the League of Nations, of which she has always been an obedient servant. She has suffered in particular from her association with France, under whose guidance and policy she has been actuated for so long. The very measures taken by His Majesty's Government in the Anglo-French Agreement to give her the best chance possible, namely, the 50 per cent clean-cut in certain districts instead of a plebiscite, have turned to her detriment, because there is to be a plebiscite too in wide areas, and those other Powers who had claims have also come down upon the helpless victim. Those municipal elections upon whose voting the basis is taken for the 50 per cent cut were held on issues which had nothing to do with Germany. When I saw Herr Henlein over here he assured me that was not the desire of his people. Positive statements were made that it was only a question of home rule, of having a position of their own in the Czechoslovakian State. No one has a right to say that the plebiscite which is to be taken in areas under Saar conditions, and the clean-cut of the 50 per cent areas – that those two operations together amount in the slightest degree to a verdict of self-determination. It is a fraud and a farce to invoke that name.

We in this country, as in other Liberal and democratic countries, have a perfect right to exalt the principle of self-determination, but it comes ill out of the mouths of those in totalitarian states who deny even the smallest element of toleration to every section and creed within their bounds. But, however you put it, this particular block of land, this mass of human beings to be handed over, has never expressed the desire to go into the Nazi rule. I do not believe that even now, if their opinion could be asked, they would exercise such an opinion.

What is the remaining position of Czechoslovakia? Not only are they politically mutilated, but, economically and financially, they are in complete confusion. Their banking, their railway arrangements, are severed and broken, their industries are curtailed, and the movement of their population is most cruel. The Sudeten miners, who are all Czechs and whose families have lived in that area for centuries, must now flee into an area where there are hardly any mines left for them to work. It is a tragedy which has occurred. There must always be the most profound regret and a sense of vexation in British hearts at the treatment and the misfortune which have overcome the Czechoslovakian Republic. They have not ended here. At any moment there may be a hitch in the programme. At any moment there may be an order for Herr Goebbels to start again his propaganda of calumny and lies; at any moment an incident may be provoked, and now that the fortress line is turned what is there to stop the will of the conqueror? Obviously, we are not in a position to give them the slightest help at the present time, except what everyone is glad to know has been done, the financial aid which the Government have promptly produced.

I venture to think that in future the Czechoslovak State cannot be maintained as an independent entity. I think you will find that in a period of time which may be measured by years, but may be measured only by months, Czechoslovakia will be engulfed in the Nazi regime. Perhaps they may join it in despair or in revenge. At any rate, that story is over and told. But we cannot consider the abandonment and ruin of Czechoslovakia in the light only of what happened only last month. It is the most grievous consequence of what we have done and of what we have left undone in the last five years – five years of futile good intentions, five years of eager search for the line of least resistance, five years of uninterrupted retreat of British power, five years of neglect of our air defences. Those are the features which I stand here to expose and which marked an improvident stewardship for which Great Britain and France have dearly to pay. We have been reduced in those five years from a position of security so overwhelming and so unchallengeable that we never cared to think about it. We have been reduced from a position where the very word 'war' was considered one which could be used only by persons qualifying for a lunatic asylum. We have been reduced from a position of safety and power – power to do good, power to be generous to a beaten foe, power to make terms with Germany, power to give her proper redress for her grievances, power to stop her arming if we chose, power to take any step in strength or mercy or justice which we thought right – reduced in five years from a position safe and unchallenged to where we stand now.

When I think of the fair hopes of a long peace which still lay before Europe at the beginning of 1933 when Herr Hitler first obtained power, and of all the opportunities of arresting the growth of the Nazi power which have been thrown away, when I think of the immense combinations and resources which have been neglected or squandered, I cannot believe that a parallel exists in the whole course of history. So far as this country is concerned the responsibility must rest with those who have had the undisputed control of our political affairs. They neither prevented Germany from rearming, nor did they rearm ourselves in time. They quarrelled with Italy without saving Ethiopia. They exploited and discredited the vast institution of the League of Nations and they neglected to make alliances and combinations which might have repaired previous errors, and thus they left us in the hour of trial without adequate national defence or effective international security.

In my holiday I thought it was a chance to study the reign of King Ethelred the Unready. The House will remember that that was a period of great misfortune, in which, from the strong position which we had gained under the descendants of King Alfred, we fell very swiftly into chaos. It was the period of

Danegeld and of foreign pressure. I must say that the rugged words of the *Anglo-Saxon Chronicle*, written a thousand years ago, seem to me apposite, at least as apposite as those quotations from Shakespeare with which we have been regaled by the last speaker from the Opposition Bench. Here is what the *Anglo-Saxon Chronicle* said, and I think the words apply very much to our treatment of Germany and our relations with her. 'All these calamities fell upon us because of evil counsel, because tribute was not offered to them at the right time nor yet were they resisted; but when they had done the most evil, then was peace made with them.' That is the wisdom of the past, for all wisdom is not new wisdom.

I have ventured to express those views in justifying myself for not being able to support the Motion which is moved tonight, but I recognize that this great matter of Czechoslovakia, and of British and French duty there, has passed into history. New developments may come along, but we are not here to decide whether any of those steps should be taken or not. They have been taken. They have been taken by those who had a right to take them because they bore the highest executive responsibility under the Crown. Whatever we may think of it, we must regard those steps as belonging to the category of affairs which are settled beyond recall. The past is no more, and one can only draw comfort if one feels that one has done one's best to advise rightly and wisely and in good time. I, therefore, turn to the future, and to our situation as it is today. Here, again, I am sure I shall have to say something which will not be at all welcome.

We are in the presence of a disaster of the first magnitude which has befallen Great Britain and France. Do not let us blind ourselves to that. It must now be accepted that all the countries of Central and Eastern Europe will make the best terms they can with the triumphant Nazi power. The system of alliances in Central Europe upon which France has relied for her safety has been swept away, and I can see no means by which it can be reconstituted. The road down the Danube Valley to the Black Sea, the road which leads as far as Turkey, has been opened. In fact, if not in form, it seems to me that all those countries of

Middle Europe, all those Danubian countries, will, one after another, be drawn into this vast system of power politics – not only power military politics but power economic politics – radiating from Berlin, and I believe this can be achieved quite smoothly and swiftly and will not necessarily entail the firing of a single shot. If you wish to survey the havoc of the foreign policy of Britain and France, look at what is happening and is recorded each day in the columns of *The Times*. Why, I read this morning about Yugoslavia – and I know something about the details of that country –

> The effects of the crisis for Yugoslavia can immediately be traced. Since the elections of 1935, which followed soon after the murder of King Alexander, the Serb and Croat Opposition to the Government of Dr Stoyadinovitch have been conducting their entire campaign for the next elections under the slogan: 'Back to France, England, and the Little Entente; back to democracy.' The events of the past fortnight have so triumphantly vindicated Dr Stoyadinovitch's policy ... [his is a policy of close association with Germany] that the Opposition has collapsed practically ... overnight; the new elections, the date of which was in doubt, are now likely to be held very soon and can result only in an overwhelming victory for Dr Stoyadinovitch's Government.

Here was a country which, three months ago, would have stood in the line with other countries to arrest what has occurred.

Again, what happened in Warsaw? The British and French Ambassadors visited the Foreign Minister, Colonel Beck, or sought to visit him, in order to ask for some mitigation in the harsh measures being pursued against Czechoslovakia about Teschen. The door was shut in their faces. The French Ambassador was not even granted an audience and the British Ambassador was given a most curt reply by a political director. The whole matter is described in the Polish Press as a political indiscretion committed by those two powers, and we are today reading of the success of Colonel Beck's blow. I am not forgetting, I must say, that it is less than twenty years since British and French bayonets rescued Poland from the bondage of a century and a half. I think it is indeed a sorry episode in the history of that country, for whose freedom and right so many of us have had warm and long sympathy.

Those illustrations are typical. You will see, day after day, week after week, entire alienation of those regions. Many of those countries, in fear of the rise of the Nazi power, have already got politicians, Ministers, Governments, who were pro-German, but there was always an enormous popular movement in Poland, Rumania, Bulgaria and Yugoslavia which looked to the Western democracies and loathed the idea of having this arbitrary rule of the totalitarian system thrust upon them, and hoped that a stand would be made. All that has gone by the board. We are talking about countries which are a long way off. But what will be the position, I want to know, of France and England this year and the year afterwards? What will be the position of that Western front of which we are in full authority the guarantors? The German army at the present time is more numerous than that of France, though not nearly so matured or perfected. Next year it will grow much larger, and its maturity will be more complete. Relieved from all anxiety in the East, and having secured resources which will greatly diminish, if not entirely remove, the deterrent of a naval blockade, the rulers of Nazi Germany will have a free choice open to them as to what direction they will turn their eyes. If the Nazi dictator should choose to look westward, as he may, bitterly will France and England regret the loss of that fine army of ancient Bohemia which was estimated last week to require not fewer than thirty German divisions for its destruction.

Can we blind ourselves to the great change which has taken place in the military situation, and to the dangers we have to meet? We are in process, I believe, of adding in four years, four battalions to the British Army. No fewer than two have already been completed. Here are at least thirty divisions which must now be taken into consideration upon the French front, besides the twelve that were captured when Austria was engulfed. Many people, no doubt, honestly believe that they are only giving away the interests of Czechoslovakia, whereas I fear we shall find that we have deeply compromised, and perhaps fatally endangered, the safety and even the independence of Great Britain and France. This is not merely a question of giving up the German colonies, as I am sure we shall be asked to do. Nor is it a question only of losing influence in Europe. It goes far deeper than that. You have to consider the character of the Nazi movement and the rule which it implies. The Prime Minister desires to see cordial relations between this country and Germany. There is no difficulty at all in having cordial relations between the peoples. Our hearts go out to them. But they have no power. But never will you have friendship with the present German Government. You must have diplomatic and correct relations, but there can never be friendship between the British democracy and the Nazi power, that power which spurns Christian ethics, which cheers its onward course by a barbarous paganism, which vaunts the spirit of aggression and conquest, which derives strength and perverted pleasure from persecution, and uses, as we have seen, with pitiless brutality the threat of murderous force. That power cannot ever be the trusted friend of the British democracy.

What I find unendurable is the sense of our country falling into the power, into the orbit and influence of Nazi Germany, and of our existence becoming dependent upon their good will or pleasure. It is to prevent that that I have tried my best to urge the maintenance of every bulwark of defence – first, the timely creation of an Air Force superior to anything within striking distance of our shores; secondly, the gathering together of the collective strength of many nations; and thirdly, the making of alliances and military conventions, all within the Covenant, in order to gather together forces at any rate to restrain the onward movement of this power. It has all been in vain. Every position has been successfully undermined and abandoned on specious and plausible excuses.

We do not want to be led upon the high road to becoming a satellite of the German Nazi system of European domination. In a very few years, perhaps in a very few months, we shall be confronted with demands with which we shall no doubt be invited to comply. Those demands may affect the surrender of territory or the surrender of liberty. I foresee and foretell that the policy of submission will carry with it restrictions upon the freedom of speech and debate in Parliament, on public platforms, and discussions in the Press, for it will be said – indeed, I hear it said sometimes now – that we cannot allow the Nazi system of dictatorship to be criticized by ordinary, common English politicians. Then, with a Press under control, in part direct but more potently indirect, with every organ of public opinion doped and chloroformed into acquiescence, we shall be conducted along further stages of our journey.

It is a small matter to introduce into such a Debate as this, but during the week I heard something of the talk of Tadpole and Taper. They were very keen upon having a general election, a sort of, if I may say so, inverted khaki election. I wish the Prime Minister had heard the speech of my hon. and gallant Friend the Member for the Abbey Division of Westminster [Sir Sidney Herbert] last night. I know that no one is more patient and regular in his attendance than the Prime Minister, and it is marvellous how he is able to sit through so much of our Debates, but it happened that by bad luck he was not here at that moment. I am sure, however, that if he had heard my hon. and gallant Friend's speech he would have felt very much annoyed that such a rumour could even have been circulated. I cannot believe that the Prime Minister, or any Prime Minister, possessed of a large working majority, would be capable of such an act of historic, constitutional indecency. I think too highly of him. Of course, if I have misjudged him on the right side, and there is a dissolution on the Munich Agreement, on Anglo-Nazi friendship, of the state of our defences and so forth, everyone will have to fight according to his convictions, and only a prophet could forecast the ultimate result; but whatever the result, few things could be more fatal to our remaining chances of survival as a great Power than that this country should be torn in twain upon this deadly issue of foreign policy at a moment when, whoever the Ministers may be, united effort can alone make us safe.

I have been casting about to see how measures can be taken to protect us from this advance of the Nazi power, and to secure those forms of life which are so dear to us. What is the sole method that is open? The sole method that is open for us to regain our old island independence by acquiring that supremacy in the air which we were promised, that security in our air defences which we were assured we had, and thus to make ourselves an island once again. That, in all this grim outlook, shines out as the overwhelming fact. An effort at rearmament the like of which has not been seen ought to be made forthwith, and all the resources of this country and all its united strength should be bent to that task. I was very glad to see that Lord Baldwin yesterday in the House of Lords said that he would mobilize industry tomorrow. But I think it would have been much better if Lord Baldwin had said that two and a half years ago, when everyone demanded a Ministry of Supply. I will venture to say to hon. Gentlemen sitting here behind the Government Bench, hon. Friends of mine, whom I thank for the patience with which they have listened to what I have to say, that they have some responsibility for all this too, because, if they had given one tithe of the cheers they have lavished upon this transaction of Czechoslovakia to the small band of Members who were endeavouring to get timely rearmament set in motion, we should not now be in the position in which we are. Hon. Gentleman opposite, and hon. Members on the Liberal benches, are not entitled to throw these stones. I remember for two years having to face, not only the Government's deprecation, but their stern disapproval. Lord Baldwin has now given the signal, tardy though it may be; let us at least obey it.

After all, there are no secrets now about what happened in the air and in the mobilization of our anti-aircraft defences. These matters have been, as my hon. and gallant Friend the Member for the Abbey Division said, seen by thousands of people. They can form their own opinions of the character of the statements which have been persistently made to us by Ministers on this subject. Who pretends now that there is air parity with Germany? Who pretends now that our anti-aircraft defences were adequately manned or armed? We know that the German General Staff are well informed upon these subjects, but the

House of Commons has hitherto not taken seriously its duty of requiring to assure itself on these matters. The Home Secretary [Sir Samuel Hoare] said the other night that he would welcome investigation. Many things have been done which reflect the greatest credit upon the administration. But the vital matters are what we want to know about. I have asked again and again during these three years for a secret Session where these matters could be thrashed out, or for an investigation by a Select Committee of the House, or for some other method. I ask now that, when we meet again in the autumn, that should be a matter on which the Government should take the House into its confidence, because we have a right to know where we stand and what measures are being taken to secure our position.

I do not begrudge our loyal, brave people, who were ready to do their duty no matter what the cost, who never flinched under the strain of last week – I do not grudge them the natural, spontaneous outburst of joy and relief when they learned that the hard ordeal would no longer be required of them at the moment; but they should know the truth. They should know that there has been gross neglect and deficiency in our defences; they should know that we have sustained a defeat without a war, the consequences of which will travel far with us along our road; they should know that we have passed an awful milestone in our history, when the whole equilibrium of Europe has been deranged, and that the terrible words have for the time being been pronounced against the Western democracies: 'Thou art weighed in the balance and found wanting.' And do not suppose that this is the end. This is only the beginning of the reckoning. This is only the first sip, the first foretaste of a bitter cup which will be proferred to us year by year unless by a supreme recovery of moral health and martial vigour, we arise again and take our stand for freedom as in the olden time.

PART THREE
Mobilizing the English Language
1940

13

The New Administration

'Blood, Toil, Tears and Sweat'

House of Commons, 13 May 1940

ON THE OUTBREAK OF WAR IN SEPTEMBER 1939, Churchill was once again appointed First Lord of the Admiralty, and thus found himself occupying exactly the same post he had held in 1914. But, in May 1940, the failure of British operations in Norway (for which Churchill himself was, ironically, very largely responsible) led to a critical Commons debate in which the Government's majority was so reduced that Chamberlain felt obliged to resign. He was replaced by Churchill, who spent the next few days forming his administration.

On Whit Monday, the House of Commons met, and Churchill made this short speech, essentially asking for the approval of the House. Reactions were mixed. On entering the chamber, Chamberlain received more cheers than the new Prime Minister, and in these early days it was from the Labour benches that most of Churchill's support came. Harold Nicolson called it 'a very short statement, but to the point.' Geoffrey Dawson patronizingly dismissed it as 'quite a good little warlike speech.'

As *The Times* was quick to point out, there were echoes of Garibaldi ('hunger, thirst, forced marches, battles and death'), and of Clemenceau (*'Je fais la guerre'*). But Churchill himself had also used very similar words in a passage of *The World Crisis*: 'Their tears, their sweat, their blood, bedewed the endless plain.' Here was rhetorical recycling at its best.

147

House of Commons, 13 May 1940

O N FRIDAY EVENING LAST I RECEIVED His Majesty's Commission to form a new Administration. It was the evident wish and will of Parliament and the nation that this should be conceived on the broadest possible basis and that it should include all parties, both those who supported the late Government and also the parties of the Opposition. I have completed the most important part of this task. A War Cabinet has been formed of five Members, representing, with the Opposition Liberals, the unity of the nation. The three party Leaders have agreed to serve, either in the War Cabinet or in high executive office. The three Fighting Services have been filled. It was necessary that this should be done in one single day, on account of the extreme urgency and rigour of events. A number of other key positions were filled yesterday, and I am submitting a further list to His Majesty tonight. I hope to complete the appointment of the principal Ministers during tomorrow. The appointment of the other Ministers usually takes a little longer, but I trust that when Parliament meets again this part of my task will be completed, and that the administration will be complete in all respects.

I considered it in the public interest to suggest that the House should be summonded to meet today. Mr Speaker agreed, and took the necessary steps, in accordance with the powers conferred upon him by the Resolution of the House. At the end of the proceedings today, the Adjournment of the House will be proposed until Tuesday, 21 May, with, of course, provision for earlier meeting if need be. The business to be considered during that week will be notified to Members at the earliest opportunity. I now invite the House, by the Resolution which stands in my name, to record its approval of the steps taken and to declare its confidence in the new Government.

To form an Administration of this scale and complexity is a

serious undertaking in itself, but it must be remembered that we are in the preliminary stage of one of the greatest battles in history, that we are in action at many points in Norway and in Holland, that we have to be prepared in the Mediterranean, that the air battle is continuous and that many preparations have to be made here at home. In this crisis I hope I may be pardoned if I do not address the House at any length today. I hope that any of my friends and colleagues, or former colleagues, who are affected by the political reconstruction, will make all allowance for any lack of ceremony with which it has been necessary to act. I would say to the House, as I said to those who have joined the Government: 'I have nothing to offer but blood, toil, tears and sweat.'

We have before us an ordeal of the most grievous kind. We have before us many, many long months of struggle and of suffering. You ask, what is our policy? I will say: It is to wage war, by sea, land and air, with all our might and with all the strength that God can give us: to wage war against a monstrous tyranny, never surpassed in the dark, lamentable catalogue of human crime. That is our policy. You ask, What is our aim? I can answer in one word: Victory – victory at all costs, victory in spite of all terror, victory, however long and hard the road may be; for without victory, there is no survival. Let that be realized; no survival for the British Empire; no survival for all that the British Empire has stood for, no survival for the urge and impulse of the ages, that mankind will move forward towards its goal. But I take up my task with buoyancy and hope. I feel sure that our cause will not be suffered to fail among men. At this time I feel entitled to claim the aid of all, and I say, 'Come, then, let us go forward together with our united strength.'

14

The Impending Ordeal
'Be Ye Men of Valour'

BBC, London, 19 May 1940

IN THE EARLY HOURS OF 10 MAY, the Germans invaded Holland and Belgium, and within four days they had broken through the French defences at Sedan. On 15 May, Holland surrendered, and Churchill flew to Paris to confer with the French leaders. It soon became clear that French resistance would not long continue, and that the position of the British troops on the Continent was perilous. At a meeting of the War Cabinet on 18 May, Chamberlain urged the Prime Minister to broadcast to the nation, to indicate 'that we were in a tight fix, and that no personal considerations must be allowed to stand in the way of the measures necessary for victory.'

On the following day, after only three hours in which to compose it, Churchill broadcast this speech live, his first as Prime Minister. He held out the hope that France might continue to resist, warned his listeners that a German assault on Britain might be imminent, and made plain his resolve 'to call forth from our people the last ounce and the last inch of effort of which they are capable.'

It seems clear that this broadcast caught the nation's imagination. Anthony Eden told Churchill he had never 'done anything as good or as great.' The *Evening Standard* thought it a speech 'of imperishable resolve.' Even Lord Halifax considered it 'worth a lot.' Churchill's war of words had begun in earnest.

'Be Ye Men of Valour' 1940

BBC, London, 19 May 1940

I SPEAK TO YOU FOR THE FIRST TIME as Prime Minister in a solemn hour for the life of our country, of our Empire, of our Allies, and, above all, of the cause of Freedom. A tremendous battle is raging in France and Flanders. The Germans, by a remarkable combination of air bombing and heavily armoured tanks, have broken through the French defences north of the Maginot Line, and strong columns of their armoured vehicles are ravaging the open country, which for the first day or two was without defenders. They have penetrated deeply and spread alarm and confusion in their track. Behind them there are now appearing infantry in lorries, and behind them, again, the large masses are moving forward. The regroupment of the French armies to make head against, and also to strike at, this intruding wedge has been proceeding for several days, largely assisted by the magnificent efforts of the Royal Air Force.

We must not allow ourselves to be intimidated by the presence of these armoured vehicles in unexpected places behind our lines. If they are behind our Front, the French are also at many points fighting actively behind theirs. Both sides are therefore in an extremely dangerous position. And if the French Army, and our own Army, are well handled, as I believe they will be; if the French retain that genius for recovery and counter-attack for which they have so long been famous; and if the British Army shows the dogged endurance and solid fighting power of which there have been so many examples in the past – then a sudden transformation of the scene might spring into being.

It would be foolish, however, to disguise the gravity of the hour. It would be still more foolish to lose heart and courage or to suppose that well-trained, well-equipped armies numbering three or four millions of men can be overcome in the space of a few weeks, or even months, by a scoop, or raid of mechanized vehicles, however formidable. We may look with confidence to the stabilization of the Front in France, and to the general engagement of the masses, which will enable the qualities of the French and British soldiers to be matched squarely against those of their adversaries. For myself, I have invincible confidence in the French Army and its leaders. Only a very small part of that splendid army has yet been heavily engaged; and only a very small part of France has yet been invaded. There is good evidence to show that practically the whole of the specialized and mechanized forces of the enemy have been already thrown into the battle; and we know that very heavy losses have been inflicted upon them. No officer or man, no brigade or division, which grapples at close quarters with the enemy, wherever encountered, can fail to make a worthy contribution to the general result. The Armies must cast away the idea of resisting behind concrete lines or natural obstacles, and must realize that mastery can only be regained by furious and unrelenting assault. And this spirit must not only animate the High Command, but must inspire every fighting man.

In the air – often at serious odds – often at odds hitherto thought overwhelming – we have been clawing down three or four to one of our enemies; and the relative balance of the British and German Air Forces is now considerably more favourable to us than at the beginning of the battle. In cutting down the German bombers, we are fighting our own battle as well as that of France. My confidence in our ability to fight it out to the finish with the German Air Force has been strengthened by the fierce encounters which have taken place and are taking place. At the same time, our heavy bombers are striking nightly at the tap-root of German mechanized power, and have already inflicted serious damage upon the oil refineries on which the Nazi effort to dominate the world directly depends.

We must expect that as soon as stability is reached on the Western Front, the bulk of that hideous apparatus of aggression which gashed Holland into ruin and slavery in a few days, will be turned upon us. I am sure I speak for all when I say we are ready to face it; to endure it; and to retaliate against it – to any extent that the unwritten laws of war permit. There will be many men, and many women, in this island who when the ordeal comes upon them, as come it will, will feel comfort, and even a pride – that they are sharing the perils of our lads at the Front – soldiers, sailors and airmen, God bless them – and are drawing away from them a part at least of the onslaught they have to bear. Is not this the appointed time for all to make the utmost exertions in their power? If the battle is to be won, we must provide our men with ever-increasing quantities of the weapons and ammunition they need. We must have, and have quickly, more aeroplanes, more tanks, more shells, more guns. There is imperious need for these vital munitions. They increase our strength against the powerfully armed enemy. They replace the wastage of the obstinate struggle; and the knowledge that wastage will speedily be replaced enables us to draw more readily upon our reserves and throw them in now that everything counts so much.

Our task is not only to win the battle – but to win the War. After this battle in France abates its force, there will come the battle for our island – for all that Britain is, and all that Britain means. That will be the struggle. In that supreme emergency we shall not hesitate to take every step, even the most drastic, to call forth from our people the last ounce and the last inch of effort of which they are capable. The interests of property, the hours of labour, are nothing compared with the struggle for life and honour, for right and freedom, to which we have vowed ourselves.

I have received from the Chiefs of the French Republic, and in particular from its indomitable Prime Minister, M. Reynaud, the most sacred pledges that whatever happens they will fight to the end, be it bitter or be it glorious. Nay, if we fight to the end, it can only be glorious.

Having received His Majesty's commission, I have found an administration of men and women of every party and of almost every point of view. We have differed and quarrelled in the past; but now one bond unites us all – to wage war until victory is won, and never to surrender ourselves to servitude and shame, whatever the cost and the agony may be. This is one of the most awe-striking periods in the long history of France and Britain. It is also beyond doubt the most sublime. Side by side, unaided except by their kith and kin in the great Dominions and by the wide Empires which rest beneath their shield – side by side, the British and French peoples have advanced to rescue not only Europe but mankind from the foulest and most soul-destroying tyranny which has ever darkened and stained the pages of history. Behind them – behind us – behind the armies and fleets of Britain and France – gather a group of shattered States and bludgeoned races: the Czechs, the Poles, the Norwegians, the Danes, the Dutch, the Belgians – upon all of whom the long night of barbarism will descend, unbroken even by a star of hope, unless we conquer, as conquer we must; as conquer we shall.

Today is Trinity Sunday. Centuries ago words were written to be a call and a spur to the faithful servants of Truth and Justice: 'Arm yourselves, and be ye men of valour, and be in readiness for the conflict; for it is better for us to perish in battle than to look upon the outrage of our nation and our altar. As the Will of God is in Heaven, even so let it be.'

15

Dunkirk

'Wars Are Not Won by Evacuations'

House of Commons, 4 June 1940

MEANWHILE, THE BRITISH EXPEDITIONARY FORCE has retreated before the German onslaught to the Dunkirk bridgehead. With the fate of France still uncertain, the evacuation began on 26 May. The sea was calm, thousands of privately owned small boats made the hazardous journey across the Channel, and the RAF fought heroically to deny the enemy air supremacy. By 4 June, over 330,000 Allied troops had reached England, including 26,000 French soldiers, a far higher figure than had ever been hoped for.

On the same day, Churchill reported to the Commons, in a speech lasting just over half an hour. He sought to temper the mood of national relief and euphoria in the aftermath of such an unexpected deliverance, to warn that in the future, Britain might well be forced to fight alone, and to make the first of many appeals, in his peroration, to the United States.

By common consent, this was an outstandingly successful performance. 'This afternoon', Harold Nicolson reported 'Winston made the finest speech I have ever heard. The House was deeply moved.' Josiah Wedgwood, the Labour MP, thought it 'worth a thousand guns, and the speeches of a thousand years.' Even Henry Channon, an inveterate appeaser and an ardent Chamberlain supporter, was impressed. 'He was eloquent and oratorical, and used magnificent English; several Labour members cried.' So did Churchill.

House of Commons, 4 June 1940

FROM THE MOMENT THAT the French defences at Sedan and on the Meuse were broken at the end of the second week of May, only a rapid retreat to Amiens and the south could have saved the British and French Armies who had entered Belgium at the appeal of the Belgian King; but this strategic fact was not immediately realized. The French High Command hoped they would be able to close the gap, and the Armies of the north were under their orders. Moreover, a retirement of this kind would have involved almost certainly the destruction of the fine Belgian Army of over twenty divisions and the abandonment of the whole of Belgium. Therefore, when the force and scope of the German penetration were realized and when a new French Generalissimo, General Weygand, assumed command in place of General Gamelin, an effort was made by the French and British Armies in Belgium to keep on holding the right hand of the Belgians and to give their own right hand to a newly created French Army which was to have advanced across the Somme in great strength to grasp it.

However, the German eruption swept like a sharp scythe around the right and rear of the Armies of the north. Eight or nine armoured divisions, each of about four hundred armoured vehicles of different kinds, but carefully assorted to be complementary and divisible into small self-contained units, cut off all communications between us and the main French Armies. It severed our own communications for food and ammunition, which ran first to Amiens and afterwards through Abbeville, and it shore its way up the coast to Boulogne and Calais, and almost to Dunkirk. Behind this armoured and mechanized onslaught came a number of German divisions in lorries, and behind them again there plodded comparatively slowly the dull brute mass of the ordinary German Army and German people, always so ready to be led to the trampling down in other lands of liberties and comforts which they have never known in their own.

I have said this armoured scythe-stroke almost reached Dunkirk – almost but not quite. Boulogne and Calais were the scenes of desperate fighting. The Guards defended Boulogne for a while and were then withdrawn by orders from this country. The Rifle Bridage, the 60th Rifles, and the Queen Victoria's Rifles, with a battalion of British tanks and 1,000 Frenchmen, in all about four thousand strong, defended Calais to the last. The British Brigadier was given an hour to surrender. He spurned the offer, and four days of intense street fighting passed before silence reigned over Calais, which marked the end of a memorable resistance. Only thirty unwounded survivors were brought off by the Navy and we do not know the fate of their comrades. Their sacrifice, however, was not in vain. At least two armoured divisions, which otherwise would have been turned against the British Expeditionary Force, had to be sent to overcome them. They have added another page to the glories of the light divisions, and the time gained enabled the Graveline waterline to be flooded and to be held by the French troops.

Thus it was that the port of Dunkirk was kept open. When it was found impossible for the Armies of the north to reopen their communications to Amiens with the main French Armies, only one choice remained. It seemed, indeed, forlorn. The Belgian, British and French Armies were almost surrounded. Their sole line of retreat was to a single port and to its neighbouring beaches. They were pressed on every side by heavy attacks and far outnumbered in the air.

When a week ago today I asked the House to fix this afternoon as the occasion for a statement, I feared it would be my hard lot to announce the greatest military disaster in our long history. I thought – and some good judges agreed with me – that perhaps 20,000 or 30,000 men might be re-embarked. But it certainly seemed that the whole of the French First Army and the whole of the British Expeditionary Force north of the Amiens-Abbeville gap, would be broken up in the open field or else would have to capitulate for lack of food and ammunition. These were the hard and heavy tidings for which I called upon the House and the nation to prepare themselves a week ago. The whole root and core and brain of the British Army, on which and around which we were to build, and are to build, the great British Armies in the later years of the war, seemed about to perish upon the field or to be led into an ignominious and starving captivity.

That was the prospect a week ago. But another blow which might well have proved final was yet to fall upon us. The King of the Belgians had called upon us to come to his aid. Had not this Ruler and his Government severed themselves from the Allies, who rescued their country from extinction in the late war, and had they not sought refuge in what has proved to be a fatal neutrality, the French and British Armies might well at the outset have saved not only Belgium but perhaps even Poland. Yet at the last moment when Belgium was already invaded, King Leopold called upon us to come to his aid, and even at the last moment we came. He and his brave, efficient Army, nearly half a million strong, guarded our left flank and thus kept open our only line of retreat to the sea. Suddenly, without prior consultation, with the least possible notice, without the advice of his Ministers and upon his own personal act, he sent a plenipotentiary to the German Command, surrendered his Army and exposed our whole flank and means of retreat.

I asked the House a week ago to suspend its judgement because the facts were not clear, but I do not feel that any reason now exists why we should not form our own opinions upon this pitiful episode. The surrender of the Belgium Army compelled the British at the shortest notice to cover a flank to the sea more than 30 miles in length. Otherwise all would have been cut off, and all would have shared the fate to which King Leopold had condemned the finest Army his country had ever formed. So in doing this and in exposing this flank, as anyone who followed the operations on the map will see, contact was lost between the British and two out of the three corps forming the First French Army, who were still farther from the coast than we were, and it seemed impossible that any large number of Allied troops could reach the coast.

The enemy attacked on all sides with great strength and fierceness, and their main power, the power of their far more numerous air force, was thrown into the battle or else concentrated upon Dunkirk and the beaches. Pressing in upon the narrow exit, both from the east and from the west, the enemy began to fire with cannon upon the beaches by which alone the shipping could approach or depart. They sowed magnetic mines in the channels and seas; they sent repeated waves of hostile aircraft, sometimes more than a hundred strong in one formation, to cast their bombs upon the single pier that remained, and upon the sand dunes upon which the troops had their eyes for shelter. Their U-boats, one of which was sunk, and their motor launches took their toll of the vast traffic which now began. For four or five days an intense struggle reigned. All their armoured divisions – or what was left of them – together with great masses of infantry and artillery, hurled themselves in vain upon the ever-narrowing, ever-contracting appendix within which the British and French Armies fought.

Meanwhile, the Royal Navy, with the willing help of countless merchant seamen, strained every nerve to embark the British and Allied troops; 220 light warships and 650 other vessels were engaged. They had to operate upon the difficult coast, often in adverse weather, under an almost ceaseless hail of bombs and an increasing concentration of artillery fire. Nor were the seas, as I have said, themselves free from mines and torpedoes. It was in conditions such as these that our men carried on, with little or no rest, for days and nights on end, making trip after trip across the dangerous waters, bringing with them always men whom they had rescued. The numbers they have brought back are the measure of their devotion and their courage. The hospital ships, which brought off many thousands of British and French wounded, being so plainly marked were a special target for Nazi bombs; but the men and women on board them never faltered in their duty.

Meanwhile, the Royal Air Force, which had already been intervening in the battle, so far as its range would allow, from home bases, now used part of its main metropolitan fighter strength, and struck at the German bombers, and at the fighters which in large numbers protected them. This struggle was protracted and fierce. Suddenly the scene has cleared, the crash and thunder has for the moment – but only for the moment – died away. A miracle of deliverance, achieved by valour, by perseverance, by perfect discipline, by faultless service, by resource, by skill, by unconquerable fidelity, is manifest to us all. The enemy was hurled back to the retreating British and French troops. He was so roughly handled that he did not hurry their departure seriously. The Royal Air Force engaged the main strength of the German Air Force, and inflicted upon them losses of at least four to one; and the Navy, using nearly 1,000 ships of all kinds, carried over 335,000 men, French and British, out of the jaws of death and shame, to their native land and to the tasks which lie immediately ahead. We must be very careful not to assign to this deliverance the attributes of a victory. Wars are not won by evacuations. But there was a victory inside this deliverance, which should be noted. It was gained by the Air Force. Many of our soldiers coming back have not seen the Air Force at work; they saw only the bombers which escaped its protective attack. They underrate its achievements. I have heard much talk of this; that is why I go out of my way to say this. I will tell you about it.

This was a great trial of strength between the British and German Air Forces. Can you conceive a greater objective for the Germans in the air than to make evacuation from these beaches impossible, and to sink all these ships which were displayed, almost to the extent of thousands? Could there have been an objective of greater military importance and significance for the whole purpose of the war than this? They tried hard, and they were beaten back; they were frustrated in their task. We got the Army away; and they have paid fourfold for any losses which they have inflicted. Very large formations of German aeroplanes – and we know that they are a very brave race – have turned on several occasions from the attack of one-quarter of their number of the Royal Air Force, and have dispersed in different directions. Twelve aeroplanes have been hunted by two. One aeroplane was driven into the water and cast away, by the mere charge of a British aeroplane, which had no more ammunition. All of our types – Hurricane, the Spitfire and the new Defiant – and all our pilots have been vindicated as superior to what they have at present to face.

When we consider how much greater would be our advantage in defending the air above this island against an overseas attack, I must say that I find in these facts a sure basis upon which practical and reassuring thoughts may rest. I will pay my tribute to these young airmen. The great French Army was very largely, for the time being, cast back and disturbed by the onrush of a few thousands of armoured vehicles. May it not also be that the cause of civilization itself will be defended by the skill and devotion of a few thousand airmen. There never had been, I suppose, in all the world, in all the history of war, such an opportunity for youth. The Knights of the Round Table, the Crusaders, all fall back into the past: not only distant but prosaic; these young men, going forth every morn to guard their native land and all that we stand for, holding in their hands these instruments of colossal and shattering power, of whom it may be said that

> *Every morn brought forth a noble chance*
> *And every chance brought forth a noble knight,*

deserve our gratitude, as do all of the brave men who, in so many ways and on so many occasions, are ready, and continue ready, to give life and all for their native land.

I return to the Army. In the long series of very fierce battles, now on this front, now on that, fighting on three fronts at once, battles fought by two or three divisions against an equal or somewhat larger number of the enemy, and fought fiercely on some of the old grounds that so many of us knew so well, in these battles our losses in men have exceeded 30,000 killed, wounded and missing. I take occasion to express the sympathy of the House to all who have suffered bereavement or who are still anxious. The President of the Board of Trade [Sir Andrew Duncan] is not here today. His son has been killed, and many in the House have felt the pangs of affliction in the sharpest form. But I will say this about the missing. We have had a large number of wounded come home safely to this country, but I would say about the missing that there may be very many reported missing who will come back home, some day, in one way or another. In the confusion of this fight it is inevitable that many have been left in positions where honour required no further resistance from them.

Against this loss of over 30,000 men, we can set a far heavier loss certainly inflicted upon the enemy. But our losses in material are enormous. We have perhaps lost one-third of the men we lost in the opening days of the battle of 21 March 1918, but we have lost nearly as many guns – nearly one thousand – and all our transport, all the armoured vehicles that were with the Army in the north. This loss will impose a further delay on the expansion of our military strength. That expansion had not been proceeding as fast as we had hoped. The best of all we had to give had gone to the British Expeditionary Force, and although they had not the numbers of tanks and some articles of equipment which were desirable, they were a very well- and finely equipped Army. They had the first fruits of all that our industry had to give, and that is gone. And now here is this further delay. How long it will be, how long it will last, depends upon the exertions which we make in this island. An effort the like of which has never been seen in our records is now being made. Work is proceeding everywhere, night and day, Sundays and weekdays. Capital and labour have cast aside their interests, rights and customs and put them into the common stock. Already the flow of munitions has leapt forward. There is no reason why we should not in a few months overtake the sudden and serious loss that has come upon us, without retarding the development of our general programme.

Nevertheless, our thankfulness at the escape of our Army and so many men, whose loved ones have passed through an agonizing week, must not blind us to the fact that what has happened in France and Belgium is a colossal military disaster. The French Army has been weakened, the Belgian Army has been lost, a large part of those fortified lines upon which so much faith had been reposed is gone, many valuable mining districts and factories have passed into the enemy's possession, the whole of the Channel ports are in his hands, with all the tragic consequences that follow from that, and we must expect another blow to be struck almost immediately at us or at France. We are told that Herr Hitler has a plan for invading the British Isles. This has often been thought of before. When Napoleon lay at Boulogne for a year with his flat-bottomed boats and his Grand Army, he was told by someone 'There are bitter weeds in England.' There are certainly a great many more of them since the British Expeditionary Force returned.

The whole question of home defence against invasion is, of course, powerfully affected by the fact that we have for the time being in this island incomparably more powerful military forces than we have ever had at any moment in this war or the last. But this will not continue. We shall not be content with a defensive war. We have our duty to our Ally. We have to reconstitute and build up the British Expeditionary Force once again, under its gallant Commander-in-Chief, Lord Gort. All this is in train; but in the interval we must put our defences in this island into such a high state of organization that the fewest possible numbers will be required to give effective security and that the largest possible potential of offensive effort may be realized. On this we are now engaged. It will be very convenient, if it be the desire of the House, to enter upon this subject in a secret Session. Not that the Government would necessarily be able to reveal in very great detail military secrets, but we like to have our discussions free, without the restraint imposed by the fact that they will be read the next day by the enemy; and the Government would benefit by views freely expressed in all parts of the House by Members with their knowledge of so many different parts of the country. I understand that some request is to be made upon this subject; which will be readily acceded to by His Majesty's Government.

We have found it necessary to take measures of increasing stringency, not only against enemy aliens and suspicious characters of other nationalities, but also against British subjects who may become a danger or a nuisance should the war be transported to the United Kingdom. I know there are a great many people affected by the orders which we have made who are the passionate enemies of Nazi Germany. I am very sorry for them, but we cannot, at the present time and under the present stress, draw all the distinctions which we should like to do. If parachute landings were attempted and fierce fighting attendant upon them followed, these unfortunate people would be far better out of the way, for their own sakes as well as for ours. There is, however, another class, for which I feel not the slightest sympathy. Parliament has given us the powers to put down Fifth Column activities with a strong hand, and we shall use those powers, subject to the supervision and correction of the House, without the slightest hesitation until we are satisfied, and more than satisfied, that this malignancy in our midst has been effectively stamped out.

Turning once again, and this time more generally, to the question of invasion, I would observe that there has never been a period in all these long centuries of which we boast when an absolute guarantee against invasion, still less against serious raids, could have been given to our people. In the days of Napoleon the same wind which would have carried his transports across the Channel might have driven away the blockading fleet. There was always the chance, and it is that chance which has excited and befooled the imaginations of many Continental tyrants. Many are the tales that are told. We are assured that novel methods will be adopted, and when we see the originality of malice, the ingenuity of aggression, which our enemy displays, we may certainly prepare ourselves for every kind of novel strategem and every kind of brutal and treacherous manœuvre. I think that no idea is so outlandish that it should not be considered and viewed with a searching, but at the same time, I hope, with a steady eye. We must never forget the solid assurances of sea-power and those which belong to air power if it can be locally exercised.

I have, myself, full confidence that if all do their duty, if nothing is neglected, and if the best arrangements are made, as they are being made, we shall prove ourselves once again able to

1 The young politician, 1904.

"WORDS, WORDS, WORDS."

2 'Mr Winston Churchill's volubility has been the subject of considerable Parliamentary comment. On Tuesday evening he made four speeches in one hour.' Cartoon from the *Manchester Dispatch*, 4 August 1904.

POLITICAL COUNTERBLASTS.

FIRST INSTRUMENTALIST : "What do you want here? I haven't finished my turn yet !"
SECOND INSTRUMENTALIST : "You get out ! Your turn's over. This is where I come in."

3 Haranguing the hustings, December 1909. Cartoon from the *Manchester Evening Chronicle*, on Lord Curzon's visit to Oldham.

4 The Navy's task, 1911. Churchill and Lord Fisher arriving at HMS *Centurion*.

5 'Let us go forward together.' Budget Day, 1929.

6 'The locust years'. Churchill in his study
at Chartwell, 1936.

7 (OPPOSITE, ABOVE) Churchill addressing sailors
from HMS *Hardy* and *Eclipse*, in Horseguards Parade,
London, 19 April 1940.

8 (OPPOSITE, BELOW) After Dunkirk. Reviewing coastal
defences, 31 July 1940.

9 (OPPOSITE, ABOVE) The Battle of Britain. Churchill and
Admiral Ramsey, 28 August 1940.
10 (OPPOSITE, BELOW) 'Are we downhearted?' Inspecting
bomb damage, 10 September 1940.

11 Broadcasting to a world at war, 1941.

12 Churchill with King George VI and Queen Elizabeth
at Buckingham Palace, September 1940.

13 'The stony path we have to tread.'
The House of Commons bombed,
10 May 1941.

14 (ABOVE) Divine Service on board USS *Augusta* in Placentia Bay, Newfoundland, 9 August 1941. Churchill and Roosevelt's first wartime meeting.

15 (LEFT) 'The greatest champion of freedom'. Winston Churchill and his daughter Sarah attend the Roosevelt Memorial Service in London, April 1945.

16 (OPPOSITE, ABOVE) 'Advance Britannia.' Churchill broadcasting to the nation on 8 May 1945, the day before the German forces surrendered.

17 (OPPOSITE, BELOW) Churchill and the Royal Family on the balcony at Buckingham Palace, 9 May 1945.

18 (OPPOSITE) With the jubilant crowds
in Whitehall, 14 May 1945.

19 Final review of the war.
Eden, Churchill, Attlee and Morrison,
15 August 1945.

20 'The iron curtain'. The speech at Westminster College, Fulton, Missouri, 5 March 1946.

21 Tribute to King George VI. Churchill returns from the Privy Council meeting, 4 February 1952.

22 Addressing the Party. Churchill at
the Conservative Party Conference,
October 1953.

23 'This superb honour'. On his eightieth birthday
Churchill replies to the address of Clement Attlee,
the Leader of the Opposition, on the presentation of
Graham Sutherland's portrait. 30 November 1954.

defend our island home, to ride out the storm of war, and to outlive the menace of tyranny, if necessary for years, if necessary alone. At any rate, that is what we are going to try to do. That is the resolve of His Majesty's Government – every man of them. That is the will of Parliament and the nation. The British Empire and the French Republic, linked together in their cause and in their need, will defend to the death their native soil, aiding each other like good comrades to the utmost of their strength. Even though large tracts of Europe and many old and famous States have fallen or may fall into the grip of the Gestapo and all the odious apparatus of Nazi rule, we shall not flag or fail. We shall go on to the end, we shall fight in France, we shall fight on the seas and oceans, we shall fight with growing confidence and growing strength in the air, we shall defend our island, whatever the cost may be, we shall fight on the beaches, we shall fight on the landing grounds, we shall fight in the fields and in the streets, we shall fight in the hills; we shall never surrender, and even if, which I do not for a moment believe, this island or a large part of it were subjugated and starving, then our Empire beyond the seas, armed and guarded by the British Fleet, would carry on the struggle, until in God's good time, the new world, with all its power and might, steps forth to the rescue and the liberation of the old.

16

Alone

'Their Finest Hour'

House of Commons, 18 June 1940

DESPITE ALL CHURCHILL'S EFFORTS, the crumbling French resistance could not be maintained much longer. On 10 June, the government left Paris; two last-minute visits by Churchill were to no avail; on 16 June Marshal Petain formed a new government; and on the next day France sued for peace. As the Prime Minister correctly predicted in this famous speech, the Battle of France was over, and the Battle of Britain was about to begin.

This great oration was delivered partly to report these recent and tumultuous events, and partly to reassure domestic and international opinion of the Government's resolve to fight on alone. As a parliamentary performance, it was generally reckoned inferior to his speech on Dunkirk, but the peroration was widely – and rightly – regarded as magnificent.

Four hours later, the same speech was broadcast, and this was the version heard and remembered by several million listeners. Churchill had hoped that the speech might be transmitted live from the Commons, so as to save him valuable time and effort; but there was opposition to the proposal, and so he did not pursue the idea. Again, it was not an outstanding declamatory performance. But of all Churchill's wartime speeches, it remains perhaps the best remembered. 'Rhetoric', he later wrote, 'was no guarantee of survival.' But in the aftermath of the fall of France, no other guarantee was available.

House of Commons, 18 June 1940

I SPOKE THE OTHER DAY of the colossal military disaster which occurred when the French High Command failed to withdraw the Northern Armies from Belgium at the moment when they knew that the French front was decisively broken at Sedan and on the Meuse. This delay entailed the loss of fifteen or sixteen French divisions and threw out of action for the critical period the whole of the British Expeditionary Force. Our Army and 120,000 French troops were indeed rescued by the British Navy from Dunkirk but only with the loss of their cannon, vehicles and modern equipment. This loss inevitably took some weeks to repair, and in the first two of those weeks the battle in France has been lost. When we consider the heroic resistance made by the French Army against heavy odds in this battle, the enormous losses inflicted upon the enemy and the evident exhaustion of the enemy, it may well be thought that these twenty-five divisions of the best-trained and best-equipped troops might have turned the scale. However, General Weygand had to fight without them. Only three British divisions or their equivalent were able to stand in the line with their French comrades. They had suffered severely, but they had fought well. We sent every man we could to France as fast as we could re-equip and transport their formations.

I am not reciting these facts for the purpose of recrimination. That I judge to be utterly futile and even harmful. We cannot afford it. I recite them in order to explain why it was we did not have, as we could have had, between twelve and fourteen British divisions fighting in the line in this great battle instead of only three. Now I put all this aside. I put it on the shelf, from which the historians, when they have time, will select their documents to tell their stories. We have to think of the future and not of the past. This also applies in a small way to our own affairs at home. There are many who would hold an inquest in the House of

Commons on the conduct of the Governments – and of Parliaments, for they are in it, too – during the years which led up to this catastrophe. They seek to indict those who were responsible for the guidance of our affairs. This also would be a foolish and pernicious process. There are too many in it. Let each man search his conscience and search his speeches. I frequently search mine.

Of this I am quite sure, that if we open a quarrel between the past and the present, we shall find that we have lost the future. Therefore, I cannot accept the drawing of any distinctions between Members of the present Government. It was formed at a moment of crisis in order to unite all the parties and all sections of opinion. It has received the almost unanimous support of both Houses of Parliament. Its Members are going to stand together, and, subject to the authority of the House of Commons, we are going to govern the country and fight the war. It is absolutely necessary at a time like this that every Minister who tries each day to do his duty shall be respected; and their subordinates must know that their chiefs are not threatened men, men who are here today and gone tomorrow, but that their directions must be punctually and faithfully obeyed. Without this concentrated power we cannot face what lies before us. I should not think it would be very advantageous for the House to prolong this Debate this afternoon under conditions of public stress. Many facts are not clear that will be clear in a short time. We are to have a Secret Session on Thursday, and I should think that would be a better opportunity for the many earnest expressions of opinion which Members will desire to make and for the House to discuss vital matters without having everything read the next morning by our dangerous foes.

The disastrous military events which have happened during the past fortnight have not come to me with any sense of surprise. Indeed, I indicated a fortnight ago as clearly as I could to the House that the worst possibilities were open; and I made it perfectly clear then that whatever happened in France would make no difference to the resolve of Britain and the British Empire to fight on, 'if necessary for years, if necessary alone.'

During the last few days we have successfully brought off the great majority of the troops we had on the lines of communication in France; and seven-eighths of the troops we have sent to France since the beginning of the war – that is to say, about 350,000 out of 400,000 men – are safely back in this country. Others are still fighting with the French, and fighting with considerable success in their local encounters against the enemy. We have also brought back a great mass of stores, rifles and munitions of all kinds which had been accumulated in France during the last nine months.

We have, therefore, in this island today a very large and powerful military force. This force comprises all our best-trained and our finest troops, including scores of thousands of those who have already measured their quality against the Germans and found themselves at no disadvantage. We have under arms at the present time in this island over a million and a quarter men. Behind these we have the Local Defence Volunteers, numbering half a million, only a portion of whom, however, are yet armed with rifles or other firearms. We have incorporated into our Defence Forces every man for whom we have a weapon. We expect very large additions to our weapons in the near future, and in preparation for this we intend forthwith to call up, drill and train further large numbers. Those who are not called up, or else are employed upon the vast business of munitions production in all its branches – and their ramifications are innumerable – will serve their country best by remaining at their ordinary work until they receive their summons. We have also over here Dominions armies. The Canadians had actually landed in France, but have now been safely withdrawn, much disappointed, but in perfect order, with all their artillery and equipment. And these very high-class forces from the Dominions will now take part in the defence of the Mother Country.

Lest the account which I have given of these large forces should raise the question: Why did they not take part in the great battle in France? I must make it clear that, apart from the divisions training and organizing at home, only twelve divisions were equipped to fight upon a scale which justified their being sent abroad. And this was fully up to the number which the French had been led to expect would be available in France at the ninth month of the war. The rest of our forces at home have a fighting value for home defence which will, of course, steadily increase every week that passes. Thus, the invasion of Great Britain would at this time require the transportation across the sea of hostile armies on a very large scale, and after they had been so transported they would have to be continually maintained with all the masses of munitions and supplies which are required for continuous battle – as continuous battle it will surely be.

Here is where we come to the Navy – and after all, we have a Navy. Some people seem to forget that we have a Navy. We must remind them. For the last thirty years I have been concerned in discussions about the possibilities of overseas invasion, and I took the responsibility on behalf of the Admiralty, at the beginning of the last war, of allowing all regular troops to be sent out of the country. That was a very serious step to take, because our Territorials had only just been called up and were quite untrained. Therefore, this island was for several months practically denuded of fighting troops. The Admiralty had confidence at that time in their ability to prevent a mass invasion even though at that time the Germans had a magnificent battle fleet in the proportion of ten to sixteen, even though they were capable of fighting a general engagement every day and any day, whereas now they have only a couple of heavy ships worth speaking of – the *Scharnhorst* and the *Gneisenau*. We are also told that the Italian Navy is to come out and gain sea superiority in these waters. If they seriously intend it, I shall only say that we shall be delighted to offer Signor Mussolini a free and safeguarded passage through the Straits of Gibraltar in order that he may play the part to which he aspires. There is a general curiosity in the British Fleet to find out whether the Italians are up to the level they were at in the last war or whether they have fallen off at all.

Therefore, it seems to me that as far as seaborne invasion on a great scale is concerned, we are far more capable of meeting it today than we were at many periods in the last war and during the early months of this war, before our other troops were trained, and while the BEF had proceeded abroad. Now, the Navy have never pretended to be able to prevent raids by bodies of 5,000 or 10,000 men flung suddenly across and thrown ashore at several points on the coast some dark night or foggy morning. The efficacy of sea-power, especially under modern conditions, depends upon the invading force being of large size. It has to be of large size, in view of our military strength, to be of any use. If it is of large size, then the Navy have something they can find and meet and, as it were, bite on. Now we must remember that even five divisions, however lightly equipped, would require 200 to 250 ships, and with modern air reconnaissance and photography it would not be easy to collect such an armada, marshal it and conduct it across the sea without any powerful naval forces to escort it; and there would be very great possibilities, to put it mildly, that this armada would be intercepted long before it reached the coast, and all the men drowned in the sea or, at the worst, blown to pieces with their equipment while they were trying to land. We also have a great system of minefields, recently strongly reinforced, through which we alone know the channels. If the enemy tries to sweep passages through these minefields, it will be the task of the Navy to destroy the minesweepers and any other forces employed to protect them. There should be no difficulty in this, owing to our great superiority at sea.

Those are the regular, well-tested, well-proved arguments on which we have relied during many years in peace and war. But the question is whether there are any new methods by which those solid assurances can be circumvented. Odd as it may seem, some attention has been given to this by the Admiralty, whose prime duty and responsibility it is to destroy any large seaborne expedition before it reaches, or at the moment when it reaches these shores. It would not be a good thing for me to go into details of this. It might suggest ideas to other people which they have not thought of, and they would not be likely to give us any of their ideas in exchange. All I will say is that untiring vigilance and mind-searching must be devoted to the subject, because the enemy is crafty and cunning and full of novel treacheries and stratagems. The House may be assured that the utmost ingenuity is being displayed and imagination is being evoked from large numbers of competent officers, well trained in tactics and thoroughly up to date, to measure and counterwork novel possibilities. Untiring vigilance and untiring searching of the mind is being, and must be, devoted to the subject, because, remember, the enemy is crafty and there is no dirty trick he will not do.

Some people will ask why, then, was it that the British Navy was not able to prevent the movement of a large army from Germany into Norway across the Skaggerak? But the conditions in the Channel and in the North Sea are in no way like those which prevail in the Skaggerak. In the Skaggerak, because of the distance, we could give no air support to our surface ships, and consequently, lying as we did close to the enemy's main air power, we were compelled to use only our submarines. We could not enforce the decisive blockade or interruption which is possible from surface vessels. Our submarines took a heavy toll but could not, by themselves, prevent the invasion of Norway. In the Channel and in the North Sea, on the other hand, our superior naval surface forces, aided by our submarines, will operate with close and effective air assistance.

This brings me, naturally, to the great question of invasion from the air, and of the impending struggle between the British and German Air Forces. It seems quite clear that no invasion on a scale beyond the capacity of our land forces to crush speedily is likely to take place from the air until our Air Force has been definitely overpowered. In the meantime, there may be raids by parachute troops and attempted descents of airborne soldiers. We should be able to give those gentry a warm reception, both in the air and on the ground, if they reach it in any condition to continue the dispute. But the great question is: Can we break Hitler's air weapon? Now, of course, it is a very great pity that we have not got an Air Force at least equal to that of the most powerful enemy within striking distance of these shores. But we have a very powerful Air Force which has proved itself far superior in quality, both in men and in many types of machine, to what we have met so far in the numerous and fierce air battles which have been fought with the Germans. In France, where we were at a considerable disadvantage and lost many machines on the ground when they were standing round the aerodromes, we were accustomed to inflict in the air losses of as much as two to two-and-a-half to one. In the fighting over Dunkirk, which was a sort of no-man's land, we undoubtedly beat the German Air Force, and gained the mastery of the local air, inflicting here a loss of three or four to one day after day. Anyone who looks at the photographs which were published a week or so ago of the re-embarkation, showing the masses of troops assembled on the beach and forming an ideal target for hours at a time, must realize that this re-embarkation would not have been possible unless the enemy had resigned all hope of recovering air superiority at that time and at that place.

In the defence of this island the advantages to the defenders will be much greater than they were in the fighting around Dunkirk. We hope to improve on the rate of three or four to one which was realized at Dunkirk; and in addition all our injured machines and their crews which get down safe – and, surprisingly, a very great many injured machines and men do get down safely in modern air fighting – all of these will fall, in an attack upon these islands, on friendly soil and live to fight another day; whereas all the injured enemy machines and their complements will be total losses as far as the war is concerned.

During the great battle in France, we gave very powerful and continuous aid to the French Army, both by fighters and bombers; but in spite of every kind of pressure we never would allow the entire metropolitan fighter strength of the Air Force to be consumed. This decision was painful, but it was also right, because the fortunes of the battle in France could not have been decisively affected even if we had thrown in our entire fighter force. That battle was lost by the unfortunate strategical opening, by the extraordinary and unforeseen power of the armoured columns and by the great preponderance of the German Army in numbers. Our fighter Air Force might easily have been exhausted as a mere accident in that great struggle, and then we should have found ourselves at the present time in a very serious plight. But as it is, I am happy to inform the House that our fighter strength is stronger at the present time relatively to the Germans, who have suffered terrible losses, than it has ever been; and consequently we believe ourselves possessed of the capacity to continue the war in the air under better conditions than we have ever experienced before. I look forward confidently to the exploits of our fighter pilots – these splendid men, this brilliant youth – who will have the glory of saving their native land, their island home, and all they love, from the most deadly of all attacks.

There remains, of course, the danger of bombing attacks, which will certainly be made very soon upon us by the bomber forces of the enemy. It is true that the German bomber force is superior in numbers to ours; but we have a very large bomber force also, which we shall use to strike at military targets in Germany without intermission. I do not at all underrate the severity of the ordeal which lies before us; but I believe our countrymen will show themselves capable of standing up to it, like the brave men of Barcelona, and will be able to stand up to it, and carry on in spite of it, at least as well as any other people in the world. Much will depend upon this; every man and every woman will have the chance to show the finest qualities of their race, and render the highest service to their cause. For all of us, at this time, whatever our sphere, our station, our occupation or our duties, it will be a help to remember the famous lines:

> *He nothing common did or mean,*
> *Upon that memorable scene.*

I have thought it right upon this occasion to give the House and the country some indication of the solid, practical grounds upon which we base our inflexible resolve to continue the war. There are a good many people who say, 'Never mind. Win or lose, sink or swim, better die than submit to tyranny – and such a tyranny.' And I do not dissociate myself from them. But I can assure them that our professional advisers of the three Services unitedly advise that we should carry on the war, and that there are good and reasonable hopes of final victory. We have fully informed and consulted all the self-governing Dominions, these great communities far beyond the oceans who have been built up on our laws and on our civilization, and who are absolutely free to choose their course, but are absolutely devoted to the ancient Motherland, and who feel themselves inspired by the same emotions which lead me to stake our all upon duty and honour. We have fully consulted them, and I have received from their Prime Ministers, Mr Mackenzie King of Canada, Mr Menzies of Australia, Mr Fraser of New Zealand, and General Smuts of South Africa – that wonderful man, with his immense profound mind, and his eye watching from a distance the whole panorama of European affairs – I have received from all these eminent men, who all have Governments behind them elected on wide franchises, who are all there because they represent the will of their people, messages couched in the most moving terms in which they endorse our decision to fight on, and declare themselves ready to share our fortunes and to persevere to the end. That is what we are going to do.

We may now ask ourselves: In what way has our position worsened since the beginning of the war? It has worsened by the fact that the Germans have conquered a large part of the coastline of Western Europe, and many small countries have been overrun by them. This aggravates the possibilities of air attack and adds to our naval preoccupations. It in no way diminishes, but on the contrary definitely increases, the power of our long-distance blockade. Similarly, the entrance of Italy into the war increases the power of our long-distance blockade. We have stopped the worst leak by that. We do not know whether military resistance will come to an end in France or not, but should it do so, then of course, the Germans will be able to concentrate their forces, both military and industrial, upon us. But for the reasons I have given to the House these will not be found so easy to apply. If invasion has become more imminent, as no doubt it has, we, being relieved from the task of maintaining a large army in France, have far larger and more efficient forces to meet it.

If Hitler can bring under his despotic control the industries of the countries he has conquered, this will add greatly to his already vast armament output. On the other hand, this will not happen immediately, and we are now assured of immense, continuous and increasing support in supplies and munitions of all kinds from the United States; and especially of airplanes and pilots from the Dominions and across the oceans, coming from regions which are beyond the reach of enemy bombers.

I do not see how any of these factors can operate to our detriment on balance before the winter comes; and the winter will impose a strain upon the Nazi regime, with almost all Europe writhing and starving under its cruel heel, which, for all their ruthlessness, will run them very hard. We must not forget that from the moment when we declared war on the 3 September it was always possible for Germany to turn all her air force upon this country, together with any other devices of invasion she might conceive, and that France could have done little or nothing to prevent her doing so. We have, therefore, lived under this danger, in principle and in a slightly modified form, during all these months. In the meanwhile, however, we have enormously improved our methods of defence, and we have learned, what we had no right to assume at the beginning, namely, that the individual aircraft and the individual British pilot have a sure and definite superiority. Therefore, in casting up this dread balance sheet and contemplating our dangers with a disillusioned eye, I see great reason for intense vigilance and exertion, but none whatever for panic or despair.

During the first four years of the last war the Allies experienced nothing but disaster and disappointment. That was our constant fear: one blow after another, terrible losses, frightful dangers. Everything miscarried. And yet at the end of those four years the morale of the Allies was higher than that of the Germans, who had moved from one aggressive triumph to another, and who stood everywhere triumphant invaders of the lands into which they had broken. During that war we repeatedly asked ourselves the question: How are we going to win? And no one was able ever to answer it with much precision, until at the end, quite suddenly, quite unexpectedly, our terrible foe collapsed before us, and we were so glutted with victory that in our folly we threw it away.

We do not yet know what will happen in France or whether the French resistance will be prolonged, both in France and in the French Empire overseas. The French Government will be throwing away great opportunities and casting adrift their future if they do not continue the war in accordance with their Treaty obligations, from which we have not felt able to release them. The House will have read the historic declaration in which, at the desire of many Frenchmen – and of our own hearts – we have proclaimed our willingness at the darkest hour in French history to conclude a union of common citizenship in this struggle. However matters may go in France or with the French Government, or other French Governments, we in this island and in the British Empire will never lose our sense of comradeship with the French people. If we are now called upon to endure what they have been suffering, we shall emulate their courage, and if final victory rewards our toils they shall share the gains, aye, and freedom shall be restored to all. We abate nothing of our just demands; not one jot or tittle do we recede. Czechs, Poles, Norwegians, Dutch, Belgians have joined their causes to our own. All these shall be restored.

What General Weygand called the Battle of France is over. I expect that the Battle of Britain is about to begin. Upon this battle depends the survival of Christian civilization. Upon it depends our own British life, and the long continuity of our institutions and our Empire. The whole fury and might of the enemy must very soon be turned on us. Hitler knows that he will have to break us in this island or lose the war. If we can stand up to him, all Europe may be free and the life of the world may move forward into broad, sunlit uplands. But if we fail, then the whole world, including the United States, including all that we have known and cared for, will sink into the abyss of a new Dark Age made more sinister, and perhaps more protracted, by the lights of perverted science. Let us therefore brace ourselves to our duties and so bear ourselves that, if the British Empire and its Commonwealth last for a thousand years, men will still say, 'This was their finest hour.'

17

The Battle of Britain
'The Few'

House of Commons, 20 August 1940

ONCE FRANCE HAD BEEN DEFEATED, the threat of a German attack on Britain was the Government's prime concern during the late summer and early autumn of 1940. In the skies, the Battle of Britain raged throughout most of August and September. Churchill himself was an occasional visitor to the Operations Room of No. 11 Fighter Command at Uxbridge, and it was on his way back from one such trip that he evolved the phrase: 'Never in the field of human conflict has so much been owed, by so many, to so few.'

It reappeared, slightly more polished, in this broad and panoramic survey of the 'dark, wide field' of war, which lasted almost one hour. He spoke of Britain's military and naval preparedness, paid his Periclean tribute to the fighter pilots, looked forward to the campaigns of 1941 and 1942, described the Destroyers for Bases deal which had recently been concluded with the United States, and ended with a majestic peroration about the Mississippi. On the way back to 10 Downing Street, he sang 'Ole Man River' in the car.

Harold Nicolson, while appreciating the reference to 'the few,' thought it merely 'a moderate and well-balanced speech'. Three weeks later, however, Asquith's daughter wrote to Churchill as follows: 'Nothing so simple, so majestic and so true has been said in so great a moment of human history. You have beaten your old enemies, "the Classics", into a cocked hat!' Indeed he had.

179

House of Commons, 20 August 1940

ALMOST A YEAR HAS PASSED since the war began, and it is natural for us, I think, to pause on our journey at this milestone and survey the dark, wide field. It is also useful to compare the first year of this second war against German aggression with its forerunner a quarter of a century ago. Although this war is in fact only a continuation of the last, very great differences in its character are apparent. In the last war millions of men fought by hurling enormous masses of steel at one another. 'Men and shells' was the cry, and prodigious slaughter was the consequence. In this war nothing of this kind has yet appeared. It is a conflict of strategy, of organization, of technical apparatus, of science, mechanics and morale. The British casualties in the first twelve months of the Great War amounted to 365,000. In this war, I am thankful to say, British killed, wounded, prisoners and missing, including civilians, do not exceed 92,000, and of these a large proportion are alive as prisoners of war. Looking more widely around, one may say that throughout all Europe for one man killed or wounded in the first year perhaps five were killed or wounded in 1914–15.

The slaughter is only a small fraction, but the consequences to the belligerents have been even more deadly. We have seen great countries with powerful armies dashed out of coherent existence in a few weeks. We have seen the French Republic and the renowned French Army beaten into complete and total submission with less than the casualties which they suffered in any one of half a dozen of the battles of 1914–18. The entire body – it might also seem at times the soul – of France has succumbed to physical effects incomparably less terrible than those which were sustained with fortitude and undaunted will power twenty-five years ago. Although up to the present the loss of life has been mercifully diminished, the decisions reached in the course of the struggle are even more profound upon the fate of nations than anything that has ever happened since barbaric times. Moves are made upon the scientific and strategic boards, advantages are gained by mechanical means, as a result of which scores of millions of men become incapable of further resistance, or judge themselves incapable of further resistance, and a fearful game of chess proceeds from check to mate by which the unhappy players seem to be inexorably bound.

There is another more obvious difference from 1914. The whole of the warring nations are engaged, not only soldiers, but the entire population, men, women and children. The fronts are everywhere. The trenches are dug in the towns and streets. Every village is fortified. Every road is barred. The front line runs through the factories. The workmen are soldiers with different weapons but the same courage. These are great and distinctive changes from what many of us saw in the struggle of a quarter of a century ago. There seems to be every reason to believe that this new kind of war is well suited to the genius and the resources of the British nation and the British Empire and that, once we get properly equipped and properly started, a war of this kind will be more favourable to us than the sombre mass slaughters of the Somme and Passchendaele. If it is a case of the whole nation fighting and suffering together, that ought to suit us, because we are the most united of all the nations, because we entered the war upon the national will and with our eyes open, and because we have been nurtured in freedom and individual responsibility and are the products, not of totalitarian uniformity but of tolerance and variety. If all these qualities are turned, as they are being turned, to the arts of war, we may be able to show the enemy quite a lot of things that they have not thought of yet. Since the Germans drove the Jews out and lowered their technical standards, our science is definitely ahead of theirs. Our geographical position, the command of the sea, and the friendship of the United States enable us to draw resources from the whole world and to manufacture weapons of war of every kind, but especially of the superfine kinds, on a scale hitherto practised only by Nazi Germany.

Hitler is now sprawled over Europe. Our offensive springs are being slowly compressed, and we must resolutely and methodically prepare ourselves for the campaigns of 1941 and 1942. Two or three years are not a long time, even in our short, precarious lives. They are nothing in the history of the nation, and when we are doing the finest thing in the world, and have the honour to be the sole champion of the liberties of all Europe, we must not grudge these years or weary as we toil and struggle through them. It does not follow that energies in future years will be exclusively confined to defending ourselves and our possessions. Many opportunities may lie open to amphibious power, and we must be ready to take advantage of them. One of the ways to bring this war to a speedy end is to convince the enemy, not by words, but by deeds, that we have both the will and the means, not only to go on indefinitely but to strike heavy and unexpected blows. The road to victory may not be so long as we expect. But we have no right to count upon this. Be it long or short, rough or smooth, we mean to reach our journey's end.

It is our intention to maintain and enforce a strict blockade not only of Germany but of Italy, France, and all the other countries that have fallen into the German power. I read in the papers that Herr Hitler has also proclaimed a strict blockade of the British Islands. No one can complain of that. I remember the Kaiser doing it in the last war. What indeed would be a matter of general complaint would be if we were to prolong the agony of all Europe by allowing food to come in to nourish the Nazis and aid their war effort, or to allow food to go in to the subjugated peoples, which certainly would be pillaged off them by their Nazi conquerors.

There have been many proposals, founded on the highest motives, that food should be allowed to pass the blockade for the relief of these populations. I regret that we must refuse these requests. The Nazis declare that they have created a new unified economy in Europe. They have repeatedly stated that they possess ample reserves of food and that they can feed their captive peoples. In a German broadcast of 27 June it was said that while Mr Hoover's plan for relieving France, Belgium and

Holland deserved commendation, the German forces had already taken the necessary steps. We know that in Norway when the German troops went in, there were food supplies to last for a year. We know that Poland though not a rich country, usually produces sufficient food for her people. Moreover, the other countries which Herr Hitler has invaded all held considerable stocks when the Germans entered and are themselves, in many cases, very substantial food producers. If all this food is not available now, it can only be because it has been removed to feed the people of Germany and to give them increased rations – for a change – during the last few months. At this season of the year and for some months to come, there is the least chance of scarcity as the harvest has just been gathered in. The only agencies which can create famine in any part of Europe now and during the coming winter, will be German exactions or German failure to distribute the supplies which they command.

There is another aspect. Many of the most valuable foods are essential to the manufacture of vital war material. Fats are used to make explosives. Potatoes make the alcohol for motor spirit. The plastic materials now so largely used in the construction of aircraft are made of milk. If the Germans use these commodities to help them to bomb our women and children, rather than to feed the populations who produce them, we may be sure that imported foods would go the same way, directly or indirectly, or be employed to relieve the enemy of the responsibilities he has so wantonly assumed. Let Hitler bear his responsibilities to the full and let the peoples of Europe who groan beneath his yoke aid in every way the coming of the day when that yoke will be broken. Meanwhile, we can and we will arrange in advance for the speedy entry of food into any part of the enslaved area, when this part has been wholly cleared of German forces, and has genuinely regained its freedom. We shall do our best to encourage the building up of reserves of food all over the world, so that there will always be held up before the eyes of the peoples of Europe, including – I say deliberately – the German and Austrian peoples, the certainty that the shattering of the Nazi power will bring to them all immediate food, freedom and peace.

Rather more than a quarter of a year has passed since the new Government came into power in this country. What a cataract of disaster has poured out upon us since then. The trustful Dutch overwhelmed; their beloved and respected Sovereign driven into exile; the peaceful city of Rotterdam the scene of a massacre as hideous and brutal as anything in the Thirty Years' War. Belgium invaded and beaten down; our own fine Expeditionary Force, which King Leopold called to his rescue, cut off and almost captured, escaping as it seemed only by a miracle and with the loss of all its equipment; our Ally, France, out; Italy in against us; all France in the power of the enemy, all its arsenals and vast masses of military material converted or convertible to the enemy's use; a puppet Government set up at Vichy which may at any moment be forced to become our foe; the whole Western seaboard of Europe from the North Cape to the Spanish frontier in German hands; all the ports, all the airfields on this immense front, employed against us as potential springboards of invasion. Moreover, the German air power, numerically so far outstripping ours, has been brought so close to our Island that what we used to dread greatly has come to pass and the hostile bombers not only reach our shores in a few minutes and from many directions, but can be escorted by their fighting aircraft. Why, Sir, if we had been confronted at the beginning of May with such a prospect, it would have seemed incredible that at the end of a period of horror and disaster, or at this point in a period of horror and disaster, we should stand erect, sure of ourselves, masters of our fate and with the conviction of final victory burning unquenchable in our hearts. Few would have believed we could survive; none would have believed that we should today not only feel stronger but should actually be stronger than we have ever been before.

Let us see what has happened on the other side of the scales. The British nation and the British Empire finding themselves alone, stood undismayed against disaster. No one flinched or wavered; nay, some who formerly thought of peace, now think only of war. Our people are united and resolved, as they have never been before. Death and ruin have become small things compared with the shame of defeat or failure in duty. We cannot tell what lies ahead. It may be that even greater ordeals lie before us. We shall face whatever is coming to us. We are sure of ourselves and of our cause and that is the supreme fact which has emerged in these months of trial.

Meanwhile, we have not only fortified our hearts but our Island. We have rearmed and rebuilt our armies in a degree which would have been deemed impossible a few months ago. We have ferried across the Atlantic, in the month of July, thanks to our friends over there, an immense mass of munitions of all kinds, cannon, rifles, machine-guns, cartridges and shell, all safely landed without the loss of a gun or a round. The output of our own factories, working as they have never worked before, has poured forth to the troops. The whole British Army is at home. More than 2,000,000 determined men have rifles and bayonets in their hands tonight and three-quarters of them are in regular military formations. We have never had armies like this in our Island in time of war. The whole Island bristles against invaders, from the sea or from the air. As I explained to the House in the middle of June, the stronger our Army at home, the larger must the invading expedition be, and the larger the invading expedition, the less difficult will be the task of the Navy in detecting its assembly and in intercepting and destroying it on passage; and the greater also would be the difficulty of feeding and supplying the invaders if ever they landed, in the teeth of continuous naval and air attack on their communications. All this is classical and venerable doctrine. As in Nelson's day, the maxim holds, 'Our first line of defence is the enemy's ports.' Now air reconnaissance and photography have brought to an old principle a new and potent aid.

Our Navy is far stronger than it was at the beginning of the war. The great flow of new construction set on foot at the outbreak is now beginning to come in. We hope our friends across the ocean will send us a timely reinforcement to bridge the gap between the peace flotillas of 1939 and the war flotillas of 1941. There is no difficulty in sending such aid. The seas and oceans are open. The U-boats are contained. The magnetic mine is, up to the present time, effectively mastered. The merchant tonnage under the British flag, after a year of unlimited U-boat war, after eight months of intensive mining attack, is larger than when we began. We have in addition, under our control at least 4,000,000 tons of shipping from the captive countries which has taken refuge here or in the harbours of the Empire. Our stocks of food of all kinds are far more abundant than in the days of peace and a large and growing programme of food production is on foot.

Why do I say all this? Not assuredly to boast; not assuredly to give the slightest countenance to complacency. The dangers we face are still enormous, but so are our advantages and resources. I recount them because the people have a right to know that there are solid grounds for the confidence which we feel, and that we have good reason to believe ourselves capable, as I said in a very dark hour two months ago, of continuing the war 'if necessary alone, if necessary for years'. I say it also because the fact that the British Empire stands invincible, and that Nazidom is still being resisted, will kindle again the spark of hope in the breasts of hundreds of millions of down-trodden or despairing men and women throughout Europe, and far beyond its bounds, and that from these sparks there will presently come cleansing and devouring flame.

The great air battle which has been in progress over this Island for the last few weeks has recently attained a high intensity. It is too soon to attempt to assign limits either to its scale or to its duration. We must certainly expect that greater efforts will be made by the enemy than any he has so far put forth. Hostile air fields are still being developed in France and the Low Countries, and the movement of squadrons and material for attacking us is still proceeding. It is quite plain that Herr Hitler could not admit defeat in his air attack on Great Britain without sustaining most serious injury. If, after all his boastings and blood-curdling threats and lurid accounts trumpeted round the world of the damage he has inflicted, of the vast numbers of our Air Force he has shot down, so he says, with so little loss to himself; if after tales of the panic-stricken British crushed in their holes cursing the plutocratic Parliament which has led them to such a plight; if after all this his whole air onslaught were forced after a while tamely to peter out, the Führer's reputation for veracity of statement might be seriously impugned. We may be sure, therefore, that he will continue as long as he has the strength to do so, and as long as any preoccupations he may have in respect of the Russian Air Force allow him to do so.

On the other hand, the conditions and course of the fighting have so far been favourable to us. I told the House two months ago that whereas in France our fighter aircraft were wont to inflict a loss of two or three to one upon the Germans, and in the fighting at Dunkirk, which was a kind of no-man's-land, a loss of about three or four to one, we expected that in an attack on this Island we should achieve a larger ratio. This has certainly come true. It must also be remembered that all the enemy machines and pilots which are shot down over our Island, or over the seas which surround it, are either destroyed or captured; whereas a considerable proportion of our machines, and also of our pilots, are saved, and soon again in many cases come into action.

A vast and admirable system of salvage, directed by the Ministry of Aircraft Production, ensures the speediest return to the fighting line of damaged machines, and the most provident and speedy use of all the spare parts and material. At the same time the splendid, nay, astounding increase in the output and repair of British aircraft and engines which Lord Beaverbrook has achieved by a genius of organization and drive, which looks like magic, has given us overflowing reserves of every type of aircraft, and an ever-mounting stream of production both in quantity and quality. The enemy is, of course, far more numerous than we are. But our new production already, as I am advised, largely exceeds his, and the American production is only just beginning to flow in. It is a fact, as I see from my daily returns, that our bomber and fighter strength now, after all this fighting, are larger than they have ever been. We believe that we shall be able to continue the air struggle indefinitely and as long as the enemy pleases, and the longer it continues the more rapid will be our approach, first towards that parity, and then into that superiority in the air, upon which in a large measure the decision of the war depends.

The gratitude of every home in our Island, in our Empire, and indeed throughout the world, except in the abodes of the guilty, goes out to the British airmen who, undaunted by odds, unwearied in their constant challenge and mortal danger, are turning the tide of the world war by their prowess and by their devotion. Never in the field of human conflict was so much owed by so many to so few. All hearts go out to the fighter pilots, whose brilliant actions we see with our own eyes day after day; but we must never forget that all the time, night after night, month after month, our bomber squadrons travel far into Germany, find their targets in the darkness by the highest navigational skill, aim their attacks, often under the heaviest fire, often with serious loss, with deliberate careful discrimination, and inflict shattering blows upon the whole of the technical and war-making structure of the Nazi power. On no part of the Royal Air Force does the weight of the war fall more heavily than on the daylight bombers who will play an invaluable part in the case of invasion and whose unflinching zeal it has been necessary in the meanwhile on numerous occasions to restrain.

We are able to verify the results of bombing military targets in Germany, not only by reports which reach us through many sources, but also, of course, by photography. I have no hesitation in saying that this process of bombing the military industries and communications of Germany and the air bases and storage depots from which we are attacked, which process will continue upon an ever-increasing scale until the end of the war, and may in another year attain dimensions hitherto undreamed of, affords one at least of the most certain, if not the shortest of all the roads to victory. Even if the Nazi legions stood triumphant on the Black Sea, or indeed upon the Caspian, even if Hitler was at the gates of India, it would profit him nothing if at the same time the entire economic and scientific apparatus of German war power lay shattered and pulverized at home.

The fact that the invasion of this Island upon a large scale has become a far more difficult operation with every week that has passed since we saved our Army at Dunkirk, and our very great preponderance of sea-power enable us to turn our eyes and to turn our strength increasingly towards the Mediterranean and against that other enemy who, without the slightest provocation, coldly and deliberately, for greed and gain, stabbed France in the back in the moment of her agony, and is now marching against us in Africa. The defection of France has, of course, been deeply damaging to our position in what is called, somewhat oddly, the Middle East. In the defence of Somaliland, for instance, we had counted upon strong French forces attacking the Italians from Jibuti. We had counted also upon the use of the French naval and air bases in the Mediterranean, and particularly upon the North African shore. We had counted upon the French Fleet. Even though metropolitan France was temporarily overrun, there was no reason why the French Navy, substantial parts of the French Army, the French Air Force and the French Empire overseas should not have continued the struggle at our side.

Shielded by overwhelming sea-power, possessed of invaluable strategic bases and of ample funds, France might have remained one of the great combatants in the struggle. By so doing, France would have preserved the continuity of her life, and the French Empire might have advanced with the British Empire to the rescue of the independence and integrity of the French Motherland. In our own case, if we had been put in the terrible position of France, a contingency now happily impossible, although, of course, it would have been the duty of all war leaders to fight on here to the end, it would also have been their duty, as I indicated in my speech of 4 June, to provide as far as possible for the Naval security of Canada and our Dominions and to make sure they had the means to carry on the struggle from beyond the oceans. Most of the other countries that have been overrun by Germany for the time being have persevered valiantly and faithfully. The Czechs, the Poles, the Norwegians, the Dutch, the Belgians are still in the field, sword in hand, recognized by Great Britain and the United States as the sole representative authorities and lawful Governments of their respective States.

That France alone should lie prostrate at this moment, is the crime, not of a great and noble nation, but of what are called 'the men of Vichy'. We have profound sympathy with the French people. Our old comradeship with France is not dead. In General de Gaulle and his gallant band, that comradeship takes an effective form. These free Frenchmen have been condemned to death by Vichy, but the day will come, as surely as the sun will rise tomorrow, when their names will be held in honour, and their names will be graven in stone in the streets and villages of a France restored in a liberated Europe to its full freedom and its ancient fame. But this conviction which I feel of the future cannot affect the immediate problems which confront us in the Mediterranean and in Africa. It had been decided some time before the beginning of the war not to defend the Protectorate of Somaliland. That policy was changed in the early months of the war. When the French gave in, and when our small forces there, a few battalions, a few guns, were attacked by all the Italian troops, nearly two divisions, which had formerly faced the French at Jibuti, it was right to withdraw our detachments, virtually intact, for action elsewhere. Far larger operations no doubt impend in the Middle East theatre, and I shall certainly not attempt to discuss or prophesy, about their probable course. We have large armies and many means of reinforcing them. We have the complete sea command of the Eastern Mediterranean. We intend to do our best to give a good account of ourselves, and to discharge faithfully and resolutely all our obligations and duties in that quarter of the world. More than that I do not think the House would wish me to say at the present time.

A good many people have written to me to ask me to make on this occasion a fuller statement of our war aims, and of the kind of peace we wish to make after the war, than is contained in the very considerable declaration which was made early in the autumn. Since then we have made common cause with Norway, Holland and Belgium. We have recognized the Czech Government of Dr Benes, and we have told General de Gaulle that our success will carry with it the restoration of France. I do not think it would be wise at this moment, while the battle rages and the war is still perhaps only in its earlier stage, to embark upon elaborate speculations about the future shape which should be given to Europe or the new securities which must be arranged to spare mankind the miseries of a third World War. The ground is not new, it has been frequently traversed and explored, and many ideas are held about it in common by all good men, and all free men. But before we can undertake the task of rebuilding we have not only to be convinced ourselves, but we have to convince all other countries that the Nazi tyranny is going to be fully broken. The right to guide the course of world history is the noblest prize of victory. We are still toiling up the hill; we have not yet reached the crest-line of it; we cannot survey the landscape or even imagine what its condition will be when that longed-for morning comes. The task which lies before us immediately is at once more practical, more simple and more stern. I hope – indeed I pray – that we shall not be found unworthy of our victory if after toil and tribulation it is granted to us. For the rest, we have to gain the victory. That is our task.

There is, however, one direction in which we can see a little more clearly ahead. We have to think not only for ourselves but for the lasting security of the cause and principles for which we are fighting and of the long future of the British Commonwealth of Nations. Some months ago we came to the conclusion that the interests of the United States and of the British Empire both required that the United States should have facilities for the naval and air defence of the Western hemisphere against the attack of a Nazi power which might have acquired temporary but lengthy control of a large part of Western Europe and its formidable resources. We had therefore decided spontaneously, and without being asked or offered any inducement, to inform the Government of the United States that we would be glad to place such defence facilities at their disposal by leasing suitable sites in our Transatlantic possessions for their greater security against the unmeasured dangers of the future. The principle of association of interests for common purposes between Great Britain and the United States had developed even before the war. Various agreements had been reached about certain small islands in the Pacific Ocean which had become important as air fuelling points. In all this line of thought we found ourselves in very close harmony with the Government of Canada.

Presently we learned that anxiety was also felt in the United States about the air and naval defence of their Atlanltic seaboard, and President Roosevelt has recently made it clear that he would like to discuss with us, and with the Dominion of Canada and with Newfoundland, the development of American naval and air facilities in Newfoundland and the West Indies. There is, of course, no question of any transference of sovereignty – that has never been suggested – or of any action being taken, without the consent or against the wishes of the various Colonies concerned, but for our part, His Majesty's Government are entirely willing to accord defence facilities to the United States on a ninety-nine years leasehold basis, and we feel sure that our interests no less than theirs, and the interests of the Colonies themselves and of Canada and Newfoundland will be served thereby. These are important steps. Undoubtedly this process means that these two great organizations of the English-speaking democracies, the British Empire and the United States, will have to be somewhat mixed up together in some of their affairs for mutual and general advantage. For my own part, looking out upon the future, I do not view the process with any misgivings. I could not stop it if I wished; no one can stop it. Like the Mississippi, it just keeps rolling along. Let it roll. Let it roll on full flood, inexorable, irresistible, benignant, to broader lands and better days.

18

On the Death of Neville Chamberlain

'An English Worthy'

House of Commons, 12 November 1940

IN SEPTEMBER 1940 IT BECAME CLEAR that Neville Chamberlain – who had served Churchill loyally in the wartime Coalition as Lord President, and who had been responsible for the domestic side of the war – was dying of cancer. He resigned his post in Government, and also as Leader of the Conservative Party. Churchill was urged to accept the Party Leadership and, despite the opposition of his wife, did so in the following month. He continued to keep Chamberlain in close touch with the war, until he died in November.

The two men had disagreed violently and publicly before 1939, and Churchill always maintained that Chamberlain bore a large responsibility for the deficiencies in Britain's defences on the outbreak of war. However, he genuinely admired Chamberlain's courage and loyalty, and felt very keenly the lack of a senior figure from the Conservative Party who could control the domestic aspects of the war effort.

Nevertheless, his eulogy was remarkable for its breadth and generosity of vision, no less than for the splendour and eloquence of its language. There was not an unjust or an unkind word, nor the slightest attempt at dissimulation. As the King's Private Secretary remarked after hearing it, 'Only the Prime Minister, of living orators, could make one realize what it must have been like to hear Burke or Chatham.' How right he was.

House of Commons, 12 November 1940

SINCE WE LAST MET, the House has suffered a very grievous loss in the death of one of its most distinguished Members, and of a statesman and public servant who, during the best part of three memorable years, was first Minister of the Crown.

The fierce and bitter controversies which hung around him in recent times were hushed by the news of his illness and are silenced by his death. In paying a tribute of respect and of regard to an eminent man who has been taken from us, no one is obliged to alter the opinions which he has formed or expressed upon issues which have become a part of history; but at the Lychgate we may all pass our own conduct and our own judgements under a searching review. It is not given to human beings, happily for them, for otherwise life would be intolerable, to foresee or to predict to any large extent the unfolding course of events. In one phase men seem to have been right, in another they seem to have been wrong. Then again, a few years later, when the perspective of time has lengthened, all stands in a different setting. There is a new proportion. There is another scale of values. History with its flickering lamp stumbles along the trail of the past, trying to reconstruct its scenes, to revive its echoes, and kindle with pale gleams the passion of former days. What is the worth of all this? The only guide to a man is his conscience; the only shield to his memory is the rectitude and sincerity of his actions. It is very imprudent to walk through life without this shield, because we are so often mocked by the failure of our hopes and the upsetting of our calculations; but with this shield, however the fates may play, we march always in the ranks of honour.

It fell to Neville Chamberlain in one of the supreme crises of the world to be contradicted by events, to be disappointed in his hopes, and to be deceived and cheated by a wicked man. But what were these hopes in which he was disappointed? What were these wishes in which he was frustrated? What was that faith that was abused? They were surely among the most noble and benevolent instincts of the human heart – the love of peace, the toil for peace, the strife for peace, the pursuit of peace, even at great peril, and certainly to the utter disdain of popularity or clamour. Whatever else history may or may not say about these terrible, tremendous years, we can be sure that Neville Chamberlain acted with perfect sincerity according to his lights and strove to the utmost of his capacity and authority, which were powerful, to save the world from the awful, devastating struggle in which we are now engaged. This alone will stand him in good stead as far as what is called the verdict of history is concerned.

But it is also a help to our country and to our whole Empire, and to our decent faithful way of living that, however long the struggle may last, or however dark may be the clouds which overhang our path, no future generation of English-speaking folks – for that is the tribunal to which we appeal – will doubt that, even at a great cost to ourselves in technical preparation, we were guiltless of the bloodshed, terror and misery which have engulfed so many lands and peoples, and yet seek new victims still. Herr Hitler protests with frantic words and gestures that he has only desired peace. What do these ravings and outpourings count before the silence of Neville Chamberlain's tomb? Long, hard, and hazardous years lie before us, but at least we entered upon them united and with clean hearts.

I do not propose to give an appreciation of Neville Chamberlain's life and character, but there were certain qualities always admired in these Islands which he possessed in an altogether exceptional degree. He had a physical and moral toughness of fibre which enabled him all through his varied career to endure misfortune and disappointment without being unduly discouraged or wearied. He had a precision of mind and an aptitude for business which raised him far above the ordinary levels of our generation. He had a firmness of spirit which was not often elated by success, seldom downcast by failure, and never swayed by panic. When, contrary to all his hopes, beliefs and exertions, the war came upon him, and when, as he himself said, all that he had worked for was shattered, there was no man more resolved to pursue the unsought quarrel to the death. The same qualities which made him one of the last to enter the war, made him one of the last who would quit it before the full victory of a righteous cause was won.

I had the most singular experience of passing in a day from being one of his most prominent opponents and critics to being one of his principal lieutenants, and on another day of passing from serving under him to become the head of a Government of which, with perfect loyalty, he was content to be a member. Such relationships are unusual in our public life. I have before told the House how on the morrow of the Debate which in the early days of May challenged his position, he declared to me and a few other friends that only a National Government could face the storm about to break upon us, and that if he were an obstacle to the formation of such a Government, he would instantly retire. Thereafter, he acted with that singleness of purpose and simplicity of conduct with at all times, and especially in great times, ought to be the ideal of us all.

When he returned to duty a few weeks after a most severe operation, the bombardment of London and of the seat of Government had begun. I was a witness during that fortnight of his fortitude under the most grievous and painful bodily afflictions, and I can testify that, although physically only the wreck of a man, his nerve was unshaken and his remarkable mental faculties unimpaired.

After he left the Government he refused all honours. He would die like his father, plain Mr Chamberlain. I sought permission of the King, however, to have him supplied with the Cabinet papers, and until a few days of his death he followed our affairs with keenness, interest and tenacity. He met the approach of death with a steady eye. If he grieved at all, it was that he could not be a spectator of our victory; but I think he died with the comfort of knowing that his country had, at least, turned the corner.

At this time our thoughts must pass to the gracious and charming lady who shared his days of triumph and adversity with a courage and quality the equal of his own. He was, like his father and his brother Austen before him, a famous Member of the House of Commons, and we here assembled this morning, Members of all parties, without a single exception, feel that we do ourselves and our country honour in saluting the memory of one whom Disraeli would have called an 'English worthy'.

PART FOUR

Waging the War of Words

1941–1945

19

Appeal to America
'Give Us the Tools'

BBC, London, 9 February 1941

IN SEPTEMBER 1940, UNKNOWN to the British Government, Hitler postponed 'Operation Sea Lion' – his plan for the invasion of England – 'until further notice'. But the fall of France and the heavy German bombing of London and major provincial centres meant that Britain's position was still perilous, and that American aid was essential if the struggle was to be carried on. Under these circumstances, it was a great relief when Franklin Roosevelt – with whom Churchill was in regular and intimate correspondence – won an unprecedented third term in the presidential election of November 1940.

Churchill's broadcast of February 1941 was his first for five months. It was, as John Colville recorded, 'triumphant and yet not over-optimistic, addressed very largely to American ears.' He rejoiced in British successes against Mussolini in the eastern Mediterranean, but also made plain the urgent need for further assistance from America – assistance which was to be forthcoming in the aftermath of the Lend-Lease Bill, passed by Congress in March 1941.

Churchill concluded his broadcast by quoting some lines from Longfellow, which Roosevelt himself had sent him in January 1941. In its range as in its rhetoric, the address was an outstanding success. As one commentator remarked, 'It is not too much to say that his characteristic choice of words and phrases make a Churchillian broadcast a world event.'

BBC, London, 9 February 1941

FIVE MONTHS HAVE PASSED since I spoke to the British nation and the Empire on the broadcast. In wartime there is a lot to be said for the motto: 'Deeds, not words'. All the same, it is a good thing to look around from time to time and take stock, and certainly our affairs have prospered in several directions during these last four or five months, far better than most of us would have ventured to hope.

We stood our ground and faced the two Dictators in the hour of what seemed their overwhelming triumph, and we have shown ourselves capable, so far, of standing up against them alone. After the heavy defeats of the German Air Force by our fighters in August and September, Herr Hitler did not dare attempt the invasion of this Island, although he had every need to do so and although he had made vast preparations. Baffled in this mighty project, he sought to break the spirit of the British nation by the bombing, first of London, and afterwards of our great cities. It has now been proved, to the admiration of the world, and of our friends in the United States, that this form of blackmail by murder and terrorism, so far from weakening the spirit of the British nation, has only roused it to a more intense and universal flame than was ever seen before in any modern community.

The whole British Empire has been proud of the Mother Country, and they long to be with us over here in even larger numbers. We have been deeply conscious of the love for us which has flowed from the Dominions of the Crown across the broad ocean spaces. *There* is the first of our war aims: to be worthy of that love, and to preserve it.

All through these dark winter months the enemy has had the power to drop three or four tons of bombs upon us for every ton we could send to Germany in return. We are arranging so that presently this will be rather the other way round; but meanwhile, London and our big cities have had to stand their pounding.

They remind me of the British squares at Waterloo. They are not squares of soldiers; they do not wear scarlet coats. They are just ordinary English, Scottish and Welsh folk – men, women and children – standing steadfastly together. But their spirit is the same, their glory is the same; and, in the end, their victory will be greater than far-famed Waterloo.

All honour to the Civil Defence Services of all kinds – emergency and regular, volunteer and professional – who have helped our people through this formidable ordeal, the like of which no civilized community has ever been called upon to undergo. If I mention only one of these services here, namely the Police, it is because many tributes have been paid already to the others. But the Police have been in it everywhere, all the time, and, as a working woman wrote to me: 'What gentlemen they are!'

More than two-thirds of the winter has now gone, and so far we have had no serious epidemic; indeed, there is no increase of illness in spite of the improvised conditions of the shelters. That is most creditable to our local, medical and sanitary authorities, to our devoted nursing staff, and to the Ministry of Health, whose head, Mr Malcolm MacDonald, is now going to Canada in the important office of High Commissioner.

There is another thing which surprised me when I asked about it. In spite of all these new wartime offences and prosecutions of all kinds; in spite of all the opportunities for looting and disorder, there has been less crime this winter and there are now fewer prisoners in our gaols than in the years of peace.

We have broken the back of the winter. The daylight grows. The Royal Air Force grows, and is already certainly master of the daylight air. The attacks may be sharper, but they will be shorter; there will be more opportunities for work and service of all kinds; more opportunities for life. So, if our first victory was the repulse of the invader, our second was the frustration of his acts of terror and torture against our people at home.

Meanwhile, abroad, in October, a wonderful thing happened. One of the two Dictators – the crafty, cold-blooded, black-hearted Italian, who had thought to gain an Empire on the cheap by stabbing fallen France in the back, got into trouble. Without the slightest provocation, spurred on by lust of power and brutish greed, Mussolini attacked and invaded Greece, only to be hurled back ignominiously by the heroic Greek Army; who, I will say, with your consent, have revived before our eyes the glories which from the classic age gild their native land. While Signor Mussolini was writhing and smarting under the Greek lash in Albania, Generals Wavell and Wilson, who were charged with the defence of Egypt and of the Suez Canal in accordance with our treaty obligations, whose task seemed at one time so difficult, had received very powerful reinforcements of men, cannon, equipment and, above all, tanks, which we had sent from our island in spite of the invasion threat. Large numbers of troops from India, Australia and New Zealand had also reached them. Forthwith began that series of victories in Libya which have broken irretrievably the Italian military power on the African Continent. We have all been entertained, and I trust edified, by the exposure and humiliation of another of what Byron called

> *Those Pagod things of sabre sway,*
> *With fronts of brass, and feet of clay.*

Here then, in Libya, is the third considerable event upon which we may dwell with some satisfaction. It is just exactly two months ago, to a day, that I was waiting anxiously, but also eagerly, for the news of the great counter-stroke which had been planned against the Italian invaders of Egypt. The secret had been well kept. The preparations had been well made. But to leap across those seventy miles of desert, and attack an army of ten or eleven divisions, equipped with all the appliances of modern war, who had been fortifying themselves for three months, that was a most hazardous adventure.

When the brilliant decisive victory at Sidi Barrani, with its tens of thousands of prisoners, proved that we had quality, manœuvring power and weapons superior to the enemy, who had boasted so much of his virility and his military virtues, it was evident that all the other Italian forces in Eastern Libya were in great danger. They could not easily beat a retreat along the coastal road without running the risk of being caught in the open by our armoured divisions and brigades ranging far out into the desert in tremendous swoops and scoops. They had to expose themselves to being attacked piecemeal.

General Wavell – nay, all our leaders, and all their lithe, active, ardent men, British, Australian, Indian, in the Imperial Army, saw their opportunity. At that time I ventured to draw General Wavell's attention to the seventh chapter of the Gospel of St Matthew, at the seventh verse, where, as you all know – or ought to know – it is written: 'Ask, and it shall be given; seek, and ye shall find; knock, and it shall be opened unto you.' The Army of the Nile has asked, and it was given; they sought, and they have found; they knocked, and it has been opened unto them. In barely eight weeks, by a campaign which will long be studied as a model of the military art, an advance of over 400 miles has been made. The whole Italian Army in the east of Libya, which was reputed to exceed 150,000 men, has been captured or destroyed. The entire province of Cyrenaica – nearly as big as England and Wales – has been conquered. The unhappy Arab tribes, who have for thirty years suffered from the cruelty of Italian rule, carried in some cases to the point of methodical extermination, these Bedouin survivors have at last seen their oppressors in disorderly flight, or led off in endless droves as prisoners of war.

Egypt and the Suez Canal are safe, and the port, the base and the airfields of Benghazi constitute a strategic point of high consequence to the whole of the war in the Eastern Mediterranean.

This is the time, I think, to speak of the leaders who, at the head of their brave troops, have rendered this distinguished service to the King. The first and foremost, General Wavell, Commander-in-Chief of all the Armies of the Middle East, had proved himself a master of war, sage, painstaking, daring and tireless. But General Wavell has repeatedly asked that others should share his fame.

General Wilson, who actually commands the Army of the

Nile, was reputed to be one of our finest tacticians – and few will now deny that quality. General O'Connor commanding the 13th Corps, with General Mackay commanding the splendid Australians, and General Creagh who trained and commanded the various armoured divisions which were employed; these three men executed the complicated and astoundingly rapid movements which were made, and fought the actions which occurred. I have just seen a telegram from General Wavell in which he says that the success at Benghazi was due to the outstanding leadership and resolution of O'Connor and Creagh, ably backed by Wilson.

I must not forget here to point out the amazing mechanical feats of the British tanks, whose design and workmanship have beaten all records and stood up to all trials; and show us how closely and directly the work in the factories at home is linked with the victories abroad.

Of course, none of our plans would have succeeded had not our pilots, under Air Chief Marshal Longmore, wrested the control of the air from a far more numerous enemy. Nor would the campaign itself have been possible if the British Mediterranean Fleet, under Admiral Cunningham, had not chased the Italian Navy into its harbours and sustained every forward surge of the Army with all the flexible resources of sea-power. How far-reaching these resources are we can see from what happened at dawn this morning, when our Western Mediterranean Fleet, under Admiral Somerville, entered the Gulf of Genoa and bombarded in a shattering manner the naval base from which perhaps a Nazi German expedition might soon have sailed to attack General Weygand in Algeria or Tunis. It is right that the Italian people should be made to feel the sorry plight into which they have been dragged by Dictator Mussolini; and if the cannonade of Genoa, rolling along the coast, reverberating in the mountains, reached the ears of our French comrades in their grief and misery, it might cheer them with the feeling that friends – active friends – are near, and that Britannia rules the waves.

The events in Libya are only part of the story: they are only part of the story of the decline and fall of the Italian Empire, that will not take a future Gibbon so long to write as the original work. Fifteen hundred miles away to the southward a strong British and Indian army, having driven the invaders out of the Sudan, is marching steadily forward through the Italian colony of Eritrea, thus seeking to complete the isolation of all the Italian troops in Abyssinia. Other British forces are entering Abyssinia from the west, while the army gathered in Kenya – in the van of which we may discern the powerful forces of the Union of South Africa, organized by General Smuts – is striking northward along the whole enormous front. Lastly, the Ethiopian patriots, whose independence was stolen five years ago, have risen in arms; and their Emperor, so recently an exile in England, is in their midst to fight for their freedom and his throne. Here, then, we see the beginnings of a process of reparation and of the chastisement of wrongdoing, which reminds us that though the mills of God grind slowly, they grind exceeding small.

While these auspicious events have been carrying us stride by stride from what many people thought a forlorn position, and was certainly a very grave position in May and June, to one which permits us to speak with sober confidence of our power to discharge our duty, heavy though it be, in the future – while this has been happening, a mighty tide of sympathy, of goodwill and of effective aid, has begun to flow across the Atlantic in support of the world cause which is at stake. Distinguished Americans have come over to see things here at the front, and to find out how the United States can help us best and soonest. In Mr Hopkins, who has been my frequent companion during the last three weeks, we have the Envoy of the President, a President who has been newly re-elected to his august office. In Mr Wendell Willkie we have welcomed the champion of the great Republican Party. We may be sure that they will both tell the truth about what they have seen over here, and more than that we do not ask. The rest we leave with good confidence to the judgement of the President, the Congress and the people of the United States.

I have been so very careful, since I have been Prime Minister, not to encourage false hopes or prophesy smooth and easy things, and yet the tale that I have to tell today is one which must justly and rightly give us cause for deep thankfulness, and also, I think, for strong comfort and even rejoicing. But now I must dwell upon the more serious, darker and more dangerous aspects of the vast scene of the war. We must all of us have been asking ourselves: what has that wicked man whose crime-stained regime and system are at bay and in the toils – what has he been preparing during these winter months? What new devilry is he planning? What new small country will he overrun or strike down? What fresh form of assault will he make upon our island home and fortress; which – let there be no mistake about it – is all that stands between him and the dominion of the world?

We may be sure that the war is soon going to enter upon a phase of greater violence. Hitler's confederate, Mussolini, has reeled back in Albania; but the Nazis – having absorbed Hungary and driven Rumania into a frightful internal convulsion – are now already upon the Black Sea. A considerable Nazi German army and air force is being built up in Rumania, and its forward tentacles have already penetrated Bulgaria. With – we must suppose – the acquiescence of the Bulgarian Government, airfields are being occupied by German ground personnel numbering thousands, so as to enable the German air force to come into action from Bulgaria. Many preparations have been made for the movement of German troops into or through Bulgaria, and perhaps this southward movement has already begun.

We saw what happened last May in the Low Countries; how they hoped for the best; how they clung to their neutrality; how woefully they were deceived, overwhelmed, plundered, enslaved and since starved. We know how we and the French suffered when, at the last moment, at the urgent belated appeal of the King of the Belgians, we went to his aid. Of course, if all the Balkan peoples stood together and acted together, aided by Britain and Turkey, it would be many months before a German army and air force of sufficient strength to overcome them could be assembled in the southeast of Europe. And in those months much might happen. Much will certainly happen as American aid becomes effective, as our air power grows, as we become a well-armed nation, and as our armies in the East increase in strength. But nothing is more certain than that, if the countries of southeastern Europe allow themselves to be pulled to pieces one by one, they will share the fate of Denmark, Holland and Belgium. And none can tell how long it will be before the hour of their deliverance strikes.

One of our difficulties is to convince some of these neutral countries in Europe that we are going to win. We think it astonishing that they should be so dense as not to see it as clearly as we do ourselves. I remember in the last war, in July 1915, we began to think that Bulgaria was going wrong, so Mr Lloyd George, Mr Bonar Law, Sir F. E. Smith and I asked the Bulgarian Minister to dinner to explain to him what a fool King Ferdinand would make of himself if he were to go in on the losing side. It was no use. The poor man simply could not believe it, or could not make his Government believe it. So Bulgaria, against the wishes of her peasant population, against all her interests, fell in at the Kaiser's tail and got sadly carved up and punished when the victory was won. I trust that Bulgaria is not going to make the same mistake again. If they do, the Bulgarian peasantry and people, for whom there has been much regard, both in Great Britain and in the United States, will for the third time in thirty years have been made to embark upon a needless and disastrous war.

In the Central Mediterranean the Italian Quisling, who is called Mussolini, and the French Quisling, commonly called Laval, are both in their different ways trying to make their countries into doormats for Hitler and his New Order, in the hope of being able to keep, or get the Nazi Gestapo and Prussian bayonets to enforce, their rule upon their fellow-countrymen. I cannot tell how the matter will go, but at any rate we shall do our best to fight for the Central Mediterranean.

I dare say you will have noticed the very significant air action which was fought over Malta a fortnight ago. The Germans sent an entire *Geschwader* of dive-bombers to Sicily. They seriously injured our new aircraft-carrier *Illustrious*, and then, as this wounded ship was sheltering in Malta harbour, they concentrated upon her all their force so as to beat her to pieces. But they were met by the batteries of Malta, which is one of the strongest defended fortresses in the world against air attack; they were met by the Fleet Air Arm and by the Royal Air Force, and, in two or three days, they had lost, out of 150 dive-bombers, upwards of ninety, fifty of which were destroyed in the air and forty on the ground. Although the *Illustrious*, in her damaged condition, was one of the great prizes of the air and naval war, the German *Geschwader* accepted the defeat; they would not come any more. All the necessary repairs were made to the *Illustrious* in Malta harbour, and she steamed safely off to Alexandria under her own power at 23 knots. I dwell upon this incident, not at all because I think it disposes of the danger in the Central Mediterranean, but in order to show you that there, as elsewhere, we intend to give a good account of ourselves.

But after all, the fate of this war is going to be settled by what happens on the oceans, in the air, and – above all – in this island. It seems now to be certain that the Government and people of the United States intend to supply us with all that is necessary for victory. In the last war the United States sent two million men across the Atlantic. But this is not a war of vast armies, firing immense masses of shells at one another. We do not need the gallant armies which are forming throughout the American Union. We do not need them this year, nor next year; nor any year that I can foresee. But we do need most urgently an immense and continuous supply of war materials and technical apparatus of all kinds. We need them here and we need to bring them here. We shall need a great mass of shipping in 1942, far more than we can build ourselves, if we are to maintain and augment our war effort in the West and in the East.

These facts are, of course, all well known to the enemy, and we must therefore expect that Herr Hitler will do his utmost to prey upon our shipping and to reduce the volume of American supplies entering these islands. Having conquered France and Norway, his clutching fingers reach out on both sides of us into the ocean. I have never underrated this danger, and you know I have never concealed it from you. Therefore, I hope you will believe me when I say that I have complete confidence in the Royal Navy, aided by the Air Force of the Coastal Command, and that in one way or another I am sure they will be able to meet every changing phase of this truly mortal struggle, and that sustained by the courage of our merchant seamen, and of the dockers and workmen of all our ports, we shall outwit, out-manœuvre, outfight and outlast the worst that the enemy's malice and ingenuity can contrive.

I have left the greatest issue to the end. You will have seen that Sir John Dill, our principal military adviser, the Chief of the Imperial General Staff, has warned us all that Hitler may be forced, by the strategic, economic and political stresses in Europe, to try to invade these islands in the near future. That is a warning which no one should disregard. Naturally, we are working night and day to have everything ready. Of course, we are far stronger than we ever were before, incomparably stronger than we were in July, August and September. Our Navy is more powerful, our flotillas are more numerous; we are far stronger, actually and relatively, in the air above these islands, than we were when our Fighter Command beat off and beat down the Nazi attack last autumn. Our Army is more numerous, more mobile and far better equipped and trained than in September, and still more than in July.

I have the greatest confidence in our Commander-in-Chief, General Brooke, and in the generals of proved ability who, under him, guard the different quarters of our land. But most of all I put my faith in the simple unaffected resolve to conquer or die which will animate and inspire nearly four million Britons with serviceable weapons in their hands. It is not an easy military operation to invade an island like Great Britain, without the command of the sea and without the command of the air, and then to face what will be waiting for the invader here. But I must drop one word of caution; for next to cowardice and treachery, over-confidence, leading to neglect or slothfulness, is the worst of martial crimes. Therefore, I drop one word of caution. A Nazi invasion of Great Britain last autumn would have been a more or less improvised affair. Hitler took it for granted that when

France gave in we should give in; but we did not give in. And he had to think again. An invasion now will be supported by a much more carefully prepared tackle and equipment of landing-craft and other apparatus, all of which will have been planned and manufactured in the winter months. We must all be prepared to meet gas attacks, parachute attacks, and glider attacks, with constancy, forethought and practised skill.

I must again emphasize what General Dill has said, and what I pointed out myself last year. In order to win the war Hitler must destroy Great Britain. He may carry havoc into the Balkan States; he may tear great provinces out of Russia; he may march to the Caspian; he may march to the gates of India. All this will avail him nothing. It may spread his curse more widely through-out Europe and Asia, but it will not avert his doom. With every month that passes the many proud and once happy countries he is now holding down by brute force and vile intrigue are learning to hate the Prussian yoke and the Nazi name as nothing has ever been hated so fiercely and so widely among men before. And all the time, masters of the sea and air, the British Empire – nay, in a certain sense, the whole English-speaking world – will be on his track, bearing with them the swords of justice.

The other day, President Roosevelt gave his opponent in the late Presidential Election a letter of introduction to me, and in it he wrote out a verse, in his own handwriting, from Longfellow, which he said, 'applies to you people as it does to us.' Here is the verse:

> ... Sail on, O Ship of State!
> Sail on, O Union, strong and great!
> Humanity with all its fears,
> With all the hopes of future years,
> Is hanging breathless on thy fate!

What is the answer that I shall give, in your name, to this great man, the thrice-chosen head of a nation of 130 millions? Here is the answer which I will give to President Roosevelt: Put your confidence in us. Give us your faith and your blessing, and, under Providence, all will be well.

'Give Us the Tools' 1941

We shall not fail or falter; we shall not weaken or tire. Neither the sudden shock of battle, nor the long-drawn trials of vigilance and exertion will wear us down. Give us the tools, and we will finish the job.

20

A Difficult Time

'Westward, Look, the Land Is Bright'

BBC, London, 27 April 1941

DESPITE THE PASSING OF LEND-LEASE, it seemed during the spring of 1941 as if the tide had turned even more discouragingly against Britain. The Germans invaded the Balkans and overran both Greece and Yugoslavia with devastating speed and success. British troops were forced on the defensive and were evacuated to Crete. At the same time, the Battle of the Atlantic was going badly, with heavy losses to Allied merchant shipping, while London and other cities were still enduring severe bombardment.

At this time, Churchill visited the provinces, accompanied by Averell Harriman, the most recent of Roosevelt's personal representatives. The impressions which he obtained were reported in the opening remarks of this broadcast, which was carefully composed to allay uneasiness and despondency. He reminded his listeners that war 'is full of disappointments and also of mistakes', and made no attempt to minimize the depressing news from the Balkans. But he also urged them to consider the vital importance of America's increasing involvement in the war.

On this occasion, he ended by quoting some lines from Arthur Hugh Clough's poem, 'Say but the struggle naught availeth', which had first been read to him 35 years before by Asquith's daughter Violet. Remembering not only the poem, but also the occasion, Churchill telephoned her after he had finished speaking. 'Did you hear my broadcast?' he asked. 'Of course,' she replied, 'Everybody in England listens when you speak.'

BBC, London, 27 April 1941

I WAS ASKED LAST WEEK whether I was aware of some uneasiness which it was said existed in the country on account of the gravity, as it was described, of the war situation. So I thought it would be a good thing to go and see for myself what this 'uneasiness' amounted to, and I went to some of our great cities and seaports which had been most heavily bombed, and to some of the places where the poorest people had got it worst. I have come back not only reassured, but refreshed. To leave the offices in Whitehall with their ceaseless hum of activity and stress, and go out to the front, by which I mean the streets and wharves of London or Liverpool, Manchester, Cardiff, Swansea or Bristol, is like going out of a hothouse on to the bridge of a fighting ship. It is a tonic which I should recommend any who are suffering from fretfulness to take in strong doses when they have need of it.

It is quite true that I have seen many painful scenes of havoc, and of fine buildings and acres of cottage homes blasted into rubble-heaps of ruin. But it is just in those very places where the malice of the savage enemy has done its worst, and where the ordeal of the men, women and children has been most severe, that I found their morale most high and splendid. Indeed, I felt encompassed by an exaltation of spirit in the people which seemed to lift mankind and its troubles above the level of material facts into that joyous serenity we think belongs to a better world than this.

Of their kindness to me I cannot speak, because I have never sought it or dreamed of it, and can never deserve it. I can only assure you that I and my colleagues, or comrades rather – for that is what they are – will toil with every scrap of life and strength, according to the lights that are granted to us, not to fail these people or be wholly unworthy of their faithful and generous regard. The British nation is stirred and moved as it has never been at any time in its long, eventful, famous history, and it is no hackneyed trope of speech to say that they mean to conquer or to die.

What a triumph the life of these battered cities is, over the worst that fire and bomb can do. What a vindication of the civilized and decent way of living we have been trying to work for and work towards in our Island. What a proof of the virtues of free institutions. What a test of the quality of our local authorities, and of institutions and customs and societies so steadily built. This ordeal by fire has even in a certain sense exhilarated the manhood and womanhood of Britain. The sublime but also terrible and sombre experiences and emotions of the battlefield which for centuries had been reserved for the soldiers and sailors, are now shared, for good or ill, by the entire population. All are proud to be under the fire of the enemy. Old men, little children, the crippled veterans of former wars, aged women, the ordinary hard-pressed citizen or subject of the King, as he likes to call himself, the sturdy workmen who swing the hammers or load the ships; skilful craftsmen; the members of every kind of ARP service, are proud to feel that they stand in the line together with our fighting men, when one of the greatest of causes is being fought out, as fought out it will be, to the end. This is indeed the grand heroic period of our history, and the light of glory shines on all.

You may imagine how deeply I feel my own responsibility to all these people; my responsibility to bear my part in bringing them safely out of this long, stern, scowling valley through which we are marching, and not to demand from them the sacrifices and exertions in vain.

I have thought in this difficult period, when so much fighting and so many critical and complicated manœuvres are going on, that it is above all things important that our policy and conduct should be upon the highest level, and that honour should be our guide. Very few people realize how small were the forces with which General Wavell, that fine Commander whom we cheered in good days and will back through bad – how small were the forces which took the bulk of the Italian masses in Libya prisoners. In none of his successive victories could General Wavell maintain in the desert or bring into action more than two divisions, or about 30,000 men. When we reached Benghazi, and what was left of Mussolini's legions scurried back along the dusty road to Tripoli, a call was made upon us which we could not resist. Let me tell you about that call.

You will remember how in November the Italian Dictator fell upon the unoffending Greeks, and without reason and without warning invaded their country, and how the Greek nation, reviving their classic fame, hurled his armies back at the double-quick. Meanwhile Hitler, who had been creeping and worming his way steadily forward, doping and poisoning and pinioning, one after the other Hungary, Rumania and Bulgaria, suddenly made it clear that he would come to the rescue of his fellow-criminal. The lack of unity among the Balkan States had enabled him to build up a mighty army in their midst. While nearly all the Greek troops were busy beating the Italians, the tremendous German military machine suddenly towered up on their other frontier. In their mortal peril the Greeks turned to us for succour. Strained as were our own resources, we could not say them nay. By solemn guarantee given before the war, Great Britain had promised them her help. They declared they would fight for their native soil even if neither of their neighbours made common cause with them, and even if we left them to their fate. But we could not do that. There are rules against that kind of thing; and to break those rules would be fatal to the honour of the British Empire, without which we could neither hope nor deserve to win this hard war. Military defeat or miscalculation can be redeemed. The fortunes of war are fickle and changing. But an act of shame would deprive us of the respect which we now enjoy throughout the world, and this would sap the vitals of our strength.

During the last year we have gained by our bearing and conduct a potent hold upon the sentiments of the people of the United States. Never, never in our history, have we been held in such admiration and regard across the Atlantic Ocean. In that great Republic, now in much travail and stress of soul, it is customary to use all the many valid, solid arguments about American interests and American safety, which depend upon the destruction of Hitler and his foul gang and even fouler doctrines. But in the long run – believe me, for I know – the action of the United States will be dictated, not by methodical calculations of profit and loss, but by moral sentiment, and by that gleaming flash of resolve which lifts the hearts of men and nations, and springs from the spiritual foundations of human life itself.

We, for our part, were of course bound to hearken to the Greek appeal to the utmost limit of our strength. We put the case to the Dominions of Australia and New Zealand, and their Governments, without in any way ignoring the hazards, told us that they felt the same as we did. So an important part of the mobile portion of the Army of the Nile was sent to Greece in fulfilment of our pledge. It happened that the divisions available and best suited to this task were from New Zealand and Australia, and that only about half the troops who took part in this dangerous expedition came from the Mother Country. I see the German propaganda is trying to make bad blood between us and Australia by making out that we have used them to do what we would not have asked of the British Army. I shall leave it to Australia to deal with that taunt.

Let us see what has happened. We knew, of course, that the forces we could send to Greece would not by themselves alone be sufficient to stem the German tide of invasion. But there was a very real hope that the neighbours of Greece would by our intervention be drawn to stand in line together with her while time remained. How nearly that came off will be known some day. The tragedy of Yugoslavia has been that these brave people had a government who hoped to purchase an ignoble immunity by submission to the Nazi will. Thus when at last the people of Yugoslovia found out where they were being taken, and rose in one spontaneous surge of revolt, they saved the soul and future of their country: but it was already too late to save its territory. They had no time to mobilize their armies. They were struck down by the ruthless and highly mechanized Hun before they could even bring their armies into the field. Great disasters have occurred in the Balkans. Yugoslavia has been beaten down. Only in the mountains can she continue her resistance. The Greeks have been overwhelmed. Their victorious Albanian army has been cut off and forced to surrender, and it has been left to the Anzacs and their British comrades to fight their way back to the sea, leaving their mark on all who hindered them.

I turn aside from the stony path we have to tread, to indulge a moment of lighter relief. I dare say you have read in the newspapers that, by a special proclamation, the Italian Dictator has congratulated the Italian army in Albania on the glorious laurels they have gained by their victory over the Greeks. Here surely is the world's record in the domain of the ridiculous and the contemptible. This whipped jackal, Mussolini, who to save his own skin has made all Italy a vassal state of Hitler's Empire, comes frisking up at the side of the German tiger with yelpings not only of appetite – that can be understood – but even of triumph. Different things strike different people in different ways. But I am sure there are a great many millions in the British Empire and in the United States, who will find a new object in life in making sure that we come to the final reckoning this absurd impostor will be abandoned to public justice and universal scorn.

While these grievous events were taking place in the Balkan Peninsula and in Greece, our forces in Libya have sustained a vexatious and damaging defeat. The Germans advanced sooner and in greater strength than we or our Generals expected. The bulk of our armoured troops, which had played such a decisive part in beating the Italians, had to be refitted, and the single armoured brigade which had been judged sufficient to hold the frontier till about the middle of May was worsted and its vehicles largely destroyed by a somewhat stronger German armoured force. Our infantry, which had not exceeded one division, had to fall back upon the very large Imperial armies that have been assembled and can be nourished and maintained in the fertile delta of the Nile.

Tobruk – the fortress of Tobruk – which flanks any German advance on Egypt, we hold strongly. There we have repulsed many attacks, causing the enemy heavy losses and taking many prisoners. That is how the matter stands in Egypt and on the Libyan front.

We must now expect the war in the Mediterranean on the sea, in the desert, and above all in the air, to become very fierce, varied and widespread. We had cleaned the Italians out of Cyrenaica, and it now lies with us to purge that province of the Germans. That will be a harder task, and we cannot expect to do it at once. You know I never try to make out that defeats are victories. I have never underrated the German as a warrior. Indeed I told you a month ago that the swift, unbroken course of victories which we had gained over the Italians could not possibly continue, and that misfortunes must be expected. There is only one thing certain about war, that it is full of disappointments and also full of mistakes. It remains to be seen, however, whether it is the Germans who have made the mistake in trampling down the Balkan States and in making a river of blood and hate between themselves and the Greek and Yugoslav peoples. It remains also to be seen whether they have made a mistake in their attempt to invade Egypt with the forces and means of supply which they have now got. Taught by experience, I make it a rule not to prophesy about battles which have yet to be fought out. This, however, I will venture to say, that I should be very sorry to see the tasks of the combatants in the Middle East exchanged, and that General Wavell's armies should be in the position of the German invaders. That is only a personal opinion, and I call well understand you may take a different view. It is certain that fresh dangers besides those which threaten Egypt may come upon us in the Mediterranean. The war may spread to Spain and Morocco. It may spread eastward to Turkey and Russia. The Huns may lay their hands for a time upon the granaries of the Ukraine and the oil-wells of the Caucasus. They may dominate the Black Sea. They may dominate the Caspian. Who can tell? We shall do our best to meet them and fight them wherever they go. But there is one thing which is certain. There is one thing which rises out of the vast welter which is sure and solid, and which no one in his senses can mistake. Hitler cannot find safety from avenging justice in the East, in the Middle East, or in the Far East. In order to win this war, he must either conquer this Island by invasion, or he must cut the ocean life-line which joins us to the United States.

Let us look into these alternatives, if you will bear with me for a few minutes longer. When I spoke to you last, early in February, many people believed the Nazi boastings that the invasion of Britain was about to begin. It has not begun yet, and with every week that passes we grow stronger on the sea, in the air, and in the numbers, quality, training and equipment of the great Armies that now guard our Island. When I compare the position at home as it is today with what it was in the summer of last year, even after making allowance for a much more elaborate mechanical preparation on the part of the enemy, I feel that we have very much to be thankful for, and I believe that provided our exertions and our vigilance are not relaxed even for a moment, we may be confident that we shall give a very good account of ourselves. More than that it would be boastful to say. Less than that it would be foolish to believe.

But how about our life-line across the Atlantic? What is to happen if so many of our merchant ships are sunk that we cannot bring in the food we need to nourish our brave people? What if the supplies of war materials and war weapons which the United States are seeking to send us in such enormous quantities should in large part be sunk on the way? What is to happen then? In February, as you may remember, that bad man in one of his raving outbursts threatened us with a terrifying increase in the numbers and activities of his U-boats and in his air-attack – not only on our Island but, thanks to his use of French and Norwegian harbours, and thanks to the denial to us of the Irish bases – upon our shipping far out into the Atlantic. We have taken and are taking all possible measures to meet this deadly attack, and we are now fighting against it with might and main. That is what is called the Battle of the Atlantic, which in order to survive we have got to win on salt water just as decisively as we had to win the Battle of Britain last August and September in the air.

WAGING THE WAR OF WORDS

Wonderful exertions have been made by our Navy and Air Force; by the hundreds of mine-sweeping vessels which with their marvellous appliances keep our ports clear in spite of all the enemy can do; by the men who build and repair our immense fleets of merchant ships; by the men who load and unload them; and need I say by the officers and men of the Merchant Navy who go out in all weathers and in the teeth of all dangers to fight for the life of their native land and for a cause they comprehend and serve. Still, when you think how easy it is to sink ships at sea and how hard it is to build them and protect them, and when you remember that we have never less than two thousand ships afloat and three or four hundred in the danger zone; when you think of the great armies we are maintaining and reinforcing in the East, and of the worldwide traffic we have to carry on – when you remember all this, can you wonder that it is the Battle of the Atlantic which holds the first place in the thoughts of those upon whom rests the responsibility for procuring the victory?

It was therefore with indescribable relief that I learned of the tremendous decisions lately taken by the President and people of the United States. The American Fleet and flying boats have been ordered to patrol the wide waters of the Western Hemisphere, and to warn the peaceful shipping of all nations outside the combat zone of the presence of lurking U-boats or raiding cruisers belonging to the two aggressor nations. We British shall therefore be able to concentrate our protecting forces far more upon the routes nearer home, and to take a far heavier toll of the U-boats there. I have felt for some time that something like this was bound to happen. The President and Congress of the United States, having newly fortified themselves by contact with their electors, have solemnly pledged their aid to Britain in this war because they deem our cause just, and because they know their own interests and safety would be endangered if we were destroyed. They are taxing themselves heavily. They have passed great legislation. They have turned a large part of their gigantic industry to making the munitions which we need. They have even given us or lent us valuable weapons of their own. I could not believe that they would allow the high purposes to which they have set themselves to be frustrated and the products of their skill and labour sunk to the bottom of the sea. U-boat warfare as conducted by Germany is entirely contrary to international agreements freely subscribed to by Germany only a few years ago. There is no effective blockade, but only a merciless murder and marauding over wide, indiscriminate areas utterly beyond the control of the German seapower. When I said ten weeks ago: 'Give us the tools and we will finish the job', I meant, *give* them to us: put them within our reach – and that is what it now seems the Americans are going to do. And that is why I feel a very strong conviction that though the Battle of the Atlantic will be long and hard, and its issue is by no means yet determined, it has entered upon a more grim but at the same time a far more favourable phase. When you come to think of it, the United States are very closely bound up with us now, and have engaged themselves deeply in giving us moral, material, and, within the limits I have mentioned, naval support.

It is worth while therefore to take a look on both sides of the ocean at the forces which are facing each other in this awful struggle, from which there can be no drawing back. No prudent and far-seeing man can doubt that the eventual and total defeat of Hitler and Mussolini is certain, in view of the respective declared resolves of the British and American democracies. There are less than seventy million malignant Huns – some of whom are curable and others killable – many of whom are already engaged in holding down Austrians, Czechs, Poles, French, and the many other ancient races they now bully and pillage. The peoples of the British Empire and of the United States number nearly two hundred millions in their homelands and in the British Dominions alone. They possess the unchallengeable command of the oceans, and will soon obtain decisive superiority in the air. They have more wealth, more technical resources, and they make more steel, than the whole of the rest of the world put together. They are determined that the cause of freedom shall not be trampled down, nor the tide of world progress turned backwards, by the criminal Dictators.

While therefore we naturally view with sorrow and anxiety

much that is happening in Europe and in Africa, and may happen in Asia, we must not lose our sense of proportion and thus become discouraged or alarmed. When we face with a steady eye the difficulties which lie before us, we may derive new confidence from remembering those we have already overcome. Nothing that is happening now is comparable in gravity with the dangers through which we passed last year. Nothing that can happen in the East is comparable with what is happening in the West.

Last time I spoke to you I quoted the lines of Longfellow which President Roosevelt had written out for me in his own hand. I have some other lines which are less well known but which seem apt and appropriate to our fortunes tonight, and I believe they will be so judged wherever the English language is spoken or the flag of freedom flies:

> *For while the tired waves, vainly breaking,*
> *Seem here no painful inch to gain,*
> *Far back, through creeks and inlets making,*
> *Comes silent, flooding in, the main.*
>
> *And not by eastern windows only,*
> *When daylight comes, comes in the light;*
> *In front the sun climbs slow, how slowly,*
> *But westward, look, the land is bright.*

21

The Widening Conflict
'A Long, Hard War'

Joint Session of Congress, Washington, 26 December 1941

IN JUNE 1941, HITLER INVADED RUSSIA, and initially the German troops once more swept all before them. At the same time, the British forces in Africa were thrown on the defensive when the Germans replaced the Italians as their prime adversary. In August, Churchill and Roosevelt met for the first time, and published the Atlantic Charter, a joint statement of democratic principles. Then, at the very end of the year, the Japanese bombed the American fleet anchored at Pearl Harbor. The war was suddenly and dramatically transformed, and an Allied victory now seemed a realistic – if still far-distant – possibility.

Churchill immediately set out for the New World, to confer with the American President, and to do his utmost to ensure that British military influence was maintained in this vastly increased global conflict, where the superior resources of the United States would eventually become overwhelming. While in Washington, he addressed a Joint Session of Congress, the first time he had ever spoken to a foreign legislature.

Although he was more than usually apprehensive about his address (which was also broadcast live), it was one of the his most triumphant performances, and he was accorded a standing ovation. 'I thought your Washington speech the best you have ever done,' his son Randolph reported from Cairo, 'particularly the delivery, which was wonderfully strong and clear.' The very same night, Churchill suffered a mild heart attack.

225

Joint Session of Congress, Washington, 26 December 1941

I FEEL GREATLY HONOURED that you should have invited me to enter the United States Senate Chamber and address the representatives of both branches of Congress. The fact that my American forebears have for so many generations played their part in the life of the United States, and that here I am, an Englishman, welcomed in your midst, makes this experience one of the most moving and thrilling in my life, which is already long and has not been entirely uneventful. I wish indeed that my mother, whose memory I cherish across the vale of years, could have been here to see. By the way, I cannot help reflecting that if my father had been American and my mother British, instead of the other way round, I might have got here on my own. In that case, this would not have been the first time you would have heard my voice. In that case I should not have needed any invitation, but if I had, it is hardly likely it would have been unanimous. So perhaps things are better as they are. I may confess, however, that I do not feel quite like a fish out of water in a legislative assembly where English is spoken.

I am a child of the House of Commons. I was brought up in my father's house to believe in democracy. 'Trust the people' – that was his message. I used to see him cheered at meetings and in the streets by crowds of working men way back in those aristocratic Victorian days when, as Disraeli said, the world was for the few, and for the very few. Therefore I have been in full harmony all my life with the tides which have flowed on both sides of the Atlantic against privilege and monopoly, and I have steered confidently towards the Gettysburg ideal of 'government of the people by the people for the people'. I owe my advancement entirely to the House of Commons, whose servant I am. In my country, as in yours, public men are proud to be the servants of the State and would be ashamed to be its masters. On any day, if they thought the people wanted it, the House of Commons could by a simple vote remove me from my office. But I am not worrying about it at all. As a matter of fact, I am sure they will approve very highly of my journey here, for which I obtained the King's permission in order to meet the President of the United States and to arrange with him all that mapping-out of our military plans, and for all those intimate meetings of the high officers of the armed services of both countries, which are indispensable to the successful prosecution of the war.

I should like to say first of all how much I have been impressed and encouraged by the breadth of view and sense of proportion which I have found in all quarters over here to which I have had access. Anyone who did not understand the size and solidarity of the foundations of the United States might easily have expected to find an excited, disturbed, self-centred atmosphere, with all minds fixed upon the novel, startling and painful episodes of sudden war as they hit America. After all, the United States have been attacked and set upon by three most powerfully armed dictator States. The greatest military power in Europe, the greatest military power in Asia, German and Japan, Italy, too, have all declared, and are making, war upon you, and a quarrel is opened, which can only end in their overthrow or yours. But here in Washington, in these memorable days, I have found an Olympian fortitude which, far from being based upon complacency, is only the mask of an inflexibile purpose and the proof of a sure and well-grounded confidence in the final outcome. We in Britain had the same feeling in our darkest days. We, too, were sure in the end all would be well. You do not, I am certain, underrate the severity of the ordeal to which you and we have still to be subjected. The forces ranged against us are enormous. They are bitter, they are ruthless. The wicked men and their factions who have launched their peoples on the path of war and conquest know that they will be called to terrible account if they cannot beat down by force of arms the peoples they have assailed. They will stop at nothing. They have a vast accumulation of war weapons of all kinds. They have highly trained, disciplined armies, navies, and air services. They have plans and

227

designs which have long been tried and matured. They will stop at nothing that violence or treachery can suggest.

It is quite true that, on our side, our resources in man-power and materials are far greater than theirs. But only a portion of your resources is as yet mobilized and developed, and we both of us have much to learn in the cruel art of war. We have therefore, without doubt, a time of tribulation before us. In this time some ground will be lost which it will be hard and costly to regain. Many disappointments and unpleasant surprises await us. Many of them will afflict us before the full marshalling of our latent and total power can be accomplished. For the best part of twenty years the youth of Britain and America have been taught that war is evil, which is true, and that it would never come again, which has been proved false. For the best part of twenty years the youth of Germany, Japan and Italy have been taught that aggressive war is the noblest duty of the citizen, and that it should be begun as soon as the necessary weapons and organization had been made. We have performed the duties and tasks of peace. They have plotted and planned for war. This, naturally, has placed us in Britain and now places you in the United States at a disadvantage, which only time, courage and strenuous, untiring exertions can correct.

We have indeed to be thankful that so much time has been granted to us. If Germany had tried to invade the British Isles after the French collapse in June 1940, and if Japan had declared war on the British Empire and the United States at about the same date, no one could say what disasters and agonies might not have been our lot. But now at the end of December 1941, our transformation form easy-going peace to total war efficiency has made very great progress. The broad flow of munitions in Great Britain has already begun. Immense strides have been made in the conversion of American industry to military purposes, and now that the United States are at war it is possible for orders to be given every day which a year or eighteen months hence will produce results in war power beyond anything that has yet been seen or foreseen in the dictator States. Provided that every effort is made, that nothing is kept back, that the whole man-power, brain power, virility, valour and civic virtue of the English-speaking world with all its galaxy of loyal, friendly, associated communities and States – provided all that is bent unremittingly to the simple and supreme task, I think it would be reasonable to hope that the end of 1942 will see us quite definitely in a better position than we are now, and that the year 1943 will enable us to assume the initiative upon an ample scale.

Some people may be startled or momentarily depressed when, like your President, I speak of a long and hard war. But our peoples would rather know the truth, sombre though it be. And after all, when we are doing the noblest work in the world, not only defending our hearths and homes but the cause of freedom in other lands, the question of whether deliverance comes in 1942, 1943 or 1944 falls into its proper place in the grand porportions of human history. Sure I am that this day – now – we are the masters of our fate; that the task which has been set us is not above our strength; that its pangs and toils are not beyond our endurance. As long as we have faith in our cause and an unconquerable will-power, salvation will not be denied us. In the words of the Psalmist, 'He shall not be afraid of evil tidings; his heart is fixed, trusting in the Lord.' Not all the tidings will be evil.

On the contrary, mighty strokes of war have already been dealt against the enemy; the glorious defence of their native soil by the Russian armies and people have inflicted wounds upon the Nazi tyranny and system which have bitten deep, and will fester and inflame not only in the Nazi body but in the Nazi mind. The boastful Mussolini has crumbled already. He is now but a lackey and serf, the merest utensil of his master's will. He has inflicted great suffering and wrong upon his own industrious people. He has been stripped of his African empire, Abyssinia has been liberated. Our armies in the East, which so weak and ill-equipped at the moment of French desertion, now control all the regions from Teheran to Benghazi, and from Aleppo and Cyprus to the sources of the Nile.

For many months we devoted ourselves to preparing to take the offensive in Libya. The very considerable battle, which has been proceeding for the last six weeks in the desert, has been most fiercely fought on both sides. Owing to the difficulties of supply on the desert flanks, we were never able to bring numerically equal forces to bear upon the enemy. Therefore, we had to rely upon a superiority in the numbers and quality of tanks and aircraft, British and American. Aided by these, for the first time, we have fought the enemy with equal weapons. For the first time we have made the Hun feel the sharp edge of those tools with which he had enslaved Europe. The armed forces of the enemy in Cyrenaica amounted to about 150,000, of whom about one-third were Germans. General Auchinleck set out to destroy totally that armed force. I have every reason to believe that his aim will be fully accomplished. I am glad to be able to place before you, members of the Senate and of the House of Representatives, at this moment when you are entering the war, proof that with proper weapons and proper organization we are able to beat the life out of the savage Nazi. What Hitler is suffering in Libya is only a sample and foretaste of what we must give him and his accomplices, wherever this war shall lead us, in every quarter of the globe.

There are good tidings also from blue water. The life-line of supplies which joins our two nations across the ocean, without which all might fail, is flowing steadily and freely in spite of all the enemy can do. It is a fact that the British Empire, which many thought eighteen months ago was broken and ruined, is now incomparably stronger, and is growing stronger with every month. Lastly, if you will forgive me for saying it, to me the best tidings of all is that the United States, united as never before, have drawn the sword for freedom and cast away the scabbard.

All these tremendous facts have led the subjugated peoples of Europe to lift up their heads again in hope. They have put aside for ever the shameful temptation of resigning themselves to the conqueror's will. Hope has returned to the hearts of scores of millions of men and women, and with that hope there burns the flame of anger against the brutal, corrupt invader, and still more fiercely burns the fires of hatred and contempt for the squalid quislings whom he has suborned. In a dozen famous ancient

States now prostrate under the Nazi yoke, the masses of the people of all classes and creeds await the hour of liberation, when they too will be able once again to play their part and strike their blows like men. That hour will strike, and its solemn peal will proclaim that the night is past and that the dawn has come.

The onslaught upon us so long and so secretly planned by Japan has presented both our countries with grievous problems for which we could not be fully prepared. If people ask me – as they have a right to ask me in England – why is it that you have not got ample equipment of modern aircraft and Army weapons of all kinds in Malaya and in the East Indies, I can only point to the victories General Auchinleck has gained in the Libyan campaign. Had we diverted and dispersed our gradually grow-ing resources between Libya and Malaya, we should have been found wanting in both theatres. If the United States have been found at a disadvantage at various points in the Pacific Ocean, we know well that it is to no small extent because of the aid you have been giving us in munitions for the defence of the British Isles and for the Libyan campaign, and, above all, because of your help in the battle of the Atlantic, upon which all depends, and which has in consequence been successfully and prosper-ously maintained. Of course it would have been much better, I freely admit, if we had enough resources of all kinds to be at full strength at all threatened points; but considering how slowly and reluctantly we brought ourselves to large-scale preparations, and how long such preparations take, we had no right to expect to be in such a fortunate position.

The choice of how to dispose of our hitherto limited resources had to be made by Britain in time of war and by the United States in time of peace; and I believe that history will pronounce that upon the whole – and it is upon the whole that these matters must be judged – the choice made was right. Now that we are together, now that we are linked in a righteous comradeship of arms, now that our two considerable nations, each in perfect unity, have joined all their life energies in a common resolve, a new scene opens upon which a steady light will glow and brighten.

Many people have been astonished that Japan should in a single day have plunged into war against the United States and the British Empire. We all wonder why, if this dark design, with all its laborious and intricate preparations, had been so long filling their secret minds, they did not choose our moment of weakness eighteen months ago. Viewed quite dispassionately, in spite of the losses we have suffered and the further punishment we shall have to take, it certainly appears to be an irrational act. It is, of course, only prudent to assume that they have made very careful calculations and think they see their way through. Nevertheless, there may be another explanation. We know that for many years past the policy of Japan has been dominated by secret societies of subalterns and junior officers of the Army and Navy, who have enforced their will upon successive Japanese Cabinets and Parliaments by the assassination of any Japanese statesman who opposed, or who did not sufficiently further, their aggressive policy. It may be that these societies, dazzled and dizzy with their own schemes of aggression and the prospect of early victories, have forced their country against its better judgement into war. They have certainly embarked upon a very considerable undertaking. For after the outrages they have committed upon us at Pearl Harbor, in the Pacific Islands, in the Philippines, in Malaya, and in the Dutch East Indies, they must now know that the stakes for which they have decided to play are mortal.

When we consider the resources of the United States and the British Empire compared to those of Japan, when we remember those of China, which has so long and valiantly withstood invasion and when also we observe the Russian menace which hangs over Japan, it becomes still more difficult to reconcile Japanese action with prudence or even with sanity. What kind of a people do they think we are? Is it possible they do not realize that we shall never cease to persevere against them until they have been taught a lesson which they and the world will never forget?

Members of the Senate and members of the House of Representatives, I turn for one moment more from the turmoil and convulsions of the present to the broader basis of the future. Here we are together facing a group of mighty foes who seek our ruin; here we are together defending all that to free men is dear. Twice in a single generation the catastrophe of world war has fallen upon us; twice in our lifetime has the long arm of fate reached across the ocean to bring the United States into the forefront of the battle. If we had kept together after the last War, if we had taken common measures for our safety, this renewal of the curse need never have fallen upon us.

Do we not owe it to ourselves, to our children, to mankind tormented, to make sure that these catastrophes shall not engulf us for the third time? It has been proved that pestilence may break out in the Old World, which carry their destructive ravages into the New World, from which, once they are afoot, the New World cannot by any means escape. Duty and prudence alike command first that the germ-centres of hatred and revenge should be constantly and vigilantly surveyed and treated in good time, and, secondly, that an adequate organization should be set up to make sure that the pestilence can be controlled at its earliest beginnings before it spreads and rages throughout the entire earth.

Five or six years ago it would have been easy, without shedding a drop of blood, for the United States and Great Britain to have insisted on fulfilment of the disarmament clauses of the treaties which Germany signed after the Great War; that also would have been the opportunity for assuring to Germany those raw materials which we declared in the Atlantic Charter should not be denied to any nation, victor or vanquished. That chance has passed. It is gone. Prodigious hammer-strokes have been needed to bring us together again, or if you will allow me to use other language, I will say that he must indeed have a blind soul who cannot see that some great purpose and design is being worked out here below, of which we have the honour to be the faithful servants. It is not given to us to peer into the mysteries of the future. Still, I avow my hope and faith, sure and inviolate, that in the days to come the British and American peoples will for their own safety and for the good of all walk together side by side in majesty, in justice and in peace.

22

A No-Confidence Motion Repulsed

'I Offer No Excuses'

House of Commons, 29 January 1942

WHILE CHURCHILL WAS AWAY IN NORTH AMERICA, optimistically planning for ultimate victory, the military situation further deteriorated. In the Far East, the *Prince of Wales* and the *Repulse* were sunk, and Japanese troops overran Malaya and threatened Singapore itself. At the same time, the German forces in North Africa, brilliantly led by Rommel, were advancing inexorably towards Egypt. Churchill returned to find Parliament restive and determined to force a Commons debate on a vote of confidence in his government and his leadership.

On 27 January 1942, he spoke for two hours. 'One can actually feel the wind of opposition dropping sentence by sentence,' Harold Nicolson recorded. The debate continued for two more days but, as Churchill later recalled, 'the tone was to me unexpectedly friendly'. On 29 January, he delivered this concluding speech. Nicolson thought it 'genial and self-confident'. Even Henry Channon described it as 'conciliatory, tactful – and, finally, successful'.

The eventual vote was 464 in support of the Government and only one against. But there was soon to be further bad news from North Africa and the Far East, and in July 1942 Churchill had to face a further no-confidence debate. Once again, he emerged triumphant, and thereafter his parliamentary position remained essentially secure for the duration of the war.

234

'I Offer No Excuses' 1942

House of Commons, 29 January 1942

NO ONE CAN SAY that this has not been a full and free Debate. No one can say that criticism has been hampered or stifled. No one can say that it has not been a necessary Debate. Many will think it has been a valuable Debate. But I think there will be very few who upon reflection will doubt that a Debate of this far-reaching character and memorable importance, in times of hard and anxious war, with the state of the world what it is, our relationships to other countries being what they are, and our own safety so deeply involved – very few people will doubt that it should not close without a solemn and formal expression of the opinion of the House in relation both to the Government and to the prosecution of the war.

In no country in the world at the present time could a Government conducting a war be exposed to such a stress. No dictator country fighting for its life would dare allow such a discussion. They do not even allow the free transmission of news to their peoples, or even the reception of foreign broadcasts, to which we are all now so hardily inured. Even in the great democracy of the United States the Executive does not stand in the same direct, immediate, day-to-day relation to the Legislative body as we do. The President, in many vital respects independent of the Legislature, Commander-in-Chief of all the Forces of the Republic, has a fixed term of office, during which his authority can scarcely be impugned. But here in this country the House of Commons is master all the time of the life of the Administration. Against its decisions there is only one appeal, the appeal to the nation, an appeal it is very difficult to make under the conditions of a war like this, with a register like this, with air raids and invasion always hanging over us.

Therefore, I say that the House of Commons has a great responsibility. It owes it to itself and it owes it to the people and

235

the whole Empire, and to the world cause, either to produce an effective, alternative Administration by which the King's Government can be carried on, or to sustain that Government in the enormous tasks and trials which it has to endure. I feel myself very much in need of that help at the present time, and I am sure I shall be accorded it in a manner to give encouragement and comfort, as well as guidance and suggestion. I am sorry that I have not been able to be here throughout the whole Debate, but I have read every word of the Debate, except what has been spoken and has not yet been printed, and I can assure the House that I shall be ready to profit to the full from many constructive and helpful lines of thought which have been advanced, even when they come from the most hostile quarters. I shall not be like that saint to whom I have before referred in this House, but whose name I have unhappily forgotten, who refused to do right because the devil prompted him. Neither shall I be deterred from doing what I am convinced is right by the fact that I have thought differently about it in some distant, or even in some recent past.

When events are moving at hurricane speed and when scenes change with baffling frequency, it would be disastrous to lose that flexibility of mind in dealing with new situations on which I have often been complimented, which is the essential counterpart of a consistent and unswerving purpose. Let me take an instance. During my visit to America, events occurred which altered in a decisive way the question of creating a Minister of Production. President Roosevelt has appointed Mr Donald Nelson to supervise the whole field of American production. All the resources of our two countries are now pooled, in shipping, in munitions and in raw materials, and some similar office, I will not say with exactly the same scope, but of similar scope, must be created here, if harmonious working between Great Britain and the United States is to be maintained upon this very high level. I have been for some weeks carefully considering this, and the strong opinions which have been expressed in the House, even though I do not share their reasoning in all respects, have reinforced the conclusions with which I returned from the

United States. I will not of course anticipate any advice that it may be my duty to tender to the Crown.

I was forced to inflict upon the House two days ago a very lengthy statement, which cost me a great deal of time and trouble, in the intervals of busy days and nights, to prepare. I do not desire to add to it to any important extent. It would not be possible for me to answer all the criticisms and inquiries which have been made during this Debate. I have several times pointed out to the House the disadvantage I lie under, compared with the leaders of other countries who are charged with general war direction, in having to make so many public statements, and the danger that in explaining fully our position to our friends we may also be stating it rather too fully to our enemies. Moreover, the Lord Privy Seal, in his excellent speech yesterday, has already replied to a number of the controversial issues which were raised. There are therefore only a few points with which I wish to deal today, but they are important points.

The first is the advantage, not only to Britain but·to the Empire, of the arrival of powerful American Army and Air Forces in the United Kingdom. First of all, this meets the desire of the American people and of the leaders of the Republic that the large mass of trained and equipped troops which they have under arms in the United States shall come into contact with the enemy as close and as soon as possible. Secondly, the presence of these forces in these Islands imparts a greater freedom of movement overseas, to theatres where we are already engaged, of the mature and seasoned divisions of the British Home Army. It avoids the difficulty of reinforcing theatres where we are engaged with troops of another nation, and all the complications of armament and command which arise therefrom. Therefore, we must consider this arrival of the American Army as giving us a latitude of manœuvre which we have not hitherto possessed. Thirdly, the presence in our Islands of a Force of heavy but unknown strength, and the establishment of a broader bridgehead between us and the New World, constituted an additional deterrent to invasion at a time when the successful invasion of these Islands is Hitler's last remaining hope of total victory.

Fourthly – and here I address myself to what has been said about aiding and succouring Australia and New Zealand – the fact that well-equipped American divisions can be sent into these Islands so easily and rapidly will enable substantial supplies of weapons and munitions, now being made in the United States for our account, to be sent direct on the other side of the world to Australia and New Zealand, to meet the new dangers of home defence which are cast upon them by the Japanese war. Lastly, this whole business cannot do Mr de Valera any harm, and it may even do him some good. It certainly offers a measure of protection to Southern Ireland, and to Ireland as a whole, which she could not otherwise enjoy. I feel sure that the House will find these reasons, or most of them, solid and satisfactory.

The course of this Debate has mainly turned upon the admitted inadequacy of our preparations to meet the full onslaught of the new and mighty military opponent who has launched against us his whole force, his whole energies and fury in Malaya and in the Far East. There is not very much I wish to add, and that only by way of illustration, to the connected argument which I deployed to the House on Tuesday. The speeches of the hon. Members for Kidderminster [Sir J. Wardlaw-Milne] and Seaham [Mr Shinwell] dwelt from different angles upon this all-important issue. I do not, of course, pretend that there may not have been avoidable shortcomings or mistakes, or that some oversight may not have been shown in making use of our resources, limited though those resources were. While I take full responsibility for the broad strategic dispositions, that does not mean that scandals, or inefficiency or misbehaviour of functionaries at particular moments and particular places, occurring on the spot, will not be probed or will be covered by the general support I gave to our commanders in the field.

I am by no means claiming that faults have not been committed in the minor sphere, and faults for which the Government are blameworthy. But when all is said and done, the House must not be led into supposing that even if everything on the spot had gone perfectly – which is rare in war – they must not be led into supposing that this would have made any decisive difference to the heavy British and American forfeits which followed inexorably from the temporary loss of sea-power in the Pacific, combined with the fact of our being so fully extended elsewhere. Even that is not exhaustive, because, before the defeat of Pearl Harbor – I am speaking of eight or nine months ago – our ability to defend the Malay Peninsula was seriously prejudiced by the incursion of the Japanese into French Indo-China and the steady building-up of very powerful forces and bases there. Even at the time when I went to meet the President in Newfoundland the invasion of Siam seemed imminent, and probably it was due to the measures which the President took as the result of our conversations that this attack was staved off for so long, and might well have been staved off indefinitely. In ordinary circumstances, if we had not been engaged to the last ounce in Europe and the Nile Valley, we should ourselves, of course, have confronted the Japanese aggression into Indo-China with the strongest possible resistance from the moment when they began to build up a large military and air power. We were not in a position to do this.

If we had gone to war with Japan to stop the Japanese coming across the long ocean stretches from their own country, and establishing themselves within close striking distance of the Malay Peninsula and Singapore, we should have had to fight alone, perhaps for a long time, the whole of the Japanese attacks upon our loosely knit establishments and possessions in this vast Oriental region. As I said on Tuesday, we have never had the power, and we never could have had the power, to fight Germany, Italy and Japan single-handed at the same time. We therefore had to watch the march of events with an anxiety which increased with the growth of the Japanese concentrations, but at the same time was offset by the continuous approach of the United States ever nearer to the confines of the War. It must not be supposed that endless, repeated consultations and discussions were not held by the Staffs, by the Defence Committee, by Ministers, and that Staff conferences were not held at Singapore.

Contact was maintained with Australia and New Zealand, and with the United States to a lesser degree.

All this went on; but, when all was said and done, there was the danger, and the means of meeting it had yet to be found. Ought we not in that interval to have considered the question which the House must ask itself – I want to answer the case quite fairly – whether, in view of that menace, apart from minor precautions, many of which were taken and some of which were not, we ought not to have reduced our aid in munitions to Russia? A part of what we sent to Russia would have made us, I will not say safe, because I do not think that that was possible, in view of what happened at sea, but far better prepared in Burma and Malaya than we were. Figures were mentioned by the hon. Member for Seaham yesterday. He will not expect me to confirm or deny those figures, but, taking them as a basis, half of that would have made us far better off, and would have dazzled the eyes of Sir Robert Brooke-Popham, who so repeatedly asked for more supplies of all those commodities of which we were most short. We did not make such a reduction in Russian supplies, and I believe that the vast majority of opinion in all parts of the House, and in the country, endorses our decision now, even after the event. If they had to go back, they would take it again, even although they see now what consequences have arisen.

I entirely agree about the vital importance of the Burma Road and of fighting with every means in our power to keep a strong hand-grasp with the Chinese Armies and the closest contact with their splendid leader Chiang Kai-shek. Nothing has prevented the employment of Indian troops in that area, except the use of them in other theatres and the immense difficulties of transport in those regions. So much for the Russian policy, which, for good or for ill, has played a very great part in the thoughts and actions of the people of this country in this struggle, and I believe has played a very important – not by any means a decisive part, but a very important part – in the crushing defeats which have been inflicted on the German army and the possible demoralization of the wicked regime which uses that army.

But, apart from Russia, what about the campaign in Libya?

What were the reasons which made that a necessary operation? First, we had to remove, and probably we have removed, the menace to the Nile Valley from the West for a considerable time, thus liberating important forces and still more important transport to meet what seemed to be an impending attack through the Caucasus from the North. Secondly, this was the only place where we could open a second front against the enemy. Everyone will remember, conveniently short as memories may be, the natural and passionate impatience which our prolonged inactivity aroused in all our hearts while Russia seemed to be being battered to pieces by the fearful machinery of the German army. There is no doubt whatever that, although our offensive in Libya was on a small scale compared with the mighty struggle on the Russian front, it nevertheless drew important German air forces from that front. They were moved at a most critical moment in that battle and transferred to the Mediterranean theatre. Thirdly, this second front in the Western Desert afforded us the opportunity of fighting a campaign against Germany and Italy on terms most costly to them. If there be any place where we can fight them with marked advantage, it is in the Western Desert and Libya, because not only, as I have explained, have we managed to destroy two-thirds of their African army and a great amount of its equipment and air power, but also to take a formidable toll of all their reinforcements of men and materials, and above all of their limited shipping across the Mediterranean by which they were forced to maintain themselves. The longer they go on fighting in this theatre the longer that process will go on, and there is no part of the world where you have a chance of getting better results for the blood and valour of your soldiers.

For these reasons, I am sure that it was a sound decision, and one with which all our professional advisers agreed, to take the offensive in the Western Desert and to do our utmost to make it a success. We have been over this ground in Cyrenaica already. The first time we took a quarter of a million Italian prisoners without serious loss to ourselves. The second time we have accounted for 60,000 men, including many Germans, for the loss of only one-third to ourselves. Even if we have to do part of it a third time, as seems possible, in view of the tactical successes of the enemy attacks upon our armoured brigade last week, there seems no reason why the campaign should not retain its profitable character in the war in North East Africa and become a festering sore, a dangerous drain, upon the German and Italian resources.

This is the question: Should we have been right to sacrifice all this, to stand idly on the defensive in the Western Desert and send all our available Forces to garrison Malaya and guard against a war against Japan which nevertheless might not have taken place, and which, I believe, did take place only through the civil Government being overwhelmed by a military *coup d'état*? That is a matter of opinion, and it is quite easy for those who clamoured eagerly for opening an offensive in Libya to dilate upon our want of foresight and preparedness in the Far East. That is a matter on which anyone can form an opinion, and those are lucky who do not have to form one before the course of events is known.

I come now to this battle which is raging in Johore. I cannot tell how it will go or how the attack upon the Island of Singapore will go, but a steady stream of reinforcements, both air and troops, has flowed into the island for several weeks past. The forces which have been sent were, of course, set in motion within a few days, and some within a few hours, of the Japanese declaration of war. To sum up, I submit to the House that the main strategic and political decision to aid Russia, to deliver an offensive in Libya and to accept a consequential state of weakness in the then peaceful theatre of the Far East, was sound, and will be found to have played a useful part in the general course of the War, and that this is in no wise invalidated by the unexpected naval misfortunes and the heavy forfeits which we have paid, and shall have to pay, in the Far East. For this Vote of Confidence, on that I rest.

There is, however, one episode of a tactical rather than a strategic character about which many questions have been asked, both here and in another place, and to which it is not easy to refer. I mean, of course, the dispatch from this country of

242

the *Prince of Wales* during November last and, secondly, the operation which led to the sinking of the *Prince of Wales* and of the *Repulse,* which had started earlier. This sinking took place on 9th December. It was the policy of the War Cabinet and the Defence Committee, initiated by the Naval Staff, to build up in the Indian Ocean, and base mainly on Singapore, a battle squadron to act, it was hoped, in co-operation with the United States fleet in general protective work in Far Eastern waters. I am not at liberty to state how these plans stand at the present time, but the House may be assured that nothing has been left undone, which was in our power, to repair the heavy losses which have been sustained. My right hon. Friend the Member for East Edinburgh [Mr Pethick-Lawrence] has asked very properly why the *Prince of Wales* and *Repulse* were sent to Eastern waters if they could not be properly protected by aircraft. The answer to this question is that the decision to send those ships in advance to the Far East was taken in the hope, primarily, of deterring the Japanese from going to war at all, or, failing that, of deterring her from sending convoys into the Gulf of Siam, having regard to the then position of the strong American fleet at Hawaii.

After long and careful consideration it was decided, in view of the importance of having in Far Eastern waters at least one ship which could catch or kill any individual vessel of the enemy – the Americans then not having a new battleship available – to send the *Prince of Wales.* Moreover, she was the only ship available at the moment which could reach the spot in time for any deterrent effect to be produced. The intention was that these two fast ships, whose arrival at Cape Town was deliberately not concealed, should not only act as a deterrent upon Japan coming into the war but a deterrent upon the activities of individual heavy ships of the enemy, our ships being able to choose their moment to fight. The suggestion of the hon. and gallant Member for Epsom [Sir A. Southby] that the Naval Staff desired to send an aircraft-carrier and were overruled by me is as mischievous as it is untrue. It was always the intention that any fast ships proceeding to the Far East should be accompanied by an aircraft-carrier. Unfortunately, at the time, with the exception of an aircraft-carrier in home waters, not a single ship of this type was available. Through a succession of accidents, some of very slight consquence, all of them, except the one with the Home Fleet, were under repair. Accordingly, the *Prince of Wales* and the *Repulse* arrived at Singapore, and it was hoped they would shortly leave again for secret bases and the broad waters, which would enable them to put a continuous restraining preoccupation on all the movements of the enemy. That is the first phase of the story.

I now come to the further question of why, the presence of the two ships having failed to achieve the deterrent object, Pearl Harbor having occurred, and the Japanese having begun war, they were sent North from Singapore to oppose the Japanese landings from the Gulf of Siam on the Kra Peninsula. Admiral Tom Phillips, as Vice-Chief of the Naval Staff, was fully acquainted with the whole policy I have described, and had sailed in the *Prince of Wales* to carry it out. On 8th December he decided, after conferring with his captain and staff officers, that in the circumstances, and in view of the movement of Japanese transports with a weak fighting escort towards the Kra Peninsula, drastic and urgent naval action was required. This action, if successful, would have presented the Army with a good prospect of defeating the landings and possibly of paralysing the invasion of Malaya at its birth. The stakes on both sides were very high. The prize was great if gained; if lost, our danger most grievous. Admiral Phillips was fully aware of the risk, and he took steps for air reconnaissance to see whether there was an enemy aircraft-carrier about, and for fighter protection up to the limit of the short-range fighters available. Only after he left harbour was he informed that fighter protection could not be provided in the area in which he intended to operate, but in view of the low visibility he decided to stand on. Later, in accordance with his predetermined plans, he turned back, because the weather began to clear, and he knew he had been sighted. However, later still, during his retirement, a further landing more to the south of the peninsula was reported, presenting an even more serious threat to Malaya, and he decided to investigate this. It was on returning from this investigation, which proved to be negative, that his force was attacked, not, as has been supposed, by torpedo or bomber aircraft flown off a carrier, but by very long-range, shore-based, heavy, two-engined torpedo bombers from the main Japanese aerodromes 400 miles away.

In the opinion of the Board of Admiralty, which it is my duty to pronounce, the risks which Admiral Phillips took were fair and reasonable, in the light of the knowledge which he had of the enemy, when compared with the very urgent and vital issues at stake on which the whole safety of Malaya might have depended. I have given an account of this episode. No doubt the Admiralty will have its own inquiry for the purpose of informing itself and of studying the lessons, but I could not bring myself, on the first day that this matter was mentioned, when the information I had was most scanty, to pronounce condemnation on the audacious, daring action of Admiral Tom Phillips in going forward, although he knew of the risks he ran, when the prize might have been 20,000 of the enemy drowned in the sea, and a relief from the whole catalogue of misfortunes which have since come upon us, and have still to come.

I have finished, and it only remains for us to act. I have tried to lay the whole position before the House as far as public interest will allow, and very fully have we gone into matters. On behalf of His Majesty's Government, I make no complaint of the Debate, I offer no apologies, I offer no excuses, I make no promises. In no way have I mitigated the sense of danger and impending misfortunes of a minor character and of a severe character which still hang over us, but at the same time I avow my confidence, never stronger than at this moment, that we shall bring this conflict to an end in a manner agreeable to the interests of our country, and in a manner agreeable to the future welfare of the world. I have finished. Let every man act now in accordance with what he thinks is his duty in harmony with his heart and conscience.

23

On the Death of Lloyd George

'A Man of Action, Resource and Creative Energy'

House of Commons, 28 March 1945

CHURCHILL HAD FIRST MET LLOYD GEORGE immediately after he had delivered his own maiden speech in the Commons in February 1901. Initially, they were political opponents, but after Churchill joined the Liberals they became firm friends and close colleagues, and were almost continuously in office together from 1905 to 1922. Thereafter, their paths diverged. In 1940, Lloyd George refused to take office in Churchill's coalition; and for much of the war he was one of the Prime Minister's most persistent (and defeatist) critics.

As with his eulogy of Neville Chamberlain, however, Churchill's tribute was a model of its kind, as one great war leader acclaimed and saluted another. Indeed, many of its phrases apply with equal truth to Churchill himself: 'He aroused intense and sometimes needless antagonisms. He had fierce and bitter quarrels at various times with all the parties.' And, above all, this: 'As a man of action, resource and creative energy he stood, when at his zenith, without a rival.'

John Colville thought the tribute 'eloquent in parts and well delivered' but not 'as good as that he paid to Neville Chamberlain'. Clementine Churchill, on her way to Moscow, wrote to her husband that 'I loved your speech about LG. It recalled forgotten blessings which he showered on the meek and lowly.' Unlike Colville, and unlike her husband, she remained at heart a lifelong Liberal.

246

House of Commons, 28 March 1945

SHORTLY AFTER DAVID LLOYD GEORGE first took Cabinet office as President of the Board of Trade, the Liberals, who had been in eclipse for twenty years, obtained, in January 1906, an overwhelming majority over all other parties. They were independent of the Irish; the Labour Party was in its infancy; the Conservatives were reduced to little more than 100. But this moment of political triumph occurred in a period when the aspirations of nineteenth-century Liberalism had been largely achieved. Most of the great movements and principles of Liberalism had become the common property of enlightened men all over the civilized world. The chains had been struck from the slave; a free career was open to talent; the extension of the franchise was moving irresistibly forward; the advance in education was rapid and continuous, not only in this Island but in many lands. Thus at the moment when the Liberal Party became supreme, the great and beneficent impulses which had urged them forward were largely assuaged by success. Some new and potent conception had to be found by those who were called into power.

It was Lloyd George who launched the Liberal and Radical forces of this country effectively into the broad stream of social betterment and social security along which all modern parties now steer. There was no man so gifted, so eloquent, so forceful, who knew the life of the people so well. His warm heart was stirred by the many perils which beset the cottage homes: the health of the bread-winner, the fate of his widow, the nourishment and upbringing of his children, the meagre and haphazard provision of medical treatment and sanatoria, and the lack of any organized accessible medical service of a kind worthy of the age, from which the mass of the wage earners and the poor suffered. All this excited his wrath. Pity and compassion lent their powerful wings. He knew the terror with which old age threatened the toiler – that after a life of exertion he could be no more than a burden at the fireside and in the family of a struggling son. When I first became Lloyd George's friend and active associate, now more than forty years ago, this deep love of the people, the profound knowledge of their lives and of the undue and needless pressures under which they lived, impressed itself indelibly upon my mind.

Then there was his dauntless courage, his untiring energy, his oratory, persuasive, provocative, now grave, now gay. His swift, penetrating, comprehensive mind was always grasping at the root, or what he thought to be the root, of every question. His eye ranged ahead of the obvious. He was always hunting in the field beyond. I have often heard people come to him with a plan, and he would say 'That is all right, but what happens when we get over the bridge? What do we do then?'

In his prime, his power, his influence, his initiative, were unequalled in the land. He was the champion of the weak and the poor. Those were great days. Nearly two generations have passed. Most people are unconscious of how much their lives have been shaped by the laws for which Lloyd George was responsible. Health Insurance and Old Age Pensions were the first large-scale State-conscious efforts to set a balustrade along the crowded causeway of the people's life, and, without pulling down the structures of society, to fasten a lid over the abyss into which vast numbers used to fall, generation after generation, uncared-for and indeed unnoticed. Now we move forward confidently into larger and more far-reaching applications of these ideas. I was his lieutenant in those bygone days, and shared in a minor way in the work. I have lived to see long strides taken, and being taken, and going to be taken, on this path of insurance by which the vultures of utter ruin are driven from the dwellings of the nation. The stamps we lick, the roads we travel, the system of progressive taxation, the principal remedies that have so far been used against unemployment – all these to a very great extent were part not only of the mission but of the actual achievement of Lloyd George; and I am sure that as time passes his name will not only live but shine on account of the great, laborious, constructive work he did for the social and domestic life of our country.

When the calm, complacent, self-satisfied tranquillities of the Victorian era had exploded into the world convulsions and wars of the terrible twentieth century, Lloyd George had another part to play on which his fame will stand with equal or even greater firmness. Although unacquainted with the military arts, although by public repute a pugnacious pacifist, when the life of our country was in peril he rallied to the war effort and cast aside all other thoughts and aims. He was the first to discern the fearful shortages of ammunition and artillery and all the other appliances of war which would so soon affect, and in the case of Imperial Russia mortally affect, the warring nations on both sides. He saw it before anyone. Here I must say that my hon. and gallant Friend the Member for Wycombe [Sir A. Knox] was a truthful and vigilant prophet and guide in all that information which we received. He was our military representative in Russia. But it was Mr Lloyd George who fixed on these papers, brought them forth before the eyes of the Cabinet, and induced action to be taken with the utmost vigour possible at that late hour.

Lloyd George left the Exchequer, when the Coalition Government was formed, for the Ministry of Munitions. Here he hurled himself into the mobilization of British industry. In 1915 he was building great war factories that could not come into operation for two years. There was the usual talk about the war being over in a few months, but he did not hesitate to plan on a vast scale for two years ahead. It was my fortune to inherit the output of those factories in 1917 – the vast, overflowing output which came from them. Presently Lloyd George seized the main power in the State and the leadership of the Government. [*Hon. Members: 'Seized?'*] Seized. I think it was Carlyle who said of Oliver Cromwell: 'He coveted the place; perhaps the place was his.' He imparted immediately a new surge of strength, of impulse, far stronger than anything that had been known up to that time, and extending over the whole field of wartime Government, every part of which was of equal interest to him.

I have already written about him at this time, when I watched him so closely and enjoyed his confidence and admired him so much, and I have recorded two characteristics of his which seemed to me invaluable in those days: first, his power to live in the present yet without taking short views; and secondly, his power of drawing from misfortune itself the means of future success. All this was illustrated by the successful development of the war; by the adoption of the convoy system, which he enforced upon the Admiralty and by which the U-boats were defeated; by the unified command on the Western Front which gave Marshal Foch the power to lead us all to victory; and in many other matters which form a part of the story of those sombre and tremendous years, the memory of which forever abides with me, and to which I have often recurred in thought during our present, second heavy struggle against German aggression, now drawing towards its victorious close.

Thus the statesman and guide whose gentle passing in the fullness of his years we mourn today served our country, our Island and our age, both faithfully and well in peace and in war. His long life was, from almost the beginning to almost the end, spent in political strife and controversy. He aroused intense and sometimes needless antagonisms. He had fierce and bitter quarrels at various times with all the parties. He faced undismayed the storms of criticism and hostility. In spite of all obstacles, including those he raised himself, he achieved his main purposes. As a man of action, resource and creative energy he stood, when at his zenith, without a rival. His name is a household word throughout our Commonwealth of Nations. He was the greatest Welshman which that unconquerable race has produced since the age of the Tudors. Much of his work abides, some of it will grow greatly in the future, and those who come after us will find the pillars of his life's toil upstanding, massive and indestructible; and we ourselves, gathered here today, may indeed be thankful that he voyaged with us through storm and tumult with so much help and guidance to bestow.

24

On the Death of Franklin Roosevelt

'The Greatest Champion of Freedom'

House of Commons, 17 April 1945

THIS WAS THE THIRD GREAT SET-PIECE EULOGY which Churchill delivered during the war. He regarded the President's death as almost 'a physical blow'. Their long and cordial association had been unique in the annals of Western statesmanship. In the spring of 1945, with Hitler's Germany in full retreat, but with Stalin's Russia advancing inexorably from the east, Churchill deeply regretted this sudden weakening in Anglo-American leadership and collaboration.

His first thought was to fly to Washington for the funeral, where he hoped to establish close and cordial relations with the new President. Eventually, he decided not to go – a decision which he later regretted. His eulogy was feverishly composed over lunch, between the memorial service held for Roosevelt at St Paul's in the morning and the meeting of the Commons in the afternoon. The House was crowded to hear him, but he was held up for an hour by a trivial but distracting debate concerning the admission of a recently elected Scottish Nationalist MP.

Thus delayed, and with the early inspiration gone, Churchill eventually delivered his eulogy. His restive audience was clearly less impressed than usual. John Colville considered it 'adequate, but not one of his finest efforts.' And Harold Nicolson agreed: 'I did not think him very good – nothing like so good as when he made the funeral oration on Neville Chamberlain, which was truly Periclean.' Nevertheless, the speech reads magnificently.

House of Commons, 17 April 1945

MY FRIENDSHIP WITH THE GREAT MAN to whose work and fame we pay our tribute today began and ripened during this war. I had met him, but only for a few minutes, after the close of the last war, and as soon as I went to the Admiralty in September 1939, he telegraphed, inviting me to correspond with him direct on naval or other matters if at any time I felt inclined. Having obtained the permission of the Prime Minister, I did so. Knowing President Roosevelt's keen interest in sea warfare, I furnished him with a stream of information about our naval affairs, and about the various actions, including especially the action of the Plate River, which lighted the first gloomy winter of the war.

When I became Prime Minister, and the war broke out in all its hideous fury, when our own life and survival hung in the balance, I was already in a position to telegraph to the President on terms of an association which had become most intimate and, to me most agreeable. This continued through all the ups and downs of the world struggle until Thursday last, when I received my last messages from him. These messages showed no falling-off in his accustomed clear vision and vigour upon perplexing and complicated matters. I may mention that this correspondence which, of course, was greatly increased after the United States' entry into the war, comprises, to and fro between us, over 1,700 messages. Many of these were lengthy messages, and the majority dealt with those difficult points which come to be discussed upon the level of Heads of Governments only after official solutions have not been reached at other stages. To this correspondence there must be added our nine meetings – at Argentia, three in Washington, at Casablanca, at Teheran, two at Quebec and, last of all, at Yalta, comprising in all about 120 days of close personal contact, during a great part of which I stayed with him at the White House, or at his home at Hyde Park or in his retreat in the Blue Mountains, which he called 'Shangri-la'.

I conceived an admiration for him as a statesman, a man of affairs, and a war leader. I felt the utmost confidence in his upright, inspiring character and outlook, and a personal regard – affection I must say – for him beyond my power to express today. His love of his own country, his respect for its constitution, his power of gauging the tides and currents of its mobile public opinion, were always evident, but added to these were the beatings of that generous heart which was always stirred to anger and to action by spectacles of aggression and oppression by the strong against the weak. It is, indeed, a loss, a bitter loss to humanity that those heart-beats are stilled for ever.

President Roosevelt's physical affliction lay heavily upon him. It was a marvel that he bore up against it through all the many years of tumult and storm. Not one man in ten millions, stricken and crippled as he was, would have attempted to plunge into a life of physical and mental exertion and of hard, ceaseless political controversy. Not one in ten millions would have tried, not one in a generation would have succeeded, not only in entering this sphere, not only in acting vehemently in it, but in becoming indisputable master of the scene. In this extraordinary effort of the spirit over the flesh, of will-power over physical infirmity, he was inspired and sustained by that noble woman his devoted wife, whose high ideals marched with his own, and to whom the deep and respectful sympathy of the House of Commons flows out today in all fullness.

There is no doubt that the President foresaw the great dangers closing in upon the pre-war world with far more prescience than most well-informed people on either side of the Atlantic, and that he urged forward with all his power such precautionary military preparations as peace-time opinion in the United States could be brought to accept. There never was a moment's doubt, as the quarrel opened, upon which side his sympathies lay. The fall of France, and what seemed to most people outside this Island the impending destruction of Great Britain, were to him an agony, although he never lost faith in us. They were an agony to him not only on account of Europe, but because of the serious perils to which the United States herself would have been exposed had we been overwhelmed or the survivors cast down under the German yoke. The bearing of the British nation at that time of stress, when we were all alone, filled him and vast numbers of his countrymen with the warmest sentiments towards our people. He and they felt the blitz of the stern winter of 1940–41, when Hitler set himself to rub out the cities of our country, as much as any of us did, and perhaps more indeed, for imagination is often more torturing than reality. There is no doubt that the bearing of the British and, above all, of the Londoners, kindled fires in American bosoms far harder to quench than the conflagrations from which we were suffering. There was also at that time, in spite of General Wavell's victories – all the more, indeed, because of the reinforcements which were sent from this country to him – the apprehension widespread in the United States that we should be invaded by Germany after the fullest preparation in the spring of 1941. It was in February that the President sent to England the late Mr Wendell Willkie, who, although a political rival and an opposing candidate, felt as he did on many important points. Mr Willkie brought a letter from Mr Roosevelt, which the President had written in his own hand, and this letter contained the famous lines of Longfellow:

> . . . *Sail on, O ship of State!*
> *Sail on, O Union, strong and great!*
> *Humanity with all its fears,*
> *With all the hopes of future years,*
> *Is hanging breathless on thy fate!*

At about that same time he devised the extraordinary measure of assistance called Lend-Lease, which will stand forth as the most unselfish and unsordid financial act of any country in all history. The effect of this was greatly to increase British fighting power, and for all the purposes of the war effort to make us, as it were, a much more numerous community. In that autumn I met the President for the first time during the war at Argentia in

Newfoundland, and together we drew up the Declaration which has since been called the Atlantic Charter, and which will, I trust, long remain a guide for both our peoples and for other peoples of the world.

All this time, in deep and dark and deadly secrecy, the Japanese were preparing their act of treachery and greed. When next we met in Washington, Japan, Germany and Italy had declared war upon the United States, and both our countries were in arms, shoulder to shoulder. Since then we have advanced over the land and over the sea through many difficulties and disappointments, but always with a broadening measure of success. I need not dwell upon the series of great operations which have taken place in the Western Hemisphere, to say nothing of that other immense war proceeding on the other side of the world. Nor need I speak of the plans which we made with our great Ally, Russia, at Teheran, for these have now been carried out for all the world to see.

But at Yalta I noticed that the President was ailing. His captivating smile, his gay and charming manner, had not deserted him, but his face had a transparency, an air of purification, and often there was a faraway look in his eyes. When I took my leave of him in Alexandria harbour I must confess that I had an indefinable sense of fear that his health and his strength were on the ebb. But nothing altered his inflexible sense of duty. To the end he faced his innumerable tasks unflinching. One of the tasks of the President is to sign maybe a hundred or two State papers with his own hand every day, commissions and so forth. All this he continued to carry out with the utmost strictness. When death came suddenly upon him 'he had finished his mail.' That portion of his day's work was done. As the saying goes, he died in harness, and we may well say in battle harness, like his soldiers, sailors, and airmen, who side by side with ours are carrying on their task to the end all over the world. What an enviable death was his! He had brought his country through the worst of its perils and the heaviest of its toils. Victory had cast its sure and steady beam upon him.

In the days of peace he had broadened and stabilized the

foundations of American life and union. In war he had raised the strength, might and glory of the great Republic to a height never attained by any nation in history. With her left hand she was leading the advance of the conquering Allied Armies into the heart of Germany, and with her right, on the other side of the globe, she was irresistibly and swiftly breaking up the power of Japan. And all the time ships, munitions, supplies and food of every kind were aiding on a gigantic scale her Allies, great and small, in the course of the long struggle.

But all this was no more than wordly power and grandeur, had it not been that the causes of human freedom and of social justice, to which so much of his life had been given, added a lustre to this power and pomp and warlike might, a lustre which will long be discernible among men. He has left behind him a band of resolute and able men handling the numerous inter-related parts of the vast American war machine. He has left a successor who comes forward with firm step and sure conviction to carry on the task to its appointed end. For us, it remains only to say that in Franklin Roosevelt there died the greatest American friend we have ever known, and the greatest champion of freedom who has ever brought help and comfort from the new world to the old.

25

Victory in Europe

'Forward, Till the Whole Task Is Done'

BBC, London, 13 May 1945

WITHIN WEEKS OF ROOSEVELT'S DEATH, the war in Europe came to an end. By late April, Russian and American forces had linked up, Berlin was surrounded, Hitler had committed suicide, and Mussolini had been shot by Italian partisans. On 7 May, the unconditional surrender was signed by General Jodl, the German Chief of Staff, to take effect at midnight on 8/9 May. Churchill made a brief broadcast, received a great ovation in the Commons, and appeared on the balcony of Buckingham Palace together with the Royal Family – the last politician ever to do so.

On 13 May, he delivered this 40-minute victory broadcast, his last great speech as leader of the Coalition Government. Its theme was that of triumph and tragedy, the very words he was to use as the title of the last volume of his history of the war. He spoke with understandable pride of the improvement in Britain's position during the five years he had been Prime Minister, and he fully acknowledged the contributions of the Empire, the Americans and the Russians to ultimate victory.

He also made what Harold Nicolson called 'an envenomed attack on de Valera', expressed his fears for the future of freedom in many parts of Europe, and reminded his audience that the war against Japan had still to be fought and won. Although Churchill was by this time a very tired man, his speech was a masterly survey of the course of the war, richly informed by his own passionate belief in Britain's historic destiny.

257

BBC, London, 13 May 1945

IT WAS FIVE YEARS AGO on Thursday last that His Majesty the King commissioned me to form a National Government of all parties to carry on our affairs. Five years is a long time in human life, especially when there is no remission for good conduct. However, this National Government was sustained by Parliament and by the entire British nation at home and by all our fighting men abroad, and by the unswerving co-operation of the Dominions far across the oceans and of our Empire in every quarter of the globe. After various episodes had occurred it became clear last week that so far things have worked out pretty well, and that the British Commonwealth and Empire stands more united and more effectively powerful than at any time in its long romantic history. Certainly we are – this is what may well, I think, be admitted by any fair-minded person – in a far better state to cope with the problems and perils of the future than we were five years ago.

For a while our prime enemy, our mighty enemy, Germany, overran almost all Europe. France, who bore such a frightful strain in the last great war, was beaten to the ground and took some time to recover. The Low Countries, fighting to the best of their strength, were subjugated. Norway was overrun. Mussolini's Italy stabbed us in the back when we were, as he thought, at our last gasp. But for ourselves – our lot, I mean – the British Commonwealth and Empire, we were absolutely alone.

In July, August and September 1940, forty or fifty squadrons of British fighter aircraft in the Battle of Britain broke the teeth of the German air fleet at odds of seven or eight to one. May I repeat again the words I used at that momentous hour: 'Never in the field of human conflict was so much owed by so many to so few.' The name of Air Chief Marshal Lord Dowding will always be linked with this splendid event. But conjoined with the Royal Air Force lay the Royal Navy, ever ready to tear to pieces the barges, gathered from the canals of Holland and Belgium, in which a German invading army could alone have been transported. I was never one to believe that the invasion of Britain, with the tackle that the enemy had at that time, was a very easy task to accomplish. With the autumn storms, the immediate danger of invasion in 1940 passed.

Then began the blitz, when Hitler said he would 'rub out our cities.' That's what he said 'rub out our cities.' This blitz was borne without a word of complaint or the slightest sign of flinching, while a very large number of people – honour to them all – proved that London could 'take it', and so could our other ravaged centres. But the dawn of 1941 revealed us still in jeopardy. The hostile aircraft could fly across the approaches to our Island, where forty-six millions of people had to import half their daily bread and all the materials they needed for peace or war: these hostile aircraft could fly across the approaches from Brest to Norway and back again in a single flight. They could observe all the movements of our shipping in and out of the Clyde and Mersey, and could direct upon our convoys the large and increasing numbers of U-boats with which the enemy bespattered the Atlantic – the survivors or successors of which U-boats are now being collected in British harbours.

The sense of envelopment, which might at any moment turn to strangulation, lay heavy upon us. We had only the North-Western approach between Ulster and Scotland through which to bring in the means of life and to send out the forces of war. Owing to the action of Mr de Valera, so much at variance with the temper and instinct of thousands of Southern Irishmen who hastened to the battle-front to prove their ancient valour, the approaches which the Southern Irish ports and airfields could so easily have guarded were closed by the hostile aircraft and U-boats. This was indeed a deadly moment in our life, and if it had not been for the loyalty and friendship of Northern Ireland we should have been forced to come to close quarters with Mr de Valera or perish for ever from the earth. However, with a restraint and poise to which, I say, history will find few parallels, His Majesty's Government never laid a violent hand upon them, though at times it would have been quite easy and quite natural, and we left the de Valera Government to frolic with the Germans and later with the Japanese representatives to their hearts' content.

When I think of these days I think also of other episodes and personalities. I think of Lieutenant-Commander Esmonde, VC, of Lance-Corporal Kenneally, VC, and Captain Fegen, VC, and other Irish heroes that I could easily recite, and then I must confess that bitterness by Britain against the Irish race dies in my heart. I can only pray that in years which I shall not see the shame will be forgotten and the glories will endure, and that the peoples of the British Isles as of the British Commonwealth of Nations will walk together in mutual comprehension and forgiveness.

My friends, when our minds turn to the North-Western approaches, we will not forget the devotion of our merchant seamen, and our minesweepers out every night, and so rarely mentioned in the headlines. Nor will we forget the vast, inventive, adaptive, all-embracing and, in the end, all-controlling power of the Royal Navy, with its ever more potent new ally, the air. These have kept the life-line open. We were able to breathe; we were able to live; we were able to strike. Dire deeds we had to do. We had to destroy or capture the French fleet which, had it ever passed undamaged into German hands, would, together with the Italian fleet, have perhaps enabled the German Navy to face us on the high seas. This we did. We had to make the dispatch to General Wavell all round the Cape, at our darkest hour, of the tanks – practically all we had in the Island – and this enabled us as far back as November 1940, to defend Egypt against invasion and hurl back with the loss of a quarter of a million captives and with heavy slaughter the Italian armies at whose tail Mussolini had already planned to ride into Cairo or Alexandria.

Great anxiety was felt by President Roosevelt, and indeed by thinking men throughout the United States, about what would happen to us in the early part of 1941. The President felt to the depths of his being that the destruction of Britain would not only be an event fearful in itself, but that it would expose to mortal danger the vast and as yet largely unarmed potentialities and the future destiny of the United States. He feared greatly that we should be invaded in that spring of 1941, and no doubt he had behind him military advice as good as any that is known in the world, and he sent his recent Presidential opponent, the late Mr Wendell Willkie, to me with a letter in which he had written in his own hand the famous lines of Longfellow which I quoted in the House of Commons the other day.

We were, however, in a fairly tough condition by the early months of 1941, and felt very much better about ourselves than in those months immediately after the collapse of France. Our Dunkirk army and field force troops in Britain, almost a million strong, were nearly all equipped or re-equipped. We had ferried over the Atlantic a million rifles and a thousand cannon from the United States, with all their ammunition, since the previous June. In our munition works, which were becoming very power-ful, men and women had worked at their machines till they dropped senseless from fatigue. Nearly one million of men, growing to two millions at the peak, although working all day, had been formed into the Home Guard. They were armed at least with rifles, and armed also with the spirit 'Conquer or Die.'

Later in 1941, when we were still alone, we sacrificed unwil-lingly, to some extent unwittingly, our conquests of the winter in Cyrenaica and Libya in order to stand by Greece; and Greece will never forget how much we gave, albeit unavailingly, of the little we had. We did this for honour. We repressed the German-instigated rising in Iraq. We defended Palestine. With the assistance of General de Gaulle's indomitable Free French we cleared Syria and the Lebanon of Vichyites and of German aviators and intriguers. And then in June, 1941, another tremen-dous world event occurred.

You have no doubt noticed in your reading of British history – and I hope you will take pains to read it, for it is only from the past that one can judge the future, and it is only from reading the story of the British nation, of the British Empire, that you can feel a well-grounded sense of pride to dwell in these islands – you have sometimes noticed in your reading of British history that we have had to hold out from time to time all alone, or to be the mainspring of coalitions, against a continental tyrant or dictator, and we have had to hold out for quite a long time: against the Spanish Armada, against the might of Louis XIV, when we led Europe for nearly twenty-five years under William III and Marlborough, and 150 years ago, when Nelson, Pitt and Wellington broke Napoleon, not without assistance from the heroic Russians of 1812. In all these world wars our Island kept the lead of Europe or else held out alone.

And if you hold out alone long enough, there always comes a time when the tyrant makes some ghastly mistake which alters the whole balance of the struggle. On June 22 1941, Hitler master as he thought himself of all Europe – nay, indeed, soon to be master of the world, so he thought – treacherously, without warning, without the slightest provocation, hurled himself on Russia and came face to face with Marshal Stalin and the numberless millions of the Russian people. And then at the end of the year Japan struck a felon blow at the United States at Pearl Harbor, and at the same time attacked us in Malaya and Singapore. Thereupon Hitler and Mussolini declared war on the Republic of the United States.

Years have passed since then. Indeed every year seems to me almost a decade. But never since the United States entered the war have I had the slightest doubt but that we should be saved, and that we only had to do our duty in order to win. We have played our part in all this process by which the evil-doers have been overthrown, and I hope I do not speak vain or boastful words, but from Alamein in October 1942, through the Anglo-American invasion of North Africa, of Sicily, of Italy, with the capture of Rome, we marched many miles and never knew defeat. And then last year, after two years' patient preparation and marvellous devices of amphibious warfare – and mark you, our scientists are not surpassed in any nation in the world, especially when their thought is applied to naval matters – last year on June 6 we seized a carefully selected little toe of German-occupied France and poured millions in from this

Island and from across the Atlantic, until the Seine, the Somme and the Rhine all fell behind the advancing Anglo-American spearheads. France was liberated. She produced a fine army of gallant men to aid her own liberation. Germany lay open.

Now from the other side the mighty military achievements of the Russian people, always holding many more German troops on their front than we could do, rolled forward to meet us in the heart and centre of Germany. At the same time, in Italy, Field-Marshal Alexander's army of so many nations, the largest part of which was British or British Empire, struck their final blow and compelled more than a million enemy troops to surrender. This Fifteenth Army Group, as we call it, British and Americans joined together in almost equal numbers, are now deep in Austria, joining their right hand with the Russians and their left with the United States armies of General Eisenhower's command. It happened, as you may remember – but memories are short – that in the space of three days we received the news of the unlamented departures of Mussolini and Hitler, and in three days also surrenders were made to Field-Marshal Alexander and Field-Marshal Montgomery of over 2,500,000 soldiers of this terrible warlike German army.

I shall make it clear at this moment that we never failed to recognize the immense superiority of the power used by the United States in the rescue of France and the defeat of Germany. For our part, British and Canadians, we have had about one-third as many men over there as the Americans, but we have taken our full share of the fighting, as the scale of our losses shows. Our Navy has borne incomparably the heaviest burden in the Atlantic Ocean, in the narrow seas and the Arctic convoys to Russia, while the United States Navy has had to use its immense strength mainly against Japan. We made a fair division of the labour, and we can each report that our work is either done or going to be done. It is right and natural that we should extol the virtues and glorious services of our own most famous commanders, Alexander and Montgomery, neither of whom was ever defeated since they began together at Alamein. Both of them have conducted in Africa, in Italy, in Normandy and in Germany, battles of the first magnitude and of decisive consequence. At the same time we know how great is our debt to the combining and unifying command and high strategic direction of General Eisenhower.

And here is the moment when I pay my personal tribute to the British Chiefs of the Staff, with whom I worked in the closest intimacy throughout these heavy, stormy years. There have been very few changes in this small, powerful and capable body of men who, sinking all Service differences and judging the problems of the war as a whole, have worked together in perfect harmony with each other. In Field-Marshal Brooke, in Admiral Pound, succeeded after his death by Admiral Andrew Cunningham, and in Marshal of the Air Portal, a team was formed who deserved the highest honour in the direction of the whole British war strategy and in its relations with that of our Allies.

It may well be said that our strategy was conducted so that the best combinations, the closest concert, were imparted into the operations by the combined staffs of Britain and the United States, with whom, from Teheran onwards, the war leaders of Russia were joined. And it may also be said that never have the forces of two nations fought side by side and intermingled in the lines of battle with so much unity, comradeship and brotherhood as in the great Anglo-American Armies. Some people say: Well, what would you expect, if both nations speak the same language, have the same laws, have a great part of their history in common, and have very much the same outlook upon life with all its hope and glory? Isn't it just the sort of thing that would happen? And others may say: It would be an ill day for all the world and for the pair of them if they did not go on working together and marching together and sailing together and flying together, whenever something has to be done for the sake of freedom and fair play all over the world. That is the great hope of the future.

There was one final danger from which the collapse of Germany has saved us. In London and the southeastern counties we have suffered for a year from various forms of flying-bombs – perhaps you have heard about this – and rockets, and our Air Force and our ack-ack batteries have done wonders against them. In particular the Air Force turned on in good time on what then seemed very slight and doubtful evidence, hampered and vastly delayed all German preparations. But it was only when our Armies cleaned up the coast and overran all the points of discharge, and when the Americans captured vast stores of rockets of all kinds near Leipzig, which only the other day added to the information we had, and when all the preparations being made on the coasts of France and Holland could be examined in detail, in scientific detail, that we knew how grave had been the peril, not only from rockets and flying-bombs but from multiple long-range artillery which was being prepared against London. Only just in time did the Allied armies blast the viper in his nest. Otherwise the autumn of 1944, to say nothing of 1945, might well have seen London as shattered as Berlin.

For the same period the Germans had prepared a new U-boat fleet and novel tactics which, though we should have eventually destroyed them, might well have carried anti-U-boat warfare back to the high peak days of 1942. Therefore we must rejoice and give thanks, not only for our preservation when we were all alone, but for our timely deliverance from new suffering, new perils not easily to be measured.

I wish I could tell you tonight that all our toils and troubles were over. Then indeed I could end my five years' service happily, and if you thought that you had had enough of me and that I ought to be put out to grass, I tell you I would take it with the best of grace. But, on the contrary, I must warn you, as I did when I began this five years' task – and no one knew then that it would last so long – that there is still a lot to do, and that you must be prepared for further efforts of mind and body and further sacrifices to great causes if you are not to fall back into the rut of inertia, the confusion of aim, and the craven fear of being great. You must not weaken in any way in your alert and vigilant frame of mind. Though holiday rejoicing is necessary to the human spirit, yet it must add to the strength and resilience with which every man and woman turns again to the work they have to do, and also to the outlook and watch they have to keep on public affairs.

On the continent of Europe we have yet to make sure that the simple and honourable purposes for which we entered the war are not brushed aside or overlooked in the months following our success, and that the words 'freedom', 'democracy' and 'liberation' are not distorted from their true meaning as we have understood them. There would be little use in punishing the Hitlerites for their crimes if law and justice did not rule, and if totalitarian or police governments were to take the place of the German invaders. We seek nothing for ourselves. But we must make sure that those causes which we fought for find recognition at the peace table in facts as well as words, and above all we must labour that the world organization which the United Nations are creating at San Francisco does not become an idle name, does not become a shield for the strong and a mockery for the weak. It is the victors who must search their hearts in their glowing hours, and be worthy by their nobility of the immense forces that they wield.

We must never forget that beyond all lurks Japan, harassed and failing but still a people of a hundred millions, for whose warriors death has few terrors. I cannot tell you tonight how much time or what exertions will be required to compel the Japanese to make amends for their odious treachery and cruelty. We – like China, so long undaunted – have received horrible injuries from them ourselves, and we are bound by the ties of honour and fraternal loyalty to the United States to fight this great war at the other end of the world at their side without flagging or failing. We must remember that Australia and New Zealand and Canada were and are all directly menaced by this evil Power. They came to our aid in our dark times, and we must not leave unfinished any task which concerns their safety and their future. I told you hard things at the beginning of these last five years; you did not shrink, and I should be unworthy of your confidence and generosity if I did not still cry: Forward, unflinching, unswerving, indomitable, till the whole task is done and the whole world is safe and clean.

PART FIVE

Speaking with Different Tongues

1945–1955

26

Electioneering Once More

'Some Form of Gestapo'

BBC, London, 4 June 1945

THE END OF THE WAR IN EUROPE soon brought with it the end of Churchill's great wartime administration. The Labour Party were not prepared to continue in the Coalition until Japan had been defeated and so, on 23 May, Churchill formally resigned, and was at once invited to form a caretaker government. Parliament was dissolved on 15 June, the General Election was held on 5 July, ten days later both Churchill and Attlee flew to Potsdam, and the results were declared on 26 July.

During the course of the campaign, Churchill gave four broadcasts as Conservative Party leader. Of these, his first was made memorable by its vicious and deplorable attack on the Labour Party. Clementine Churchill vainly begged him to delete the 'Gestapo' passage, and *The Times* also regretted his 'uncomfortably abrupt' transition from national leader to partisan demagogue. Sir Charles Wilson, Churchill's doctor, thought it showed that his illustrious patient had once again lost his touch, 'and so he falls back on vituperation.'

Although Attlee gave a very effective reply on the following evening, it is not at all clear that this notorious broadcast profoundly influenced the outcome of the election. Indeed, some Conservatives actually approved of it. But it greatly damaged Churchill's reputation for generosity and magnanimity, was a disquieting reminder of his well-known lack of judgement, and did not bode well for what were to be his years as Opposition leader.

BBC, London, 4 June 1945

I AM SORRY TO HAVE LOST so many good friends who served with me in the five years' Coalition. It was impossible to go on in a state of 'electionitis' all through the summer and autumn. This election will last quite long enough for all who are concerned in it, and I expect many of the general public will be sick and tired of it before we get to polling day.

My sincere hope was that we could have held together until the war against Japan was finished. On the other hand, there was a high duty to consult the people after all these years. I could only be relieved of that duty by the full agreement of the three parties, further fortified, perhaps, by a kind of official Gallup Poll, which I am sure would have resulted in an overwhelming request that we should go on to the end and finish the job. That would have enabled me to say at once, 'There will be no election for a year', or words to that effect.

I know that many of my Labour colleagues would have been glad to carry on. On the other hand, the Socialist Party as a whole had been for some time eager to set out upon the political warpath, and when large numbers of people feel like that it is not good for their health to deny them the fight they want. We will therefore give it to them to the best of our ability.

Party, my friends, has always played a great part in our affairs. Party ties have been considered honourable bonds, and on one could doubt that when the German war was over and the immediate danger to this country, which had led to the Coalition, had ceased, conflicting loyalties would arise. Our Socialist and Liberal friends felt themselves forced, therefore, to put party before country. They have departed, and we have been left to carry the nation's burden.

I have therefore formed, exactly as I said I would two years ago, another form of National Government, resting no longer on the agreement of the three official party machines, but on the Conservative Party, together with all the men of good will of any party or no party who have been ready to give their services. I claim the support of all throughout the country who sincerely put the nation first in their thoughts. This is a National Government. I shall stand myself as a Conservative and National candidate. Others may choose to call themselves National or National Liberal, and those who give us their support should vote National rather than Party on polling day.

Why do I claim the right to call this Government National? First of all, because those who have left us have left us on party grounds alone. Secondly, because the Conservative Party, which has for many years been the strongest party in this country, has been willing to abandon party feeling to such an extent that more than one-third of the members of Cabinet rank in this new Government are not members of the Conservative Party. Many of these very able men, without whose aid we could not have got through the war, would prefer not to call themselves Conservative in a party sense. They prefer to call themselves National. And many Conservatives who might have looked forward to high office have accepted cheerfully the interruption of their political careers in order to aid the nation in its time of trouble.

Particularly do I regret the conduct of the Liberal Party. Between us and the orthodox Socialists there is a great doctrinal gulf, which yawns and gapes. Of this continental conception of human society called Socialism, or in its more violent form Communism, I shall say more later. There is no such gulf between the Conservative and National Government I have formed and the Liberals. There is scarcely a Liberal sentiment which animated the great Liberal leaders of the past which we do not inherit and defend. Above all, there is our championship of freedom at home and abroad. All the guiding principles of the British Constitution are proclaimed and enforced by us in their highest degree.

When could any Liberal Party in the past have been offered a political programme of social reform so massive, so warm, so adventurous as that which is contained in our Four Years' Plan?

Indeed, I feel that Mr Gladstone would have recoiled from a great deal of it. He would have thought it was going too far. But we still have a Rosebery and a Lloyd George to carry forward the flags of their fathers.

Why, then, should the Liberal Party spurn us? Why then should they leave the fighting line? Why could not they, at any rate, stay with us till we have beaten down the cruel domination of Japan and until we have set on foot some tolerable way of life for agonized Europe? I am sorry to tell you that they have yielded to the tactical temptation, natural to politicians, to acquire more seats in the House of Commons, if they can, at all costs. It is also obvious that the more equally the two large parties can be brought together at the polls, the greater will be the Liberal bargaining power. That is, no doubt, why all the criticisms of the Sinclair–Beveridge Liberals, who have been very active against us, are directed upon us. It is us they abuse.

I am sorry, indeed, to see such a line developed by men and women who are my friends, by a party many of whose ideals I cherish and will always strive to achieve or guard to the best of my strength. I do not wonder at all that a very large part of the Liberal Party have chosen the national course and still remain in office with us, bearing the heavy burden.

But I appeal to Liberals in all parts of the land, and I call upon them to search their hearts as to whether their differences with a British Government which will put through the Four Years' Plan, a Government which is animated by the love of freedom, which is vowed to that harmonious medium of justice and generosity so befitting to the conqueror, has not more claim on their ancestral loyalties than has a Socialist Party administration, whose principles are the absolute denial of traditional Liberalism. Let them think it out carefully in the light of the speeches of the famous Liberal leaders of the past. Let them think it out carefully in the warmth which may come to the weary Liberal combatant when he sees his ideas increasingly accepted by enlightened peoples and victorious nations.

My friends, I must tell you that a Socialist policy is abhorrent to the British ideas of freedom. Although it is now put forward in the main by people who have a good grounding in the Liberalism and Radicalism of the early part of this century, there can be no doubt that Socialism is inseparably interwoven with Totalitarianism and the abject worship of the State. It is not alone that property, in all its forms, is struck at, but that liberty, in all its forms, is challenged by the fundamental conceptions of Socialism.

Look how even today they hunger for controls of every kind, as if these were delectable foods instead of wartime inflictions and monstrosities. There is to be one State to which all are to be obedient in every act of their lives. This State is to be the arch-employer, the arch-planner, the arch-administrator and ruler, and the arch-caucus-boss.

How is an ordinary citizen or subject of the King to stand up against this formidable machine, which, once it is in power, will prescribe for every one of them where they are to work; what they are to work at; where they may go and what they may say; what views they are to hold and within what limits they may express them; where their wives are to go to queue up for the State ration; and what education their children are to receive to mould their views of human liberty and conduct in the future?

A Socialist State once thoroughly completed in all its details and its aspects – and that is what I am speaking of – could not afford to suffer opposition. Here in old England, in Great Britain, of which old England forms no inconspicuous part, in this glorious Island, the cradle and citadel of free democracy throughout the world, we do not like to be regimented and ordered about and have every action of our lives prescribed for us. In fact we punish criminals by sending them to Wormwood Scrubs and Dartmoor, where they get full employment, and whatever board and lodging is appointed by the Home Secretary.

Socialism is, in its essence, an attack not only upon British enterprise, but upon the right of the ordinary man or woman to breathe freely without having a harsh, clumsy, tyrannical hand clapped across their mouths and nostrils. A Free Parliament – look at that – a Free Parliament is odious to the Socialist doctrinaire. Have we not heard Mr Herbert Morrison descant upon his plans to curtail Parliamentary procedure and pass laws

273

simply by resolutions of broad principle in the House of Commons, afterwards to be left by Parliament to the executive and to the bureaucrats to elaborate and enforce by departmental regulations? As for Sir Stafford Cripps on 'Parliament in the Socialist State', I have not time to read you what he said, but perhaps it will meet the public eye during the election campaign.

But I will go farther. I declare to you, from the bottom of my heart, that no Socialist system can be established without a political police. Many of those who are advocating Socialism or voting Socialist today will be horrified at this idea. That is because they are short-sighted, that is because they do not see where their theories are leading them.

No Socialist Government conducting the entire life and industry of the country could afford to allow free, sharp, or violently worded expressions of public discontent. They would have to fall back on some form of Gestapo, no doubt very humanely directed in the first instance. And this would nip opinion in the bud; it would stop criticism as it reared its head, and it would gather all the power to the supreme party and the party leaders, rising like stately pinnacles above their vast bureaucracies of Civil servants, no longer servants and on longer civil. And where would the ordinary simple folk – the common people, as they like to call them in America – where would they be, once this mighty organism had got them in its grip?

I stand for the sovereign freedom of the individual within the laws which freely elected Parliaments have freely passed. I stand for the rights of the ordinary man to say what he thinks of the Government of the day, however powerful, and to turn them out, neck and crop, if he thinks he can better his temper or his home thereby, and if he can persuade enough others to vote with him.

But, you will say, look at what has been done in the war. Have not many of those evils which you have depicted been the constant companions of our daily life? It is quite true that the horrors of war do not end with the fighting-line. They spread far away to the base and the homeland, and everywhere people give up their rights and liberties for the common cause. But this is because the life of their country is in mortal peril, or for the sake of the cause of freedom in some other land. They give them freely as a sacrifice. It is quite true that the conditions of Socialism play a great part in wartime. We all submit to being ordered about to save our country. But when the war is over and the imminent danger to our existence is removed, we cast off these shackles and burdens which we imposed upon ourselves in times of dire and mortal peril, and quit the gloomy caverns of war and march out into the breezy fields, where the sun is shining and where all may walk joyfully in its warm and golden rays.

Our present opponents or assailants would be, I am sure, knowing many of them, shocked to see where they are going, and where they are trying to lead us. So they adopt temporary expedients. They say, let us just nationalize anything we can get hold of according to the size of our majority and get the Bank of England into the hands of trustworthy Socialist politicians, and we will go ahead and see what happens next. Indeed you would see what happens next.

But let me tell you that once a Socialist Government begins monkeying with the credit of Britain and trying, without regard to facts, figures or confidence, to manipulate it to Socialist requirements, there is no man or woman in this country who has, by thrift or toil, accumulated a nest-egg, however small, who will not run the risk of seeing it shrivel before their eyes.

Mr Greenwood said two years ago – and I rebuked him for it then – 'Pounds, shillings and pence are meaningless symbols.' All this 'meaningless symbol' talk is very dangerous, and would enable a Socialist Government which had got control of the Bank of England to issue notes that would destroy the value of any scrap of savings or nest-egg that anyone had accumulated in this country.

The new National Government stands decisively for the maintenance of the purchasing power of the pound sterling, and we would rather place upon all classes, rich and poor alike, the heaviest burden of taxation they can bear than slide into the delirium of inflation.

I warn you that if you vote for me and those who are acting with me, we give no guarantee of lush and easy times ahead. On the other hand, you need not expect pounds, shillings and pence to become a 'meaningless symbol'. On the contrary, our resolve will be that what has been earned by sweat, toil and skill or saved by self-denial shall command the power to buy the products of peace at an equal value in sweat, toil and skill. We will also take good care against unfair rake-offs and monopolies, and we will protect the common man by law against them by controlling monopolies whose operations are any restraint on trade or oppressive to the smaller producer or distributor.

My friends, I have been forced into a discussion between the Socialist and individualist theories of life and government. That is because for the first time the challenge has been made, in all formality, 'Socialism versus the rest'. But now I must come back to the job which stands in front of us. What have we got to do? What have we got to do now?

We have to bring home the soldiers who have borne the brunt of the war, and make sure, by every scrap of strength and brains we possess, that they find waiting for them food, homes and work. The Demobilization Scheme has been drawn up with all the advantages of seeing what mistakes were made last time. Mr Bevin has worked out a scheme which aims at being fair and square between one soldier and another, besides avoiding undue complications. But what a terrific business he has left us to carry through!

And then you have to add to it that out of this demobilizing army has got to be formed at the same time a new army to go out and finish off, at the side of our American brothers, the Japanese tyrants at the other side of the world. Here is a tremendous task.

And then come along serious people who say that we have got to get our mills going to provide new clothes and articles of all kinds for home and for our export trade. And what about our food, of which we grow only about two-thirds, even under war-time pressure? We have got anyhow to buy food and raw materials oversea, and how are we going to pay for these? We gave our foreign investments largely to the common cause. We sold every asset we could lay hands on in that year, that memorable, grim year, when we stood alone against the might of

Hitler, with Mussolini at his tail. We gave all and we have given all to the prosecution of this war, and we have reached one of the great victorious halting-posts.

Then we have our Four-Year Plan, with all its hopes and benefits, and with all the patient work that it means to pass it into law and bring it into action. All these are definite, practical, gigantic tasks. They will take every scrap of strength, good management and, above all, good comradeship that we can possibly screw out of ourselves.

What a mad thing it would be to slash across this whole great business of resettlement and reorganization with these inflaming controversies of Socialistic agitation! How foolish to plunge us into the bitter political and party fighting which must accompany the attempt to impose a vast revolutionary change on the whole daily life and structure of Britain! Surely at least we can wait till another Election? The world is not coming to an end in the next few weeks or years. The progress of free discussion can show whose fears or whose hopes are well founded. Can we not get Europe settled up, and Britain settled down? Before we plunge out on this hateful internal struggle, let us concentrate on practical and immediate action, and make sure that in gazing at the stars we do not fail in our duty to our fellow-mortals.

On with the forward march! Leave these Socialist dreamers to their Utopias or their nightmares. Let us be content to do the heavy job that is right on top of us. And let us make sure that the cottage home to which the warrior will return is blessed with modest but solid prosperity, well fenced and guarded against misfortune, and that Britons remain free to plan their lives for themselves and for those they love.

27

Final Review of the War

'Why Should We Fear for Our Future?'

House of Commons, 16 August 1945

ON 26 JULY 1945 IT SOON BECAME APPARENT that the Conservatives had suffered a massive electoral defeat and Churchill immediately tendered his resignation. But he was determined to carry on as Leader of the Opposition, and when Parliament reassembled on 1 August the Conservatives gave him a great ovation. Yet even the shock of Churchill's abrupt dismissal was soon overtaken by events in the Far East. Within two weeks, atomic bombs had been dropped on Hiroshima and Nagasaki, and on 15 August the Japanese Government surrendered.

On the following day, Clement Attlee, now Prime Minister, paid generous tribute in the Commons to Churchill's work and words: 'In undying phrases, he crystallized the unspoken feeling of all.' In reply, Churchill delivered what was, in effect, the last of his great wartime speeches. It was eloquent, humorous, high-minded, statesmanlike and magnanimous – an Olympian survey of war and peace, of the international and domestic scene and the very antithesis of his recent 'Gestapo' broadcast.

Clementine Churchill described it as 'a brilliant, moving, gallant speech on the opening of Parliament. He was right back in his 1940–41 calibre. The new house of rather awestruck, shy, nervous members was riveted and fascinated.' It was a performance all the more remarkable because Churchill himself was extremely depressed at this time, resenting his defeat, missing his work and hating the deprivations of private citizenship.

House of Commons, 16 August 1945

OUR DUTY IS TO CONGRATULATE His Majesty's Government on the very great improvement in our prospects at home, which comes from the complete victory gained over Japan and the establishment of peace throughout the world. Only a month ago it was necessary to continue at full speed and at enormous cost all preparations for a long and bloody campaign in the Far East. In the first days of the Potsdam Conference President Truman and I approved the plans submitted to us by the combined Chiefs of Staff for a series of great battles and landings in Malaya, in the Netherlands East Indies, and in the homeland of Japan itself. These operations involved an effort not surpassed in Europe, and no one could measure the cost in British and American life and treasure they would require. Still less could it be known how long the stamping-out of the resistance of Japan in the many territories she had conquered, and especially in her homeland, would take. All the while the whole process of turning the world from war to peace would be hampered and delayed. Every form of peace activity was half-strangled by the overriding priorities of war. No clear-cut decisions could be taken in the presence of this harsh dominating uncertainty.

During the last three months an element of baffling dualism has complicated every problem of policy and administration. We had to plan for peace and war at the same time. Immense armies were being demobilized; another powerful army was being prepared and dispatched to the other side of the globe. All the personal stresses among millions of men eager to return to civil life, and hundreds of thousands of men who would have to be sent to new and severe campaigns in the Far East, presented themselves with growing tension. This dualism affected also every aspect of our economic and financial life. How to set people free to use their activities in reviving the life of Britain, and at the same time to meet the stern demands of the war against Japan, constituted one of the most perplexing and distressing puzzles that in a long lifetime of experience I have ever faced.

I confess it was with great anxiety that I surveyed this prospect a month ago. Since then I have been relieved of the burden. At the same time that burden, heavy though it still remains, has been immeasurably lightened. On 17th July there came to us at Potsdam the eagerly awaited news of the trial of the atomic bomb in the Mexican desert. Success beyond all dreams crowned this sombre, magnificent venture of our American Allies. The detailed reports of the Mexican desert experiment, which were brought to us a few days later by air, could leave no doubt in the minds of the very few who were informed, that we were in the presence of a new factor in human affairs, and possessed of powers which were irresistible. Great Britain had a right to be consulted in accordance with Anglo-American agreements. The decision to use the atomic bomb was taken by President Truman and myself at Potsdam, and we approved the military plans to unchain the dread, pent-up forces.

From that moment our outlook on the future was transformed. In preparation for the results of this experiment, the statements of the President and of Mr Stimson and my own statement, which by the courtesy of the Prime Minister was subsequently read out on the broadcast, were framed in common agreement. Marshal Stalin was informed by President Truman that we contemplated using an explosive of incomparable power against Japan, and action proceeded in the way we all now know. It is to this atomic bomb more than to any other factor that we may ascribe the sudden and speedy ending of the war against Japan.

Before using it, it was necessary first of all to send a message in the form of an ultimatum to the Japanese which would apprise them of what unconditional surrender meant. This document was published on 26th July – the same day that another event, differently viewed on each side of the House, occurred [the result of the General Election and the resignation of Churchill from the Premiership]. The assurances given to Japan about her future after her unconditional surrender had been made were generous in the extreme. When we remember the cruel and treacherous nature of the utterly unprovoked attack made by the Japanese warlords upon the United States and Great Britain, these assurances must be considered magnanimous in a high degree. In a nutshell, they implied 'Japan for the Japanese', and even access to raw materials, apart from their control, was not denied to their densely populated homeland. We felt that in view of the new and fearful agencies of war-power about to be employed, every inducement to surrender, compatible with our declared policy, should be set before them. This we owed to our consciences before using this awful weapon.

Secondly, by repeated warnings, emphasized by heavy bombing attacks, an endeavour was made to procure the general exodus of the civil population from the threatened cities. Thus everything in human power, prior to using the atomic bomb, was done to spare the civil population of Japan. There are voices which assert that the bomb should never have been used at all. I cannot associate myself with such ideas. Six years of total war have convinced most people that had the Germans or Japanese discovered this new weapon, they would have used it upon us to our complete destruction with the utmost alacrity. I am surprised that very worthy people, but people who in most cases had no intention of proceeding to the Japanese front themselves, should adopt the position that rather than throw this bomb, we should have sacrificed a million American, and a quarter of a million British lives in the desperate battles and massacres of an invasion of Japan. Future generations will judge these dire decisions, and I believe that if they find themselves dwelling in a happier world from which war has been banished, and where freedom reigns, they will not condemn those who struggled for their benefit amid the horrors and miseries of this gruesome and ferocious epoch.

The bomb brought peace, but men alone can keep that peace, and henceforward they will keep it under penalties which threaten the survival, not only of civilization but of humanity itself. I may say that I am in entire agreement with the President that the secrets of the atomic bomb should so far as possible not be imparted at the present time to any other country in the world. This is in no design or wish for arbitrary power, but for the common safety of the world. Nothing can stop the progress of research and experiment in every country, but although research will no doubt proceed in many places, the construction of the immense plants necessary to transform theory into action cannot be improvised in any country.

For this and for many other reasons the United States stand at this moment at the summit of the world. I rejoice that this should be so. Let them act up to the level of their power and their responsibility, not for themselves but for others, for all men in all lands, and then a brighter day may dawn upon human history. So far as we know, there are at least three and perhaps four years before the concrete progress made in the United States can be overtaken. In these three years we must remould the relationships of all men, wherever they dwell, in all the nations. We must remould them in such a way that these men do not wish or dare to fall upon each other for the sake of vulgar and out-dated ambitions or for passionate differences in ideology, and that international bodies of supreme authority may give peace on earth and decree justice among men. Our pilgrimage has brought us to a sublime moment in the history of the world. From the least to the greatest, all must strive to be worthy of these supreme opportunities. There is not an hour to be wasted; there is not a day to be lost.

It would in my opinion be a mistake to suggest that the Russian declaration of war upon Japan was hastened by the use of the atomic bomb. My understanding with Marshal Stalin in the talks which I had with him had been, for a considerable time past, that Russia would declare war upon Japan within three months of the surrender of the German armies. The reason for the delay of three months was, of course, the need to move over the trans-Siberian Railway the large reinforcements necessary to convert the Russian-Manchurian army from a defensive to an offensive strength. Three months was the time mentioned, and the fact that the German armies surrendered on 8th May, and the

Russians declared war on Japan on 8th August, is no mere co-incidence, but another example of the fidelity and punctuality with which Marshal Stalin and his valiant armies always keep their military engagements.

I now turn to the results of the Potsdam Conference so far as they have been made public in the agreed communiqué and in President Truman's very remarkable speech of a little more than a week ago. There has been general approval of the arrangements proposed for the administration of Germany by the Allied Control Commission during the provisional period of military government. This regime is both transitional and indefinite. The character of Hitler's Nazi party was such as to destroy almost all independent elements in the German people. The struggle was fought to the bitter end. The mass of the people were forced to drain the cup of defeat to the dregs. A headless Germany has fallen into the hands of the conquerors. It may be many years before any structure of German national life will be possible, and there will be plenty of time for the victors to consider how the interests of world peace are affected thereby.

In the meanwhile, it is in my view of the utmost importance that responsibility should be effectively assumed by German local bodies for carrying on under Allied supervision all the processes of production and of administration necessary to maintain the life of a vast population. It is not possible for the Allies to bear responsibility by themselves. We cannot have the German masses lying down upon our hands and expecting to be fed, organized and educated over a period of years by the Allies. We must do our best to help to avert the tragedy of famine. But it would be in vain for us in our small Island, which still needs to import half its food, to imagine that we can make any further appreciable contribution in that respect. The rationing of this country cannot be made more severe without endangering the life and physical strength of our people, all of which will be needed for the immense tasks we have to do. I, therefore, most strongly advise the encouragement of the assumption of responsibility by trustworthy German local bodies in proportion as they can be brought into existence.

The Council which was set up at Potsdam of the Foreign Secretaries of the three, four or five Powers, meeting in various combinations as occasion served, affords a new and flexible machinery for the continuous further study of the immense problems that lie before us in Europe and Asia. I am very glad that the request that I made to the Conference that the seat of the Council's permanent Secretariat should be London, was granted. I must say that the late Foreign Secretary [Mr Anthony Eden], who has, over a long period, gained an increasing measure of confidence from the Foreign Secretaries of Russia and the United States, and who through the European Advisory Committee which is located in London has always gained the feeling that things could be settled in a friendly and easy way, deserves some of the credit for the fact that these great Powers willingly accorded us the seat in London of the permanent Secretariat. It is high time that the place of London, one of the controlling centres of international world affairs, should at last be recognized. It is the oldest, the largest, the most battered capital, the capital which was first in the war, and the time is certainly overdue when we should have our recognition.

I am glad also that a beginning is to be made with the evacuation of Persia [Iran] by the British and Russian armed forces, in accordance with the triple treaty which we made with each other and with Persia in 1941. Although it does not appear in the communiqué, we have since seen it announced that the first stage in the process, namely the withdrawal of Russian and British troops from Teheran, has already begun or is about to begin. There are various other matters arising out of this Conference which should be noted as satisfactory. We should not, however, delude ourselves into supposing that the results of this first Conference of the victors were free from disappointment or anxiety, or that the most serious questions before us were brought to good solutions. Those which proved incapable of agreement at the Conference have been relegated to the Foreign Secretaries' Council, which, though most capable of relieving difficulties, is essentially one gifted with less far-reaching powers. Other grave questions are left for the final peace settlement, by which time many of them may have settled themselves, not necessarily in the best way.

It would be at once wrong and impossible to conceal the divergences of view which exist inevitably between the victors about the state of affairs in Eastern and Middle Europe. I do not at all blame the Prime Minister or the new Foreign Secretary, whose task it was to finish up the discussions which we had begun. I am sure they did their best. We have to realize that no one of the three leading Powers can impose its solutions upon others, and that the only solutions possible are those which are in the nature of compromise. We British have had very early and increasingly to recognize the limitations of our own power and influence, great though it be, in the gaunt world arising from the ruins of this hideous war. It is not in the power of any British Government to bring home solutions which would be regarded as perfect by the great majority of Members of this House, wherever they may sit. I must put on record my own opinion that the provisional Western Frontier agreed upon for Poland, running from Stettin on the Baltic, along the Oder and its tributary, the Western Neisse, comprising as it does one-quarter of the arable land of all Germany, is not a good augury for the future map of Europe. We always had in the Coalition Government a desire that Poland should receive ample compensation in the west for the territory ceded to Russia east of the Curzon Line. But here I think a mistake has been made, in which the Provisional Government of Poland have been an ardent partner, by going far beyond what necessity or equity required. There are few virtues that the Poles do not possess – and there are few mistakes they have ever avoided.

I am particularly concerned at this moment, with the reports reaching us of the conditions under which the expulsion and exodus of Germans from the new Poland are being carried out. Between eight and nine million persons dwelt in those regions before the war. The Polish Government say that there are still 1,500,000 of these, not yet expelled, within their new frontiers. Other millions must have taken refuge behind the British and American lines, thus increasing the food stringency in our sector.

But enormous numbers are utterly unaccounted for. Where are they gone, and what has been their fate? The same conditions may reproduce themselves in a modified form in the expulsion of great numbers of Sudeten and other Germans from Czechoslovakia. Sparse and guarded accounts of what has happened and is happening have filtered through, but it is not impossible that tragedy on a prodigious scale is unfolding itself behind the iron curtain which at the moment divides Europe in twain. I should welcome any statement which the Prime Minister can make which would relieve, or at least inform us upon this very anxious and grievous matter.

There is another sphere of anxiety. I remember that a fortnight or so before the last war, the Kaiser's friend Herr Ballin, the great shipping magnate, told me that he had heard Bismarck say towards the end of his life, 'If there is ever another war in Europe, it will come out of some damned silly thing in the Balkans.' The murder of the Archduke of Sarajevo in 1914 set the signal for the First World War. I cannot conceive that the elements for a new conflict do not exist in the Balkans today. I am not using the language of Bismarck, but nevertheless not many Members of the new House of Commons will be content with the new situation that prevails in those mountainous, turbulent, ill-organized and warlike regions. I do not intend to particularize. I am very glad to see the new Foreign Secretary [Mr Ernest Bevin] sitting on the Front Bench opposite. I should like to say with what gratification I learned that he had taken on this high and most profoundly difficult office, and we are sure he will do his best to preserve the great causes for which we have so long pulled together. But as I say, not many Members will be content with the situation in that region to which I have referred, for almost everywhere Communist forces have obtained, or are in process of obtaining, dictatorial powers. It does not mean that the Communist system is everywhere being established, nor does it mean that Soviet Russia seeks to reduce all those independent States to provinces of the Soviet Union. Marshal Stalin is a very wise man, and I would set no limits to the immense contributions that he and his associates have to make to the future.

In those countries, torn and convulsed by war, there may be, for some months to come, the need of authoritarian government. The alternative would be anarchy. Therefore, it would be unreasonable to ask or expect that liberal government – as spelt with a small 'l' – and British or United States democratic conditions, should be instituted immediately. They take their politics very seriously in those countries. A friend of mine, an officer, was in Zagreb when the results of the late General Election came in. An old lady said to him, 'Poor Mr Churchill! I suppose now he will be shot.' My friend was able to reassure her. He said the sentence might be mitigated to one of the various forms of hard labour which are always open to His Majesty's subjects. Nevertheless we must know where we stand, and we must make clear where we stand, in these affairs of the Balkans and of Eastern Europe, and indeed of any country which comes into this field. Our ideal is government of the people by the people, for the people – the people being free without duress to express, by secret ballot without intimidation, their deep-seated wish as to the form and conditions of the Government under which they are to live.

At the present time – I trust a very fleeting time – 'police governments' rule over a great number of countries. It is a case of the odious 18B, carried to a horrible excess. The family is gathered round the fireside to enjoy the scanty fruits of their toil and to recruit their exhausted strength by the little food that they have been able to gather. There they sit. Suddenly there is a knock at the door and a heavily armed policeman appears. He is not, of course, one who resembles in any way those functionaries whom we honour and obey in the London streets. It may be that the father or son, or a friend sitting in the cottage, is called out and taken off into the dark, and no one knows whether he will ever come back again, or what his fate has been. All they know is that they had better not inquire. There are millions of humble homes in Europe at the moment, in Poland, in Czechoslovakia, in Austria, in Hungary, in Yugoslavia, in Rumania, in Bulgaria – where this fear is the main preoccupation of the family life. President Roosevelt laid down the four freedoms, and these are expressed in the Atlantic Charter which we agreed together. 'Freedom from fear' – but this has been interpreted as if it were only freedom from fear of invasion from a foreign country. That is the least of the fears of the common man. His patriotism arms him to withstand invasion or go down fighting; but that is not the fear of the ordinary family in Europe tonight. Their fear is of the policeman's knock. It is not fear for the country, for all men can unite in comradeship for the defence of their native soil. It is for the life and liberty of the individual, for the fundamental rights of man, now menaced and precarious in so many lands, that peoples tremble.

Surely we can agree in this new Parliament, or the great majority of us, wherever we sit – there are naturally and rightly differences and cleavages of thought – but surely we can agree in this new Parliament, which will either fail the world or once again play a part in saving it, that it is the will of the people freely expressed by secret ballot, in universal suffrage elections, as to the form of their government and as to the laws which shall prevail, which is the first solution and safeguard. Let us then march steadily along that plain and simple line. I avow my faith in Democracy, whatever course or view it may take with individuals and parties. They may make their mistakes, and they may profit from their mistakes. Democracy is now on trial as it never was before, and in these Islands we must uphold it, as we upheld it in the dark days of 1940 and 1941, with all our hearts, with all our vigilance, and with all our enduring and inexhaustible strength. While the war was on and all the Allies were fighting for victory, the word 'Democracy', like many people, had to work overtime, but now that peace has come we must search for more precise definitions. Elections have been proposed in some of these Balkan countries where only one set of candidates is allowed to appear, and where, if other parties are to express their opinion, it has to be arranged beforehand that the governing party, armed with its political police and all its propaganda, is the only one which has the slightest chance. Chance, did I say? It is a certainty.

Now is the time for Britons to speak out. It is odious to us that governments should seek to maintain their rule otherwise than by free unfettered elections by the mass of the people. Governments derive their just powers from the consent of the governed, says the Constitution of the United States. This must not evaporate in swindles and lies propped up by servitude and murder. In our foreign policy let us strike continually the notes of freedom and fair play as we understand them in these Islands. Then you will find there will be an overwhelming measure of agreement between us, and we shall in this House march forward on an honourable theme having within it all that invests human life with dignity and happiness. In saying all this, I have been trying to gather together and present in a direct form the things which, I believe, are dear to the great majority of us. I rejoiced to read them expressed in golden words by the President of the United States when he said:

> Our victory in Europe was more than a victory of arms. It was a victory of one way of life over another. It was a victory of an ideal founded on the right of the common man, on the dignity of the human being, and on the conception of the State as the servant, not the master, of its people.

I think there is not such great disagreement between us. Emphasis may be cast this way and that in particular incidents, but surely this is what the new Parliament on the whole means. This is what in our heart and conscience, in foreign affairs and world issues, we desire. Just as in the baleful glare of 1940, so now, when calmer lights shine, let us be united upon these resurgent principles and impulses of the good and generous hearts of men. Thus to all the material strength we possess and the honoured position we have acquired, we shall add these moral forces which glorify mankind and make even the weakest equals of the strong.

I now turn to the domestic sphere. I have already spoken of the enormous easement in their task which the new Government have obtained through the swift and sudden ending of the Japanese war. What thousands of millions of pounds sterling are saved from the waste of war, what scores and hundreds of thousands of lives are saved, what vast numbers of ships are set free to carry the soldiers home to all their lands, to carry about the world the food and raw materials vital to industry! What noble opportunities have the new Government inherited! Let them be worthy of their fortune, which is also the fortune of us all. To release and liberate the vital springs of British energy and inventiveness, to let the honest earnings of the nation fructify in the pockets of the people, to spread well-being and security against accident and misfortune throughout the whole nation, to plan, wherever State planning is imperative, and to guide into fertile and healthy channels the native British genius for comprehension and goodwill – all these are open to them, and all these ought to be open to all of us now. I hope we may go forward together, not only abroad but also at home, in all matters so far as we possibly can.

During the period of the 'Caretaker Government', while we still had to contemplate eighteen months of strenuous war with Japan, we reviewed the plans for demobilization in such a way as to make a very great acceleration in the whole process of releasing men and women from the Armed Forces and from compulsory industrial employment. Now, all that is overtaken by the worldwide end of the war. I must say at once that the paragraph of the Gracious Speech [The King's speech outlining the new Government's policy] referring to demobilization and to the plans which were made in the autumn of 1944 – with which I am in entire agreement in principle – gives a somewhat chilling impression. Now that we have had this wonderful windfall, I am surprised that any Government should imagine that language of this kind is still appropriate or equal to the new situation. I see that in the United States the President has said that all the American troops that the American ships can carry home in the next year will be brought home and set free. Are His Majesty's Government now able to make any statement of that kind about our Armed Forces abroad? Or what statement can they make? I do not want to harass them unduly, but perhaps some time next week some statement could be made. No doubt the Prime Minister will think of that. Great hopes have been raised in the

electoral campaign, and from those hopes has sprung their great
political victory. Time will show whether those hopes are well
founded, as we deeply trust they may be. But many decisions can
be taken now, in the completely altered circumstances in which
we find ourselves. The duty of the Government is to fix the
minimum numbers who must be retained in the next six or
twelve months' period in all the foreign theatres, and to bring the
rest home with the utmost speed that our immensely expanded
shipping resources will permit.

Even more is this releasing process important in the demobilization of the home establishment. I quite agree that the feeling
of the Class A men must ever be the dominant factor, but short of
that the most extreme efforts should be made to release people
who are standing about doing nothing. I hope the Public
Expenditure Committee will be at once reconstituted, and that
they will travel about the country examining home establishments and reporting frequently to the House. Now that the war
is over, there is no ground of military secrecy which should
prevent the publication of the exact numerical ration strengths of
our Army, Navy and Air Force in every theatre and at home, and
we should certainly have weekly, or at least monthly figures of
the progressive demobilization effected. It is an opportunity for
the new Government to win distinction. At the end of the last
war, when I was in charge of the Army and Air Force, I
published periodically very precise information. I agree with the
words used by the Foreign Secretary when he was Minister of
Labour in my Administration, namely, that the tremendous
winding-up process of the war must be followed by a methodical
and regulated unwinding. We agree that if the process is to be
pressed forward with the utmost speed it is necessary for the
Government to wield exceptional powers for the time being, and
so long as they use those powers to achieve the great administrative and executive tasks imposed upon them, we shall not attack
them. It is only if, and in so far as, those powers are used to bring
about by a side-wind a state of controlled society agreeable to
Socialist doctrinaires, but which we deem odious to British
freedom, that we shall be forced to resist them. So long as the

exceptional powers are used as part of the war emergency, His Majesty's Government may consider us as helpers and not as opponents, as friends and not as foes.

To say this in no way relieves the Government of their duty to set the nation free as soon as possible, to bring home the soldiers in accordance with the scheme with the utmost rapidity, and to enable the mass of the people to resume their normal lives and employment in the best, easiest and speediest manner. There ought not to be a long-dragged-out period of many months when hundreds of thousands of Service men and women are kept waiting about under discipline, doing useless tasks at the public expense, and other tens of thousands, more highly paid, finding them sterile work to do . What we desire is freedom; what we need is abundance. Freedom and abundance – these must be our aims. The production of new wealth is far more beneficial, and on an incomparably larger scale, than class and party fights about the liquidation of old wealth. We must try to share blessings and not miseries.

The production of new wealth must precede common wealth, otherwise there will only be common poverty. I am sorry these simple truisms should excite the hon. Member opposite – whom I watched so often during the course of the last Parliament and whose many agreeable qualities I have often admired – as if they had some sense of novelty for him.

We do not propose to join issue immediately about the legislative proposals in the Gracious Speech. We do not know what is meant by the control of investment – but apparently it is a subject for mirth. Evidently, in war you may do one thing, and in peace perhaps another must be considered. Allowance must also be made for the transitional period through which we are passing. The Debate on the Address should probe and elicit the Government's intentions in this matter. The same is true of the proposal to nationalize the coal mines. If that is really the best way of securing a larger supply of coal at a cheaper price, and at an earlier moment than is now in view, I, for one, should approach the plan in a sympathetic spirit. It is by results that the Government will be judged, and it is by results that this policy must be judged. The national ownership of the Bank of England does not in my opinion raise any matter of principle. I give my opinion – anybody else may give his own. There are important examples in the United States and in our Dominions of central banking institutions, but what matters is the use to be made of this public ownership. On this we must await the detailed statement by the Chancellor of the Exchequer, who, I am glad to say, has pledged himself to resist inflation. Meanwhile it may be helpful for me to express the opinion, as Leader of the Opposition, that foreign countries need not be alarmed by the language of the Gracious Speech on this subject, and that British credit will be resolutely upheld.

Then there is the Trade Disputes Act. We are told that this is to be repealed. Personally, I feel that we owe an inestimable debt to the Trade Unions for all they have done for the country in the long struggle against the foreign foe. But they would surely be unwise to reinstitute the political levy on the old basis. It would also be very odd if they wished to regain full facilities for legalizing and organizing a general strike. It does not say much for the confidence with which the Trades Union Council view the brave new world, or for what they think about the progressive nationalization of our industries, that they should deem it necessary on what an hon. and gallant Gentleman called 'the D-Day of the new Britain' to restore and sharpen the general strike weapon, at this particular time of all others. Apparently nationalization is not regarded by them as any security against conditions which would render a general strike imperative and justified in the interests of the workers. We are, I understand, after nationalizing the coal-mines, to deal with the railways, electricity and transport. Yet at the same time the Trade Unions feel it necessary to be heavily rearmed against State Socialism. Apparently the new age is not to be so happy for the wage-earners as we have been asked to believe. At any rate, there seems to be a fundamental incongruity in these conceptions to which the attention of the Socialist intelligentsia should speedily be directed. Perhaps it may be said that these powers will only be needed if the Tories come into office. Surely these are early days to get frightened. I will ask the Prime Minister if he will just tell us broadly what is meant by the word 'repeal'.

I have offered these comments to the House, and I do not wish to end on a sombre or even slightly controversial note. As to the situation which exists today, it is evident that not only are the two Parties in the House agreed in the main essentials of foreign policy and in our moral outlook on world affairs, but we also have an immense programme, prepared by our joint exertions during the Coalition, which requires to be brought into law and made an inherent part of the life of the people. Here and there there may be differences of emphasis and view, but in the main no Parliament ever assembled with such a mass of agreed legislation as lies before us this afternoon. I have great hopes of this Parliament, and I shall do my utmost to make its work fruitful. It may heal the wounds of war, and turn to good account the new conceptions and powers which we have gathered amid the storm. I do not underrate the difficult and intricate complications of the task which lies before us; I know too much about it to cherish vain illusions; but the morrow of such a victory as we have gained is a splendid moment both in our small lives and in our great history. It is a time not only of rejoicing but even more of resolve. When we look back on all the perils through which we have passed and at the mighty foes we have laid low and all the dark and deadly designs we have frustrated, why should we fear for our future? We have come safely through the worst.

> *Home is the sailor, home from sea,*
> *And the hunter home from the hill.*

28

The Soviet Danger:
'The Iron Curtain'

Fulton, Missouri, 5 March 1946

EARLY IN 1946, CHURCHILL DECIDED to absent himself from Parliament for a few months. He had accepted an invitation from Westminster College in Fulton, Missouri, to deliver an address, and President Truman (whose home state it was) agreed to introduce him to the audience, even though he was only speaking as a private citizen. Truman and Churchill travelled together, in the President's special train, and as usual Churchill worked on final revisions until the very last moment.

This was undoubtedly the most important, and the most influential, of all Churchill's post-war addresses. Ranging widely across the international scene, he urged that the United Nations should establish a peace-keeping force; that the Western Powers should retain their secret knowledge of the atomic bomb; that the 'special relationship' between the British Commonwealth and the United States should be strengthened; and that England and America must beware of the 'iron curtain' that had descended across the Continent of Europe.

In retrospect, with the world already at the brink of the Cold War, Churchill's words seem uncontroversially timely. But when delivered, the speech caused a furore. Stalin, predictably, denounced it; so did most American newspapers; so did *The Times* and many Labour MPs. As usual, Asquith's daughter was more appreciative: 'It is the root of the matter, whether people wish to recognize it or not.' And so, indeed, it soon proved to be.

Speaking with Different Tongues

Fulton, Missouri, 5 March 1946

I AM GLAD TO COME TO WESTMINSTER COLLEGE this afternoon, and am complimented that you should give me a degree. The name 'Westminster' is somehow familiar to me. I seem to have heard of it before. Indeed, it was at Westminster that I received a very large part of my education in politics, dialectic, rhetoric, and one or two other things. In fact we have both been educated at the same, or similar, or, at any rate, kindred establishments.

It is also an honour, perhaps almost unique, for a private visitor to be introduced to an academic audience by the President of the United States. Amid his heavy burdens, duties, and responsibilities – unsought but not recoiled from – the President has travelled a thousand miles to dignify and magnify our meeting here today and to give me an opportunity of addressing this kindred nation, as well as my own countrymen across the ocean, and perhaps some other countries too. The President has told you that it is his wish, as I am sure it is yours, that I should have full liberty to give my true and faithful counsel in these anxious and baffling times. I shall certainly avail myself of this freedom, and feel the more right to do so because any private ambitions I may have cherished in my younger days have been satisfied beyond my wildest dreams. Let me, however, make it clear that I have no official mission or status of any kind, and that I speak only for myself. There is nothing here but what you see.

I can therefore allow my mind, with the experience of a lifetime, to play over the problems which beset us on the morrow of our absolute victory in arms, and to try to make sure with what strength I have that what has been gained with so much sacrifice and suffering shall be preserved for the future glory and safety of mankind.

The United States stands at this time at the pinnacle of world

296

power. It is a solemn moment for the American Democracy. For with primacy in power is also joined an awe-inspiring accountability to the future. If you look around you, you must feel not only the sense of duty done but also you must feel anxiety lest you fall below the level of achievement. Opportunity is here now, clear and shining for both our countries. To reject it or ignore it or fritter it away will bring upon us all the long reproaches of the after-time. It is necessary that constancy of mind, persistency of purpose and the grand simplicity of decision shall guide and rule the conduct of the English-speaking peoples in peace as they did in war. We must, and I believe we shall, prove ourselves equal to this severe requirement.

When American military men approach some serious situation they are wont to write at the head of their directive the words 'overall strategic concept'. There is wisdom in this, as it leads to clarity of thought. What then is the overall strategic concept which we should inscribe today? It is nothing less than the safety and welfare, the freedom and progress, of all the homes and families of all the men and women in all the lands. And here I speak particularly of the myriad cottage or apartment homes where the wage-earner strives amid the accidents and difficulties of life to guard his wife and children from privation and bring the family up in the fear of the Lord, or upon ethical conceptions which often play their potent part.

To give security to these countless homes, they must be shielded from the two giant marauders, war and tyranny. We all know the frightful disturbances in which the ordinary family is plunged when the curse of war swoops down upon the breadwinner and those for whom he works and contrives. The awful ruin of Europe, with all its vanished glories, and of large parts of Asia glares us in the eyes. When the designs of wicked men or the aggressive urge of mighty States dissolve over large areas the frame of civilized society, humble folk are confronted with difficulties with which they cannot cope. For them all is distorted, all is broken, even ground to pulp.

When I stand here this quiet afternoon I shudder to visualize what is actually happening to millions now and what is going to happen in this period when famine stalks the earth. None can compute what has been called 'the unestimated sum of human pain'. Our supreme task and duty is to guard the homes of the common people from the horrors and miseries of another war. We are all agreed on that.

Our American military colleagues, after having proclaimed their 'over-all strategic concept' and computed available resources, always proceed to the next step – namely, the method. Here again there is widespread agreement. A world organization has already been erected for the prime purpose of preventing war. UNO, the successor of the League of Nations, with the decisive addition of the United States and all that that means, is already at work. We must make sure that its work is fruitful, that it is a reality and not a sham, that it is a force for action, and not merely a frothing of words, that it is a true temple of peace in which the shields of many nations can some day be hung up, and not merely a cockpit in a Tower of Babel. Before we cast away the solid assurances of national armaments for self-preservation we must be certain that our temple is built, not upon shifting sands or quagmires, but upon the rock. Anyone can see with his eyes open that our path will be difficult and also long, but if we persevere together as we did in the two world wars – though not, alas, in the interval between them – I cannot doubt that we shall achieve our common purpose in the end.

I have, however, a definite and practical purpose to make for action. Courts and magistrates may be set up but they cannot function without sheriffs and constables. The United Nations Organization must immediately begin to be equipped with an international armed force. In such a matter we can only go step by step, but we must begin now. I propose that each of the Powers and States should be invited to delegate a certain number of air squadrons to the service of the world organization. These squadrons would be trained and prepared in their own countries, but would move around in rotation from one country to another. They would wear the uniform of their own countries but with different badges. They would not be required to act against their own nation, but in other respects they would be

298

directed by the world organization. This might be started on a modest scale and would grow as confidence grew. I wished to see this done after the First World War, and I devoutly trust it may be done forthwith.

It would nevertheless be wrong and imprudent to entrust the secret knowledge or experience of the atomic bomb, which the United States, Great Britain and Canada now share, to the world organization, while it is still in its infancy. It would be criminal madness to cast it adrift in this still agitated and un-united world. No one in any country has slept less well in their beds because this knowledge and the method and the raw materials to apply it, are at present largely retained in American hands. I do not believe we should all have slept so soundly had the positions been reversed and if some Communist or neo-Fascist State monopolized for the time being these dread agencies. The fear of them alone might easily have been used to enforce totalitarian systems upon the free democratic world, with consequences appalling to human imagination. God has willed that this shall not be and we have at least a breathing space to set our house in order before this peril has to be encountered: and even then, if no effort is spared, we should still possess so formidable a superiority as to impose effective deterrents upon its employment, or threat of employment by others. Ultimately, when the essential brotherhood of man is truly embodied and expressed in a world organization with all the necessary practical safeguards to make it effective, these powers would naturally be confided to that world organization.

Now I come to the second danger of these two marauders which threatens the cottage, the home, and the ordinary people – namely, tyranny. We cannot be blind to the fact that the liberties enjoyed by individual citizens throughout the British Empire are not valid in a considerable number of countries, some of which are very powerful. In these States control is enforced upon the common people by various kinds of all-embracing police governments. The power of the State is exercised without restraint, either by dictators or by compact oligarchies operating through a privileged party and a political police. It is not our duty at this time when difficulties are so numerous to interfere forcibly in the internal affairs of countries which we have not conquered in war. But we must never cease to proclaim in fearless tones the great principles of freedom and the rights of man which are the joint inheritance of the English-speaking world and which through Magna Carta, the Bill of Rights, the Habeas Corpus, trial by jury, and the English common law find their most famous expression in the American Declaration of Independence.

All this means that the people of any country have the right, and should have the power by constitutional action, by free unfettered elections, with secret ballot, to choose or change the character or form of government under which they dwell; that freedom of speech and thought should reign; that courts of justice, independent of the executive, unbiased by any party, should administer laws which have received the broad assent of large majorities or are consecrated by time and custom. Here are the title deeds of freedom which should lie in every cottage home. Here is the message of the British and American peoples to mankind. Let us preach what we practise – let us practise what we preach.

I have now stated the two great dangers which menace the homes of the people: War and Tyranny. I have not yet spoken of poverty and privation which are in many cases the prevailing anxiety. But if the dangers of war and tyranny are removed, there is no doubt that science and co-operation can bring in the next few years to the world, certainly in the next few decades newly taught in the sharpening school of war, an expansion of material well-being beyond anything that has yet occurred in human experience. Now, at this sad and breathless moment, we are plunged in the hunger and distress which are the aftermath of our stupendous struggle: but this will pass and may pass quickly, and there is no reason except human folly or sub-human crime which should deny to all the nations the inauguration and enjoyment of an age of plenty. I have often used words which I learned fifty years ago from a great Irish-American orator, a friend of mine, Mr Bourke Cockran. 'There is enough for all. The earth is a generous mother; she will provide in plentiful abundance food for all her children if they will but cultivate her soil in justice and in peace.' So far I feel that we are in full agreement.

Now, while still pursuing the method of realizing our overall strategic concept, I come to the crux of what I have travelled here to say. Neither the sure prevention of war, nor the continuous rise of world organization will be gained without what I have called the fraternal association of the English-speaking peoples. This means a special relationship between the British Commonwealth and Empire and the United States. This is no time for generalities, and I will venture to be precise. Fraternal association requires not only the growing friendship and mutual understanding between our two vast but kindred systems of society, but the continuance of the intimate relationship between our military advisers, leading to common study of potential dangers, the similarity of weapons and manuals of instructions, and to the interchange of officers and cadets at technical colleges. It should carry with it the continuance of the present facilities for mutual security by the joint use of all Naval and Air Force bases in the possession of either country all over the world. This would perhaps double the mobility of the American Navy and Air Force. It would greatly expand that of the British Empire Forces and it might well lead, if and as the world calms down, to important financial savings. Already we use together a large number of islands; more may well be entrusted to our joint care in the near future.

The United States has already a Permanent Defence Agreement with the Dominion of Canada, which is so devotedly attached to the British Commonwealth and Empire. This Agreement is more effective than many of those which have often been made under formal alliances. This principle should be extended to all British Commonwealths with full reciprocity. Thus, whatever happens, and thus only, shall we be secure ourselves and able to work together for the high and simple causes that are dear to us and bode no ill to any. Eventually there may come – I feel eventually there will come – the principle of common citizenship, but that we may be content to leave to destiny, whose outstretched arm many of us can already clearly see.

There is however an important question we must ask ourselves. Would a special relationship between the United States and the British Commonwealth be inconsistent with our overriding loyalties to the World Organization? I reply that, on the contrary, it is probably the only means by which that organization will achieve its full stature and strength. There are already the special United States relations with Canada which I have just mentioned, and there are the special relations between the United States and the South American Republics. We British have our twenty years Treaty of Collaboration and Mutual Assistance with Soviet Russia. I agree with Mr Bevin, the Foreign Secretary of Great Britain, that it might well be a fifty years Treaty so far as we are concerned. We aim at nothing but mutual assistance and collaboration. The British have an alliance with Portugal unbroken since 1384, and which produced fruitful results at critical moments in the late war. None of these clash with the general interest of a world agreement, or a world organization; on the contrary they help it. 'In my father's house are many mansions.' Special associations between members of the United Nations which have no aggressive point against any other country, which harbour no design incompatible with the Charter of the United Nations, far from being harmful, are beneficial and, as I believe, indispensable.

I spoke earlier of the Temple of Peace. Workmen from all countries must build that temple. If two of the workmen know each other particularly well and are old friends, if their families are intermingled, and if they have 'faith in each other's purpose, hope in each other's future and charity towards each other's shortcomings' – to quote some good words I read here the other day – why cannot they work together at the common task as friends and partners? Why cannot they share their tools and thus increase each other's working powers? Indeed they must do so or else the temple may not be built, or, being built, it may collapse, and we shall all be proved again unteachable and have to go and try to learn again for a third time in a school of war, incomparably more rigorous than that from which we have just been released. The dark ages may return, the Stone Age may return on the gleaming wings of science, and what might now shower immeasurable material blessings upon mankind, may even bring about its total destruction. Beware, I say; time may be short. Do not let us take the course of allowing events to drift along until it is too late. If there is to be a fraternal association of the kind I have described, with all the extra strength and security which both our countries can derive from it, let us make sure that that great fact is known to the world, and that it plays its part in steadying and stabilizing the foundations of peace. There is the path of wisdom. Prevention is better than cure.

A shadow has fallen upon the scenes so lately lighted by the Allied victory. Nobody knows what Soviet Russia and its Communist international organization intends to do in the immediate future, or what are the limits, if any, to their expansive and proselytizing tendencies. I have a strong admiration and regard for the valiant Russian people and for my wartime comrade, Marshal Stalin. There is deep sympathy and goodwill in Britain – and I doubt not here also – towards the peoples of all the Russias and a resolve to persevere through many differences and rebuffs in establishing lasting friendships. We understand the Russian need to be secure on her western frontiers by the removal of all possibility of German aggression. We welcome Russia to her rightful place among the leading nations of the world. We welcome her flag upon the seas. Above all, we welcome constant, frequent and growing contacts between the Russian people and our own people on both sides of the Atlantic. It is my duty, however, for I am sure you would wish me to state the facts as I see them to you, to place before you certain facts about the present position in Europe.

From Stettin in the Baltic to Trieste in the Adriatic, an iron curtain has descended across the Continent. Behind that line lie all the capitals of the ancient states of Central and Eastern Europe. Warsaw, Berlin, Prague, Vienna, Budapest, Belgrade, Bucharest and Sofia, all these famous cities and the populations around them lie in what I must call the Soviet sphere, and all are subject in one form or another, not only to Soviet influence but to a very high and, in many cases, increasing measure of control from Moscow. Athens alone – Greece with its immortal glories – is free to decide its future at an election under British American and French observation. The Russian-dominated Polish Government has been encouraged to make enormous and wrongful inroads upon Germany, and mass expulsions of millions of Germans on a scale grievous and undreamed-of are now taking place. The Communist parties, which were very small in all these Eastern States of Europe, have been raised to pre-eminence and power far beyond their numbers and are seeking everywhere to obtain totalitarian control. Police governments are prevailing in nearly every case, and so far, except in Czechoslovakia, there is no true democracy.

Turkey and Persia [Iran] are both profoundly alarmed and disturbed at the claims which are being made upon them and at the pressure being exerted by the Moscow Government. An attempt is being made by the Russians in Berlin to build up a quasi-Communist party in their zone of Occupied Germany by showing special favours to groups of left-wing German leaders. At the end of the fighting last June, the American and British Armies withdrew westwards, in accorance with an earlier agreement, to a depth at some points of 150 miles upon a front of nearly four hundred miles, in order to allow our Russian allies to occupy this vast expanse of territory which the Western Democracies had conquered.

If now the Soviet Government tries, by separate action, to build up a pro-Communist Germany in their areas, this will cause new serious difficulties in the British and American zones, and will give the defeated Germans the power of putting themselves up to auction between the Soviets and the Western Democracies. Whatever conclusions may be drawn from these facts – and facts they are – this is certainly not the Liberated Europe we fought to build up. Nor is it one which contains the essentials of permanent peace.

The safety of the world requires a new unity in Europe, from which no nation should be permanently outcast. It is from the quarrels of the strong parent races in Europe that the world wars we have witnessed, or which occurred in former times, have sprung. Twice in our own lifetime we have seen the United States, against their wishes and their traditions, against arguments, the force of which it is impossible not to comprehend, drawn by irresistible forces, into these wars in time to secure the victory of the good cause, but only after frightful slaughter and devastation had occurred. Twice the United States has had to send several millions of its young men across the Atlantic to find the war; but now war can find any nation, wherever it may dwell between dusk and dawn. Surely we should work with conscious purpose for a grand pacification of Europe, within the structure of the United Nations and in accordance with its Charter. That I feel is an open cause of policy of very great importance.

In front of the iron curtain which lies across Europe are other causes for anxiety. In Italy the Communist Party is seriously hampered by having to support the Communist-trained Marshal Tito's claims to former Italian territory at the head of the Adriatic. Nevertheless, the future of Italy hangs in the balance. Again one cannot imagine a regenerated Europe without a strong France. All my public life I have worked for a strong France and I never lost faith in her destiny, even in the darkest hours. I will not lose faith now. However, in a great number of countries, far from the Russian frontiers and throughout the world. Communist fifth columns are established and work in complete unity and absolute obedience to the directions they receive from the Communist centre. Except in the British Commonwealth and in the United States where Communism is in its infancy, the Communist parties or fifth columns constitute a growing challenge and peril to Christian civilization. These are sombre facts for anyone to have to recite on the morrow of a victory gained by so much splendid comradeship in arms and in the cause of freedom and democracy; but we should be most unwise not to face them squarely while time remains.

The outlook is also anxious in the Far East and especially in Manchuria. The Agreement which was made at Yalta, to which I was a party, was extremely favourable to Soviet Russia, but it was made at a time when no one could say that the German war might not extend all through the summer and autumn of 1945 and when the Japanese war was expected to last for a further eighteen months from the end of the German war. In this country you are all so well informed about the Far East, and such devoted friends of China, that I do not need to expatiate on the situation there.

I have felt bound to portray the shadow which, alike in the west and in the east, falls upon the world. I was a high minister at the time of the Versailles Treaty and a close friend of Mr Lloyd George, who was the head of the British delegation at Versailles. I did not myself agree with many things that were done, but I have a very strong impression in my mind of that situation, and I find it painful to contrast it with that which prevails now. In those days there were high hopes and unbounded confidence that the wars were over, and that the League of Nations would become all-powerful. I do not see or feel that same confidence or even the same hopes in the haggard world at the present time.

On the other hand I repulse the idea that a new war is inevitable; still more that it is imminent. It is because I am sure that our fortunes are still in our own hands and that we hold the power to save the future, that I feel the duty to speak out now that I have the occasion and the opportunity to do so. I do not believe that Soviet Russia desires war. What they desire is the fruits of war and the indefinite expansion of their power and doctrines. But what we have to consider here today while time remains, is the permanent prevention of war and the establishment of conditions of freedom and democracy as rapidly as possible in all countries. Our difficulties and dangers will not be removed by closing our eyes to them. They will not be removed by mere waiting to see what happens; nor will they be removed by a policy of appeasement. What is needed is a settlement, and the longer this is delayed, the more difficult it will be and the greater our dangers will become.

From what I have seen of our Russian friends and Allies during the war, I am convinced that there is nothing they admire so much as strength, and there is nothing for which they have less respect than for weakness, especially military weakness. For

306

that reason the old doctrine of a balance of power is unsound. We cannot afford, if we can help it, to work on narrow margins, offering temptations to a trial of strength. If the Western Democracies stand together in strict adherence to the principles of the United Nations Charter, their influence for furthering those principles will be immense and no one is likely to molest them. If, however, they become divided or falter in their duty and if these all-important years are allowed to slip away then indeed catastrophe may overwhelm us all.

Last time I saw it all coming and cried aloud to my own fellow-countrymen and to the world, but no one paid any attention. Up till the year 1933 or even 1935, Germany might have been saved from the awful fate which has overtaken her and we might all have been spared the miseries Hitler let loose upon mankind. There never was a war in all history easier to prevent by timely action than the one which has just desolated such great areas of the globe. It could have been prevented in my belief without the firing of a single shot, and Germany might be powerful, prosperous and honoured today; but no one would listen and one by one we were all sucked into the awful whirlpool. We surely must not let that happen again. This can only be achieved by reaching now, in 1946, a good understanding on all points with Russia under the general authority of the United Nations Organization and by the maintenance of that good understanding through many peaceful years, by the world instrument, supported by the whole strength of the English-speaking world and all its connections. There is the solution which I respectfully offer to you in this Address to which I have given the title 'The Sinews of Peace'.

Let no man underrate the abiding power of the British Empire and Commonwealth. Because you see the forty-six millions in our island harassed about their food supply, of which they only grow one-half, even in wartime, or because we have difficulty in restarting our industries and export trade after six years of passionate war effort, do not suppose that we shall not come through these dark years of privation as we have come through the glorious years of agony, or that half a century from now, you will not see seventy or eighty millions of Britons spread about the world and united in defence of our traditions, our way of life, and of the world causes which you and we espouse. If the population of the English-speaking Commonwealths be added to that of the United States with all that such co-operation implies in the air, on the sea, all over the globe and in science and in industry, and in moral force, there will be no quivering, precarious balance of power to offer its temptation to ambition or adventure. On the contrary, there will be an overwhelming assurance of security. If we adhere faithfully to the Charter of the United Nations and walk forward in sedate and sober strength seeking no one's land or treasure, seeking to lay no arbitrary control upon the thoughts of men; if all British moral and material forces and convictions are joined with your own in fraternal association, the highroads of the future will be clear, not only for us but for all, not only for our time, but for a century to come.

29

European Unity

'Something That Will Astonish You'

Zurich, 19 September 1946

CHURCHILL SPENT MUCH OF THE LATER PART OF 1946 triumphantly visiting the nations of Western Europe, receiving honorary degrees, medals and gifts, and widespread public homage. The theme of his speeches, first expounded at Brussels in November 1945, was that the only prospect for the Continent, in the aftermath of the carnage and destruction of the Second World War, and in the shadow of the new Soviet menace, was for its inhabitants to create some form of a 'United States of Europe.'

In August and September, Churchill spent some weeks in Switzerland as the guest of the Federal Government, and he delivered this speech – which was second only to his Fulton address in its importance and its impact – on receiving an honorary degree from the University of Zurich. Once again, he made his eloquent plea for European unity. But now he went even further, and put forward his 'astonishing' proposal that there must be an end to old nationalistic antagonisms, and that there must be 'partnership between France and Germany'.

At a time when the full extent of Nazi atrocities was only just being revealed at the Nuremberg Trials, this was indeed an audacious idea. *The Times* noted that, once again, it showed Churchill was 'not afraid to startle the world with new and even, as many must find them, outrageous propositions.' But Leo Amery was more encouraging: 'You have indeed lit a torch to give its message of hope to a shattered world.'

309

SPEAKING WITH DIFFERENT TONGUES

Zurich, 19 September 1946

I WISH TO SPEAK TO YOU TODAY about the tragedy of Europe. This noble continent, comprising on the whole the fairest and the most cultivated regions of the earth, enjoying a temperate and equable climate, is the home of all the great parent races of the western world. It is the fountain of Christian faith and Christian ethics. It is the origin of most of the culture, arts, philosophy and science both of ancient and modern times. If Europe were once united in the sharing of its common inheritance, there would be no limit to the happiness, to the prosperity and glory which its three or four hundred million people would enjoy. Yet it is from Europe that have sprung that series of frightful nationalistic quarrels, originated by the Teutonic nations, which we have seen even in this twentieth century and in our own lifetime, wreck the peace and mar the prospects of all mankind.

And what is the plight to which Europe has been reduced? Some of the smaller States have indeed made a good recovery, but over wide areas a vast quivering mass of tormented, hungry, care-worn and bewildered human beings gape at the ruins of their cities and homes, and scan the dark horizons for the approach of some new peril, tyranny or terror. Among the victors there is a babel of jarring voices; among the vanquished the sullen silence of despair. That is all that Europeans, grouped in so many ancient States and nations, that is all that the Germanic Powers have got by tearing each other to pieces and spreading havoc far and wide. Indeed, but for the fact that the great Republic across the Atlantic Ocean has at length realized that the ruin or enslavement of Europe would involve their own fate as well, and has stretched out hands of succour and guidance, the Dark Ages would have returned in all their cruelty and squalor. They may still return.

Yet all the while there is a remedy which, if it were generally

310

and spontaneously adopted, would as if by a miracle transform the whole scene, and would in a few years make all Europe, or the greater part of it, as free and as happy as Switzerland is today. What is this sovereign remedy? It is to re-create the European Family, or as much of it as we can, and provide it with a structure under which it can dwell in peace, in safety and in freedom. We must build a kind of United States of Europe. In this way only will hundreds of millions of toilers be able to regain the simple joys and hopes which make life worth living. The process is simple. All that is needed is the resolve of hundreds of millions of men and women to do right instead of wrong and gain as their reward blessing instead of cursing.

Much work has been done upon this task by the exertions of the Pan-European Union which owes so much to Count Coudenhove-Kalergi and which commanded the services of the famous French patriot and statesman, Aristide Briand. There is also that immense body of doctrine and procedure, which was brought into being amid high hopes after the First World War, as the League of Nations. The League of Nations did not fail because of its principles or conceptions. It failed because these principles were deserted by those States who had brought it into being. It failed because the Governments of those days feared to face the facts and act while time remained. This disaster must not be repeated. There is, therefore, much knowledge and material with which to build; and also bitter dear-bought experience.

I was very glad to read in the newspapers two days ago that my friend President Truman had expressed his interest and sympathy with this great design. There is no reason why a regional organization of Europe should in any way conflict with the world organization of the United Nations. On the contrary, I believe that the larger synthesis will only survive if it is founded upon coherent natural groupings. There is already a natural grouping in the Western Hemisphere. We British have our own Commonwealth of Nations. These do not weaken, on the contrary they strengthen, the world organization. They are in fact its main support. And why should there not be a European group which could give a sense of enlarged patriotism and common citizenship to the distracted peoples of this turbulent and mighty continent and why should it not take its rightful place with other great groupings in shaping the destinies of men? In order that this should be accomplished there must be an act of faith in which millions of families speaking many languages must consciously take part.

We all know that the two world wars through which we have passed arose out of the vain passion of a newly united Germany to play the dominating part in the world. In this last struggle crimes and massacres have been committed for which there is no parallel since the invasions of the Mongols in the fourteenth century and no equal at any time in human history. The guilty must be punished. Germany must be deprived of the power to rearm and make another aggressive war. But when all this has been done, as it will be done, as it is being done, there must be an end to retribution. There must be what Mr Gladstone many years ago called 'a blessed act of oblivion'. We must all turn our backs upon the horrors of the past. We must look to the future. We cannot afford to drag forward across the years that are to come the hatreds and revenges which have sprung from the injuries of the past. If Europe is to be saved from infinite misery, and indeed from final doom, there must be an act of faith in the European family and an act of oblivion against all the crimes and follies of the past.

Can the free peoples of Europe rise to the height of these resolves of the soul and instincts of the spirit of man? If they can, the wrongs and injuries which have been inflicted will have been washed away on all sides by the miseries which have been endured. Is there any need for further floods of agony? Is it the only lesson of history that mankind is unteachable? Let there be justice, mercy and freedom. The peoples have only to will it, and all will achieve their hearts' desire.

I am now going to say something that will astonish you. The first step in the re-creation of the European family must be a partnership between France and Germany. In this way only can France recover the moral leadership of Europe. There can be no revival of Europe without a spiritually great France and a

312

spiritually great Germany. The structure of the United States of Europe, if well and truly built, will be such as to make the material strength of a single state less important. Small nations will count as much as large ones and gain their honour by their contribution to the common cause. The ancient states and principalities of Germany, freely joined together for mutual convenience in a federal system, might each take their individual place among the United States of Europe. I shall not try to make a detailed programme for hundreds of millions of people who want to be happy and free, prosperous and safe, who wish to enjoy the four freedoms of which the great President Roosevelt spoke, and live in accordance with the principles embodied in the Atlantic Charter. If this is their wish, they have only to say so, and means can certainly be found, and machinery erected, to carry that wish into full fruition.

But I must give you warning. Time may be short. At present there is a breathing-space. The cannon have ceased firing. The fighting has stopped; but the dangers have not stopped. If we are to form the United States of Europe or whatever name or form it may take, we must begin now.

In these present days we dwell strangely and precariously under the shield and protection of the atomic bomb. The atomic bomb is still only in the hands of a State and nation which we know will never use it except in the cause of right and freedom. But it may well be that in a few years this awful agency of destruction will be widespread and the catastrophe following from its use by several warring nations will not only bring to an end all that we call civilization, but may possibly disintegrate the globe itself.

I must now sum up the propositions which are before you. Our constant aim must be to build and fortify the strength of UNO. Under and within that world concept we must re-create the European family in a regional structure called, it may be, the United States of Europe. The first step is to form a Council of Europe. If at first all the States of Europe are not willing or able to join the Union, we must nevertheless proceed to assemble and combine those who will and those who can. The salvation of the common people of every race and of every land from war or servitude must be established on solid foundations and must be guarded by the readiness of all men and women to die rather than submit to tyranny. In all this urgent work, France and Germany must take the lead together. Great Britain, the British Commonwealth of Nations, mighty America, and I trust Soviet Russia – for then indeed all would be well – must be the friends and sponsors of the new Europe and must champion its right to live and shine.

30

Tribute to George VI

'The King Walked with Death'

BBC, London, 7 February 1952

IN FEBRUARY 1950 A GENERAL ELECTION took place and the overwhelming Labour majority was greatly reduced. No doubt chastened by his experiences in 1945, Churchill fought a more dignified, restrained and constructive campaign. Then, in October 1951, Parliament was dissolved again, and the Conservatives were returned to power. Their majority was disappointingly slight; Labour had, in fact, won a higher percentage of the popular vote. But at the age of 76 Churchill became Prime Minister for the second time, his defeat of 1945 finally avenged.

He had only been in office for a few months when George VI died in his sleep at Sandringham. Churchill was a fervent and romantic monarchist, who was, according to his wife, arguably the last believer in the divine right of kings. Although he had been a staunch supporter of Edward VIII at the time of the Abdication, he soon came to realize the error of his ways, and throughout the Second World War his relationship with his sovereign had been warm and cordial.

Churchill was deeply grieved by the king's death, and spent a whole day composing this broadcast speech. As he himself admitted, 'much was expected', and the expectations were not disappointed. In this, his last great set-piece eulogy, Churchill touched the hearts of his listeners as never before, especially with the passage including the phrase 'the king walked with death', and with his final reference to the new young queen.

315

BBC, London, 7 February 1952

MY FRIENDS, WHEN THE DEATH OF THE KING was announced to us yesterday morning there struck a deep and solemn note in our lives which, as it resounded far and wide, stilled the clatter and traffic of twentieth-century life in many lands and made countless millions of human beings pause and look around them. A new sense of values took, for the time being, possession of human minds and mortal existence presented itself to so many at the same moment in its serenity and in its sorrow, in its splendour and in its pain, in its fortitude and in its suffering.

The King was greatly loved by all his peoples. He was respected as a man and as a prince far beyond the many realms over which he reigned. The simple dignity of his life, his manly virtues, his sense of duty alike as a ruler and a servant of the vast spheres and communities for which he bore responsibility – his gay charm and happy nature, his example as a husband and a father in his own family circle, his courage in peace or war – all these were aspects of his character which won the glint of admiration, now here, now there, from the innumerable eyes whose gaze falls upon the Throne.

We thought of him as a young naval lieutenant in the great Battle of Jutland. We thought of him, when calmly, without ambition, or want of self-confidence, he assumed the heavy burden of the Crown and succeeded his brother, whom he loved, and to whom he had rendered perfect loyalty. We thought of him so faithful in his study and discharge of State affairs, so strong in his devotion to the enduring honour of our country, so self-restrained in his judgements of men and affairs, so uplifted above the clash of party politics, yet so attentive to them; so wise and shrewd in judging between what matters and what does not. All this we saw and admired. His conduct on the Throne may well be a model and a guide to constitutional sovereigns throughout the world today, and also in future generations.

The last few months of King George's life, with all the pain and physical stresses that he endured – his life hanging by a thread from day to day – and he all the time cheerful and undaunted – stricken in body but quite undisturbed and even unaffected in spirit – these have made a profound and an enduring impression and should be a help to all. He was sustained not only by his natural buoyancy but by the sincerity of his Christian faith. During these last months the King walked with death, as if death were a companion, an acquaintance, whom he recognized and did not fear. In the end death came as a friend; and after a happy day of sunshine and sport, and after 'good night' to those who loved him best, he fell asleep as every man or woman who strives to fear God and nothing else in the world may hope to do.

The nearer one stood to him the more these facts were apparent. But the newspapers and photographs of modern times have made vast numbers of his subjects able to watch with emotion the last months of his pilgrimage. We all saw him approach his journey's end. In this period of mourning and meditation, amid our cares and toils, every home in all the realms joined together under the Crown, may draw comfort for tonight and strength for the future from his bearing and his fortitude.

There was another tie between King George and his people. It was not only sorrow and affliction that they shared. Dear to the hearts and the homes of the people is the joy and pride of a united family; with this all the troubles of the world can be borne and all its ordeals at least confronted. No family in these tumultuous years was happier, or loved one another more, than the Royal Family around the King.

My friends, I suppose no Minister saw so much of the King during the war as I did. I made certain he was kept informed of every secret matter; and the care and thoroughness with which he mastered the immense daily flow of State papers made a deep mark on my mind. Let me tell you another fact. On one of the days, when Buckingham Palace was bombed, the King had just returned from Windsor. One side of the courtyard was struck, and if the windows opposite out of which he and the Queen were looking had not been, by the mercy of God, open, they would both have been blinded by the broken glass instead of being only hurled back by the explosion. Amid all that was then going on – although I saw the King so often – I never heard of this episode till a long time after. Their Majesties never mentioned it, or thought it of more significance than a soldier in their armies would of a shell bursting near him. This seems to me to be a revealing trait in the Royal character.

There is no doubt that of all the institutions which have grown up among us over the centuries, or sprung into being in our lifetime, the constitutional monarchy is the most deeply founded and dearly cherished by the whole association of our peoples. In the present generation it has acquired a meaning incomparably more powerful than anyone had dreamed possible in former times. The Crown has become the mysterious link – indeed, I may say, the magic link – which unites our loosely bound but strongly interwoven Commonwealth of nations, States and races. Peoples who would never tolerate the assertions of a written constitution which implied any diminution of their independence, are the foremost to be proud of their loyalty to the Crown.

We have been greatly blessed amid our many anxieties, and in the mighty world that has grown up all around our small island – we have been greatly blessed that this new intangible, inexpressible but for practical purposes apparently, an all-powerful element of union should have leapt into being among us. How vital it is, not only to the future of the British Commonwealth and Empire, but I believe also to the cause of world freedom and peace which we serve, that the occupant of the Throne should be equal to the august and indefinable responsibilities which this supreme office requires. For fifteen years King George VI was king; never at any moment in all the perplexities at home and abroad, in public or in private, did he fail in his duties; well does he deserve the farewell salute of all his governments and peoples.

My friends, it is at this time that our compassion and sympathy go out to his Consort and widow. Their marriage was a love match with no idea of regal pomp or splendour. Indeed, there seemed to lie before them the arduous life of royal personages denied so many of the activities of ordinary folk and having to give so much in ceremonial public service. May I say, speaking with all freedom, that our hearts go out tonight to that valiant woman with famous blood of Scotland in her veins who sustained King George through all his toils and problems and brought up, with their charm and beauty, the two daughters who mourn their father today. May she be granted strength to bear her sorrow. To Queen Mary, his mother, another of whose sons is dead – the Duke of Kent having been killed on active service – there belongs the consolation of seeing how well the King did his duty and fulfilled her hopes, and of always knowing how much he cared for her.

Now I must leave the treasures of the past and turn to the future. Famous have been the reigns of our Queens. Some of the greatest periods in our history have unfolded under their sceptres. Now that we have the second Queen Elizabeth, also ascending the Throne in her twenty-sixth year, our thoughts are carried back nearly 400 years to the magnificent figure who presided over, and in many ways embodied and inspired, the grandeur and genius of the Elizabethan Age. Queen Elizabeth the Second, like her predecessor, did not pass her childhood in any certain expectation of the Crown. But already we know her well, and we understand why her gifts, and those of her husband, the Duke of Edinburgh, have stirred the only part of our Commonwealth she has yet been able to visit. She has already been acclaimed as Queen of Canada: we make our claim, too, and others will come forward also; and tomorrow the proclamation of her sovereignty will command the loyalty of her native land and of all other parts of the British Commonwealth and Empire.

I, whose youth was passed in the august, unchallenged and tranquil glories of the Victorian Era, may well feel a thrill in invoking, once more, the prayer and the Anthem: GOD SAVE THE QUEEN.

31

Debate on the Address

'Time, Calm, Industry and Vigilance'

House of Commons, 3 November 1953

IN THE AFTERMATH OF QUEEN ELIZABETH'S triumphant coronation, and on the brink of a meeting with the Americans in Bermuda, Churchill suffered a severe stroke in June 1953. Initially, he was not even expected to survive, and for several months he remained incapacitated at Chartwell, the gravity of his condition effectively concealed from all but a very few close friends. Since Anthony Eden was himself in hospital at the time, R. A. Butler became acting Prime Minister. But to his friends' and his doctors' amazement, Churchill gradually began to recover.

In August, he was well enough to preside at a Cabinet meeting, and in early October he gave his first public speech since his stroke, to the Conservative Party Conference at Margate. Despite understandable anxieties, it was described by *The Times* as 'a personal triumph', and Churchill prepared to face his next ordeal – addressing the House of Commons. Fortified by one of Lord Moran's special pills, he made one of the most vigorous speeches of his second premiership, which ranged widely across the domestic and international scene, and ended with a majestic peroration about the menace of the hydrogen bomb.

The majority of MPs, who knew nothing of Churchill's recent illness, were genuinely impressed by the vigour and virtuosity of his oratory. Even Henry Channon conceded that it was 'one of the speeches of his lifetime', 'an Olympian spectacle', 'a supreme performance.' But there were not many left.

320

House of Commons, 3 November 1953

I THOUGHT THE LEADER OF THE OPPOSITION chose very apposite words in which to pay the traditional compliments to the mover and the seconder of the Motion. It is always difficult to find new terms in which to express the broad general feeling of the House in this matter because, after all, it happens every year and most of the good points have been taken on bygone occasions.

I think I have been a witness of these proceedings longer than anyone else, and I certainly would not guarantee to think of something entirely new. This I can say, however; that the mover stated his case with simple force, and the seconder certainly earned fully the praise of the Leader of the Opposition, in that she will have a most valuable and important contribution to make to our discussions over the social and, particularly, the health spheres. At any rate, I am obliged to the right hon. Gentleman for the way in which he has referred to these, my two hon. Friends, and I am glad that all has started in such a quiet and nice and friendly spirit. I trust that I shall not be guilty of trespassing beyond those limits further than is necessary to place the realization of the facts before the House.

The debate on the Address will continue for the rest of this week, I have to tell the House, and it is hoped that it will be completed early next week. It is our intention, Mr Speaker, under your guidance to arrange both the general debate, and the debate on any Amendments which may be tabled, so as to meet the wishes of the House. It is proposed that Private Members shall enjoy their rights in the matter of Bills and Motions in the same manner as in recent Sessions. Perhaps I may take this opportunity to give notice that my right hon. Friend the Leader of the House will tomorrow propose a Motion to provide that Private Members' business should have precedence on twenty Fridays, the first of which will be Friday 27 November.

The right hon. Gentleman referred to a few matters which are mentioned in the Gracious Speech, but not as fully as he would wish. He said that the question of Egypt was omitted. Well, the Egyptian negotiations were mentioned in the prorogation Speech and there has been no development of importance since then, but there may be as time passes.

The Overlords came in for comment. I had no experience of being Prime Minister in time of peace and I attached more importance to the grouping of Departments so that the responsible head of Government would be able to deal with a comparatively smaller number of heads than actually exists in peacetime. I think we had great advantage – although it may not be believed opposite – from the services of the three noble Lords, who did their very utmost to help forward the public service. On reflection, I have thought it better to revert to the proposal which the right hon. Gentleman himself recommended, namely, to hush it all up and manage it in the Cabinet.

That also applies in a certain sense to what the right hon. Gentleman said about atomic energy, for there too his record is one which, at any rate, may be taken as an example in some ways. He demands the control of atomic energy by the House, but we must not forget that when he was in office his Government spent more than £100 million without ever asking the House to be aware of what was going on. No doubt having been in office such a short time as we have, we have not yet learned all the tricks of the trade. The question of atomic energy being dealt with under Government authority by a corporation will be laid before the House next week when a White Paper and an Order in Council will be issued. They will give the House a very great deal of information upon a subject which, I must warn hon. Gentlemen, means quite hard reading, if one has to undertake a great deal of it.

I notice that both the mover and the seconder of the Motion and the Leader of the Opposition gave prominence in their remarks to the expression of their fervent good wishes to the Queen and the Duke of Edinburgh for the tremendous journey round the Commonwealth and Empire and round the world upon which they shortly will embark. Nothing like it has ever

322

been seen before in our history. There is no doubt of the welcome which awaits Her Majesty in Australia, New Zealand, and all the other lands which give their loyalty and allegiance to the Crown, and through which she and her husband will travel. We all join together in wishing Her Majesty and the Duke God-speed on their journey and a safe return to her loyal and devoted subjects in these islands next May.

This is the third time that I have been called upon to follow the Leader of the Opposition in the debate on the Address in this present Parliament and two years have passed since we had a General Election. When are we going to have another? [*Hon. Members: 'Tomorrow'*]. It is always difficult to foresee, and rash to forecast, the course of future events. Still, for practical purposes, one has to try from time to time to weigh the probabilities and make the best guess one can. I do not hesitate to say that, viewing the political scene as it appears to me, it looks as if a General Election was further off this afternoon than it did two years ago.

It certainly is not the wish or intention of Her Majesty's Government to take advantage of any temporary fluctuation in public opinion in the hopes of securing an electoral victory. Two years ago many thought there might soon be another trial of strength, even within a twelve month, making three quarrel-some, costly, machine-made tumults in less than three years. Now it is quite evident that different expectations prevail.

After all, we were elected for a five-year period under what is called the Quinquennial Act. I have always been in favour of the Quinquennial Act. In fact, forty-eight years ago, in 1905, I moved a Bill under the Ten Minutes Rule to establish the quinquennial period instead of the septennial, which was then the legal term. It seems to me that this 'quinquennial' strikes a happy medium between Parliaments which last too little and Parliaments which last too long.

We are not only a democracy but a Parliamentary democracy, and both aspects of our political life must be borne in mind. To have a General Election every year, as the Chartists proposed, would deprive the House of Commons of much of its dignity and authority. It would no longer be an Assembly endeavouring to find a solution for national problems and providing a stable foundation for the administration of the country, but rather a vote-catching machine looking for a springboard, in an atmosphere where party advantage and personal ambition would be by no means wholly excluded. There is no doubt, and I would like to put this general proposition to the House for their consideration, that elections exist for the sake of the House of Commons and not that the House of Commons exists for the sake of elections.

If this were true in former generations, it seems even more so in this cataclysmic twentieth century when everything is in flux and change and when, after the fearful exertions, sacrifices, and exhaustions of two world wars, the element of calm, patient study, and a sense of structure by both sides may render lasting service to our whole people and increase and consolidate their influence for good and for peace throughout the quivering, convulsive and bewildered world.

More especially is this true of a period in which the two-party system is dominant and about fourteen million vote Tory and about another fourteen million Socialist [*Hon. Members: 'Ah'*]. I looked the figures up. I have not done anybody out of anything. The two-party system is dominant. It is not really possible to assume that one of these fourteen million masses of voters possesses all the virtues and the wisdom and the other lot are dupes or fools, or even knaves or crooks. Ordinary people in the country mix about with each other in friendly, neighbourly relations, and they know it is nonsense for party politicians to draw such harsh contrasts between them. Even in his House it is very difficult for the specialists in faction to prevent Members from getting very friendly with each other and worrying about their common difficulties and the grave strain and expense of modern Parliamentary life. We have at least that in common.

On the other hand, I am sure it would be a mistake if the possibilities of dissolution were removed altogether from the mind of Parliament. In some countries Parliaments cannot be dissolved, or can hardly be dissolved, until they have run their fixed term. It is an advantage of our system that, while we aim at five-year

Parliaments – which, by etiquette, means four and a half years – extraordinary situations may arise at home or abroad which justify or even compel a precipitate appeal to the country.

Nothing I say about our desires and intentions to allow this Parliament to run its lawful course is intended to exclude necessary constitutional action if events should require it. I have fought more elections than anyone here, or indeed anyone alive in this country – Parliamentary elections – and on the whole they are great fun. But there ought to be interludes of tolerance, hard work and study of social problems between them. Having rows for the sake of having rows between politicians might be good from time to time, but it is not a good habit of political life. It does not follow that we should get further apart by staying long together.

I am not suggesting that our goal is a coalition; that, I think, would be carrying goodwill too far. But our duties, as we see them, are varied and sometimes conflicting. We have to help our respective parties, but we have also to make sure that we help our country and its people. There can be no doubt where our duty lies between these two.

I am pleading for time, calm, industry and vigilance, and also time to let things grow and prove themselves by experience. It may sometimes be necessary for Governments to undo each other's work, but this should be an exception and not the rule. We are, of course, opposed, for instance, to nationalization of industry and, to a lesser extent, to the nationalization of services. We abhor the fallacy, for such it is, of nationalization for national-ization's sake. But where we are preserving it, as in the coal-mines, the railways, air traffic, gas and electricity, we have done and are doing our utmost to make a success of it, even though this may somewhat mar the symmetry of party recrimination. It is only where we believed that a measure of nationalization was a real hindrance to our island life that we have reversed the policy, although we are generally opposed to the principle.

Here, let me say, in passing from these general remarks, that I earnestly hope the appointment of Sir Brian Robertson as head of British Railways will be distinguished not only by marked improvements in their running, but also by a feeling among the railwaymen that an element of personal contact and leadership will be developed between the management and the men so that healthy pride may play its part in the success of these national services.

In his speech, the right hon. Gentleman referred briefly both to housing and to farming. I had thought beforehand that something like this might happen, so I collected a few remarks to make upon the subjects. I have heard some talk about our policy for the repair and improvement of houses being a Tory plot to put more money into the pockets of the landlords – What, not a sound! I hope that that will not be considered – I am encouraged by the way it is received – an exhaustive exposition of the problem. It would certainly be a premature judgement, for no attempt has yet been made to explain our plans. Before I sit down this afternoon White Papers, giving full schemes for England, Wales and Scotland, will be found in the Vote Office. My right hon. Friend the Minister of Housing and Local Government will unfold his scheme in detail during our debate tomorrow, and I shall not anticipate his explanation of its structure [*Hon. Members: 'Oh'*]. But I am going to say a few words upon the subject.

We have claimed credit, as we have a right to do, for building at the rate of 300,000 new houses per year. We were frequently told, and have long known, that building new houses cannot by itself solve the urgent problem of providing homes for the people. If it were true that while 300,000 new houses were being built nearly as many were mouldering into ruin and a far larger number were devoid of modern conveniences, the gain of new building would be largely cancelled out. The Opposition have said that to us, and we concede it. The Minister of Housing and Local Government has produced – with immense work and months and months of discussions – what we believe is a practical, I will not say solution, but mitigation, of the problem.

We have to face the fact that two and a quarter million houses were built one hundred years ago and another two million are between sixty-five and one hundred years old. Even the more modern ones require regular maintenance and repair. Surely this is a matter which ought to interest – and which I am sure will interest – the whole of any House of Commons elected on the basis of universal suffrage. I hope it will not be brushed aside. I can quite see, as far as I have got, that it is not going to be treated merely as a party matter. If when the White Paper has been studied and when my right hon. Friend has commended it to the House, the Opposition have a counter proposal, let them put it forward; we shall give it our earnest attention. These are not the sort of questions which party Governments are usually anxious to tackle, but it cannot be allowed to drift any longer by any Government determined to do its duty. I would quote to the House some words spoken by an eminent and independent man, a life-long champion of Left-wing politics, highly regarded on both sides of the House, Mr Thomas Johnston. He said last year at Stirling – I really must read this to the House:

> I venture once again to draw attention to the galloping disasters coming to us in the increasing obsolescence and decay of our existing housing structures being permitted – indeed rendered inevitable – I believe through sheer political cowardice. Private house proprietors and housing trusts are unable to provide repairs, much less improvements, owing to the high cost of materials ... To allow great national assets like that to crumble and disappear prematurely does not make sense; and when it is remembered that not only no repairs but no improvements can be effected, and that hundreds of thousands of tenants are condemned for all the years of their lives to live without even the ordinary decencies of a separate family water-closet or a bath, we can see that unless existing house assets are maintained and improved side-by-side with the provision of new houses, then not only will the house problem not be solved in our day and generation, but the financial and administrative position of our local authorities will become hopeless and impossible.

He concluded:

> This is not the occasion to outline remedies, but I suggest that the first and essential condition is that the repair and maintenance and improvement of housing be taken outside the orbit of partisan politics altogether.

We shall see how we get on, but let us start with that hope.

It must be realized that houses cannot be repaired without money, and where is that money to come from? Is it to be found by the State? Or is it to be new private investment by landlords? Or will both these processes be necessary? It is quite certain that no adequate system of repairing millions of houses, let alone fitting them with baths and other basic modern requirements, will be brought into existence unless this Parliament takes effective action, and begins now.

Undoubtedly new burdens will fall upon the national finances, and this must be viewed with gravity at a time when our solvency and our independence of foreign aid, on which we count so much, stand foremost in our minds. On the other hand, we must not forget that our financial credit will be substantially enhanced by our coping with a problem which is known to have been outstanding for so long. Surely any fair and reasonable scheme for inducing private as well as public resources to be made available for these vital public purposes should not be curtly dismissed – I am sure it will not be curtly dismissed – by the House of Commons.

Would it be very wrong if I suggested, following the lines which Mr Tom Johnston indicated, that we might look into this together, with the desire to have more decent homes for the people counting much higher in our minds than ordinary partisan political gains gaining advantages for either side? War and its restrictions: aerial bombardment and its destructions: time and decay: potential improvements: all seem to make this matter worthy of the goodwill and mental effort of the House as a whole.

But this process will need time, time not only to pass the legislation but also to allow its effects to show themselves and to make people feel that benefits have been received which are welcomed by many thousands of families. Certainly we should not have embarked upon this policy to repair the crumbling homes and resume our work of cleaning up the slums unless we had intended to remain responsible long enough to be judged by results. With these introductory words, I commend the White Papers now in the Vote Office to hon. Members.

The Leader of the Opposition referred also to the farmers. The House knows that it is our theme and policy to reduce controls and restrictions as much as possible and to reverse if not to abolish the tendency to state purchase and marketing which is a characteristic of the Socialist philosophy. We hope instead to develop individual enterprise founded in the main on the laws of supply and demand and to restore to the interchange of goods and services that variety, flexibility, ingenuity and incentive on which we believe the fertility and liveliness of economic life depend. We have now reached a point when the end of wartime food rationing, with all its rigid, costly features and expensive staff, is in sight. For our farmers, the abandonment of controls will bring great opportunities.

In the agricultural field, however, another set of arguments must be borne in mind. It is the policy of both parties in the State to sustain and increase home-grown food on which this island depends so largely for a favourable trade balance and, in the ultimate issue, for its life. It is not an easy task to reconcile the beneficial liberation of our food supply from Government controls with that effective stimulus of home production which is vital [*Interruption*]. Hon. Members want the good without the evil; that is often very difficult to solve.

It is necessary for the Exchequer to subsidize in one form or another, so as to bridge the gap between the price level reached in a free market on the one hand, and the price level necessary to sustain the welfare of the farmers on the other. Moreover, the gap must not only be bridged in the industry as a whole by maintaining average returns but we must also, in the case of what are called fat stock – a technical term covering a very considerable field – provide safeguards for individual transactions where necessary.

We have laboured patiently and arduously at the difficult problems of marketing and production, and we have reached conclusions which we shall submit to the House in another White Paper – I had better not get them mixed together – this very week. We believe that these will deal equitably and encouragingly with the producers without throwing an undue burden on the taxpayer or denying the consumer – and we are all consumers – the advantages of world abundance and of widening choice in so intimate a business as meals.

The Minister of Agriculture will deal with this complicated and not entirely non-political subject when he speaks later in the debate. But I can assure the House that we intend to help the farming industry to solve their difficulties by every means compatible with the general welfare of the community, which requires the maintenance of confidence throughout the agricultural industry and that increasing flow of food which is vital to the health and stamina of the nation.

I have mentioned the larger domestic issues, which were also mentioned by the Leader of the Opposition, on which our minds this Session will be set; may I say that while controversy lends life and sparkle to Parliamentary debates, the real honour belongs to any Member, wherever he sits, who can contribute constructive suggestions and thus directly serve the people as a whole.

We shall have another debate on foreign affairs in the near future, and I shall not attempt anything like a general survey today. Comparing the outlook now with two years ago, I think it would be true to say that it is less formidable but more baffling. The issues as they had shaped themselves in the days of our predecessors were clear-cut. The vast three-year rearmament plan was just getting into its stride. The war in Korea was still raging. General Eisenhower was organizing Western Europe. A feeling of crescendo and crisis filled the air. Our Socialist Government, with the full support of the Conservative Opposition, were marching with our American allies in a vehement effort to meet the Soviet menace.

The main structure of this position is maintained, and no weakening in British purpose has resulted from the change of Government. Nevertheless, certain important events have happened which, rightly or wrongly, have somewhat veiled, and, it may be, actually modified the harshness of the scene. The fighting in Korea has shifted from the trenches to the tables. We do not know yet what will emerge from these stubborn and tangled discussions. But whatever else comes, or may come, as a result of the Korean war, one major world fact is outstanding. The United States have become again a heavily armed nation.

The second world event has been the death of Stalin and the assumption of power by a different regime in the Kremlin. It is on the second of these prodigious events that I wish to dwell for a moment. Nearly eight months have passed since it occurred and everywhere the question was, and still is asked, did the end of the Stalin epoch lead to a change in Soviet policy? Is there a new look?

I should not venture to ask the House, or any outside our doors to whom my words have access, to adopt positive conclusions on these mysteries. It may well be that there have been far-reaching changes in the temper and outlook of the immense populations, now so largely literate, who inhabit 'all the Russias', and that their mind has turned to internal betterment rather than external aggression. This may or may not be a right judgement, and we can afford, if vigilance is not relaxed and strength is not suffered again to dwindle, to await developments in a hopeful and, I trust, a helpful mood.

The only really sure guide to the actions of mighty nations and powerful Governments is a correct estimate of what are and what they consider to be their own interests. Applying this test, I feel a sense of reassurance. Studying our own strength and that of Europe under the massive American shield, I do not find it unreasonable or dangerous to conclude that internal prosperity rather than external conquest is not only the deep desire of the Russian peoples, but also the long-term interest of their rulers.

It was in this state of mind that six months ago I thought it would be a good thing if the heads of the principal States and Governments concerned met the new leaders of Russia and established that personal acquaintance and relationship which have certainly often proved a help rather than a hindrance. I still hope that such a meeting may have a useful place in international contacts.

On the other hand, one must not overlook the risk of such a four-Power conference ending in a still worse deadlock than exists at present. It certainly would be most foolish to imagine that there is any chance of making straightaway a general settlement of all the cruel problems that exist in the East as well as in the West, and that exist in Germany and in all the satellite countries. We are not likely straightaway to get them satisfactorily dealt with and laid to rest as great dangers and evils in the world by personal meetings, however friendly. Time will undoubtedly be needed – more time than some of us here are likely to see.

I am, of course, in very close touch with President Eisenhower and my hope was that at Bermuda we might have had a talk about it all. I was sorry to be prevented by conditions beyond my control. We are at present looking forward to the four-Power conference of Foreign Secretaries, and we earnestly hope it will take place soon. If it leads to improvements those themselves might again lead to further efforts on both sides. We trust we shall soon have a favourable answer to our conciliatory invitation to the Soviet.

I have mentioned two dominant events that have happened in the last two years. But there is a third which, though it happened before, has developed so prodigiously in this period that I can treat it as if it were a novel apparition which has overshadowed both those I have mentioned. I mean the rapid and ceaseless developments of atomic warfare and the hydrogen bomb.

These fearful scientific discoveries cast their shadow on every thoughtful mind, but nevertheless I believe that we are justified in feeling that there has been a diminution of tension and that the probabilities of another world war have diminished, or at least have become more remote. I say this in spite of the continual growth of weapons of destruction such as have never fallen before into the hands of human beings. Indeed, I have sometimes the odd thought that the annihilating character of these agencies may bring an utterly unforeseeable security to mankind.

When I was a schoolboy I was not good at arithmetic, but I have since heard it said that certain mathematical quantities when they pass through infinity change their signs from plus to minus – or the other way round [*Laughter*]. I do not venture to plunge too much into detail of what are called the asymptotes of hyperbolae, but any hon. Gentleman who is interested can find an opportunity for an interesting study of these matters. It may be that this rule may have a novel application and that when the advance of destructive weapons enables everyone to kill everybody else nobody will want to kill anyone at all. At any rate, it seems pretty safe to say that a war which begins by both sides suffering what they dread most – and that is undoubtedly the case at present – is less likely to occur than one which dangles the lurid prizes of former ages before ambitious eyes.

I offer this comforting idea to the House, taking care to make it clear at the same time that our only hope can spring from untiring vigilance. There is no doubt that if the human race are to have their dearest wish and be free from the dread of mass destruction, they could have, as an alternative, what many of them might prefer, namely, the swiftest expansion of material well-being that has ever been within their reach, or even within their dreams.

By material well-being I mean not only abundance but a degree of leisure for the masses such as has never before been possible in our mortal struggle for life. These majestic possibilities ought to gleam, and be made to gleam, before the eyes of the toilers in every land, and they ought to inspire the actions of all who bear responsibility for their guidance. We, and all nations, stand, at this hour in human history, before the portals of supreme catastrophe and of measureless reward. My faith is that in God's mercy we shall choose aright.

32

Eightieth Birthday

'This Superb Honour'

Westminster Hall, London, 30 November 1954

DESPITE HIS GREAT SPEECH OF NOVEMBER 1953, Churchill's health did deteriorate considerably in the aftermath of his stroke. There were murmurings of discontent in the Press, on the Tory back-benches and in the Cabinet. But he held on grimly to 10 Downing Street, partly because he could not bear the thought of quitting public life for ever, partly because he was becoming increasingly doubtful of Eden's capacity, and partly because he hankered for a final summit meeting with the Russians.

As a result, he was still in office in November 1954, when he celebrated his eightieth birthday – the first Prime Minister to reach this age in power since Gladstone. Even Churchill – egotist that he was – was deeply moved by the warmth of the reception he was given. At an unprecedented ceremony in Westminster Hall, he was presented with Parliament's gift: a portrait by Graham Sutherland, and an illuminated book containing the signatures of virtually every MP.

Although Churchill was greatly distressed by the Sutherland painting (which was eventually destroyed on the instructions of Lady Churchill), he made one of his most attractive speeches in reply. It was, John Colville noted, full 'of wit and fire. The puckish humour, the calculated asides, the perfectly modulated control of voice and that incomparable moral sturdiness made him look, and sound, years younger than his true age.' But age was catching up: it was Churchill's last great public appearance.

Westminster Hall, London, 30 November 1954

THIS IS TO ME the most memorable public occasion of my life. No one has ever received a similar mark of honour before. There has not been anything like it in British history, and indeed I doubt whether any of the modern democracies has shown such a degree of kindness and generosity to a party politician who has not yet retired and may at any time be involved in controversy. It is indeed the most striking example I have ever known of that characteristic British Parliamentary principle cherished in both Lords and Commons 'Don't bring politics into private life'. It is certainly a mark of the underlying unity of our national life which survives and even grows in spite of vehement party warfare and many grave differences of conviction and sentiment. This unity is, I believe, the child of freedom and fair play fostered in the cradle of our ancient island institutions, and nursed by tradition and custom.

I am most grateful to Mr Attlee for the agreeable words he has used about me this morning, and for the magnanimous appraisal he has given of my variegated career. I must confess, however, that this ceremony and all its charm and splendour may well be found to have seriously affected my controversial value as a party politician. However, perhaps with suitable assistance I shall get over this reaction and come round after a bit.

The Leader of the Opposition and I have been the only two Prime Ministers of this country in the last fourteen years. There are no other Prime Ministers alive. Mr Attlee was also Deputy Prime Minister with me in those decisive years of war. During our alternating tenure, tremendous events have happened abroad, and far-reaching changes have taken place at home. There have been three general elections on universal suffrage and the activity of our Parliamentary and party machinery has been absolutely free. Mr Attlee's and my monopoly of the most powerful and disputatious office under the Crown all this time is surely the fact which the world outside may recognize as a symbol of the inherent stability of our British way of life. It is not, however, intended to make it a permanent feature of the Constitution.

I am sure this is the finest greeting any Member of the House of Commons has yet received and I express my heartfelt thanks to the representatives of both Houses for the gifts which you have bestowed in their name. The portrait is a remarkable example of modern art. It certainly combines force and candour. These are qualities which no active Member of either House can do without or should fear to meet. The book with which the Father of the House of Commons [Mr David Grenfell] has presented me is a token of the goodwill and chivalrous regard of members of all parties. I have lived my life in the House of Commons, having served there for fifty-two of the fifty-four years of this tumultuous and convulsive century. I have indeed seen all the ups and downs of fate and fortune, but I have never ceased to love and honour the Mother of Parliaments, the model to the legislative assemblies of so many lands.

The care and thought which has been devoted to this beautiful volume and the fact that it bears the signatures of nearly all my fellow-Members deeply touches my heart. And may I say that I thoroughly understand the position of those who have felt it their duty to abstain. The value of such a tribute is that it should be free and spontaneous. I shall treasure it as long as I live and my family and descendants will regard it as a most precious possession. When I read the eulogy so gracefully and artistically inscribed on the title page, with its famous quotation from John Bunyan, I must confess to you that I was overpowered by two emotions – pride and humility. I have always hitherto regarded them as opposed and also corrective of one another; but on this occasion I am not able to tell you which is dominant in my mind. Indeed both seem to dwell together hand in hand. Who would not feel proud to have this happen to him and yet at the same time I never was more sure of how far it goes beyond what I deserve.

I was very glad that Mr Attlee described my speeches in the

war as expressing the will not only of Parliament but of the whole nation. Their will was resolute and remorseless and, as it proved, unconquerable. It fell to me to express it, and if I found the right words you must remember that I have always earned my living by my pen and by my tongue. It was a nation and race dwelling all round the globe that had the lion heart. I had the luck to be called upon to give the roar. I also hope that I sometimes suggested to the lion the right places to use his claws. I am now nearing the end of my journey. I hope I still have some services to render. However that may be and whatever may befall I am sure I shall never forget the emotions of this day or be able to express my gratitude to those colleagues and companions with whom I have lived my life for this superb honour they have done me.

33

Swan Song

'Never Despair'

House of Commons, 1 March 1955

DURING HIS FINAL MONTHS AS PRIME MINISTER, Churchill devoted his remaining energies to two great (and related) international problems: the threats and challenges of the hydrogen bomb, and the possibility of a summit meeting with the new Russian leaders in the aftermath of Stalin's death. But he was visibly ageing, month by month; the Americans were unenthusiastic; and there was growing pressure from ministers and MPs that he must set a date for his retirement. Eventually, in early 1955, he made a definite commitment to go at the beginning of the Easter Recess.

He was anxious to show that he was resigning of his own free will and not because of the enfeebling ravages of old age. Accordingly, he determined that his speech in the Defence Debate of early March would be (in Lord Moran's words) 'one of his great utterances, something which the House would long remember'. He spent twenty hours preparing it, dictated every word himself, and it was listened to with deep respect and almost total silence in a packed chamber.

As Christopher Soames told him immediately afterwards, it was indeed 'a very fine swan song'. The *Sunday Times* agreed that Churchill's powers, 'as he has so brilliantly demonstrated, are still of the highest order'. He made two more speeches in the House before he resigned as Prime Minister on 5 April, but the final words of this great oration were undoubtedly intended as his formal farewell – both to his audience and to his art.

338

House of Commons, 1 March 1955

WE LIVE IN A PERIOD, happily unique in human history, when the whole world is divided intellectually and to a large extent geographically between the creeds of Communist discipline and individual freedom, and when, at the same time, this mental and psychological division is accompanied by the possession by both sides of the obliterating weapons of the nuclear age.

We have antagonisms now as deep as those of the Reformation and its reactions which led to the Thirty Years' War. But now they are spread over the whole world instead of only over a small part of Europe. We have, to some extent, the geographical division of the Mongol invasion in the thirteenth century, only more ruthless and more thorough. We have force and science, hitherto the servants of man, now threatening to become his master.

I am not pretending to have a solution for a permanent peace between the nations which could be unfolded this afternoon. We pray for it. Nor shall I try to discuss the cold war which we all detest, but have to endure. I shall only venture to offer to the House some observations mainly of a general character on which I have pondered long and which, I hope, may be tolerantly received, as they are intended by me. And here may I venture to make a personal digression. I do not pretend to be an expert or to have technical knowledge of this prodigious sphere of science. But in my long friendship with Lord Cherwell I have tried to follow and even predict the evolution of events. I hope that the House will not reprove me for vanity or conceit if I repeat what I wrote a quarter of a century ago:

> We know enough [I said] to be sure that the scientific achievements of the next fifty years will be far greater, more rapid and more surprising than those we have already experienced ... High authorities tell us that new sources of power, vastly more important than

339

any we yet know, will surely be discovered. Nuclear energy is incomparably greater than the molecular energy which we use today. The coal a man can get in a day can easily do 500 times as much work as the man himself. Nuclear energy is at least one million times more powerful still. If the hydrogen atoms in a pound of water could be prevailed upon to combine together and form helium, they would suffice to drive a 1,000 horse-power engine for a whole year. If the electrons – those tiny planets of the atomic systems – were induced to combine with the nuclei in the hydrogen, the horse-power liberated would be 120 times greater still. There is no question among scientists that this gigantic source of energy exists. What is lacking is the match to set the bonfire alight, or it may be the detonator to cause the dynamite to explode.

This is no doubt not quite an accurate description of what has been discovered, but as it was published in the *Strand Magazine* of December 1931 – twenty-four years ago – I hope that my plea to have long taken an interest in the subject may be indulgently accepted by the House.

What is the present position? Only three countries possess, in varying degrees, the knowledge and the power to make nuclear weapons. Of these, the United States is overwhelmingly the chief. Owing to the breakdown in the exchange of information between us and the United States since 1946 we have had to start again independently on our own. Fortunately, executive action was taken promptly by the right hon. Gentleman the Leader of the Opposition to reduce as far as possible the delay in our nuclear development and production. By his initiative we have made our own atomic bombs.

Confronted with the hydrogen bomb, I have tried to live up to the right hon. Gentleman's standard. We have started to make that one, too. It is this grave decision which forms the core of the Defence Paper which we are discussing this afternoon. Although the Soviet stockpile of atomic bombs may be greater than that of Britain, British discoveries may well place us above them in fundamental science.

May I say that for the sake of simplicity and to avoid verbal confusion I use the expression 'atomic bombs' and also 'hydrogen bombs' instead of 'thermo-nuclear' and I keep 'nuclear' for the whole lot. There is an immense gulf between the atomic and the hydrogen bomb. The atomic bomb, with all its terrors, did not carry us outside the scope of human control or manageable events in thought or action, in peace or war. But when Mr Sterling Cole, the Chairman of the United States Congressional Committee, gave out a year ago – 17 February 1954 – the first comprehensive review of the hydrogen bomb, the entire foundation of human affairs was revolutionized, and mankind placed in a situation both measureless and laden with doom.

It is now the fact that a quantity of plutonium, probably less than would fill the Box on the Table – it is quite a safe thing to store – would suffice to produce weapons which would give indisputable world domination to any great Power which was the only one to have it. There is no absolute defence against the hydrogen bomb, nor is any method in sight by which any nation, or any country, can be completely guaranteed against the devastating injury which even a score of them might inflict on wide regions.

What ought we to do? Which way shall we turn to save our lives and the future of the world? It does not matter so much to old people; they are going soon anyway; but I find it poignant to look at youth in all its activity and ardour and, most of all, to watch little children playing their merry games, and wonder what would lie before them if God wearied of mankind.

The best defence would of course be bona fide disarmament all round. This is in all our hearts. But sentiment must not cloud our vision. It is often said that 'facts are stubborn things'. A renewed session of a sub-committee of the Disarmament Commission is now sitting in London and is rightly attempting to conduct its debates in private. We must not conceal from ourselves the gulf between the Soviet Government and the NATO Powers, which has hitherto, for so long, prevented an agreement. The long history and tradition of Russia makes it repugnant to the Soviet Government to accept any practical system of international inspection.

A second difficulty lies in the circumstance that, just as the

United States, on the one hand, has we believe, the overwhelming mastery in nuclear weapons, so the Soviets and their Communist satellites have immense superiority in what are called 'conventional' forces – the sort of arms and forces with which we fought the last war, but much improved. The problem is, therefore, to devise a balanced and phased system of disarmament which at no period enables any one of the participants to enjoy an advantage which might endanger the security of the others. A scheme on these lines was submitted last year by Her Majesty's Government and the French Government and was accepted by the late Mr Vyshinsky as a basis of discussion. It is now being examined in London.

If the Soviet Government have not at any time since the war shown much nervousness about the American possession of nuclear superiority, that is because they are quite sure that it will not be used against them aggressively, even in spite of many forms of provocation. On the other hand, the NATO Powers have been combined together by the continued aggression and advance of Communism in Asia and in Europe. That this should have eclipsed in a few years, and largely effaced, the fearful antagonism and memories that Hitlerism created for the German people is an event without parallel. But it has, to a large extent, happened. There is widespread belief throughout the free world that, but for American nuclear superiority, Europe would already have been reduced to satellite status and the Iron Curtain would have reached the Atlantic and the Channel.

Unless a trustworthy and universal agreement upon disarmament, conventional and nuclear alike, can be reached and an effective system of inspection is established and is actually working, there is only one sane policy for the free world in the next few years. That is what we call defence through deterrents. This we have already adopted and proclaimed. These deterrents may at any time become the parents of disarmament, provided that they deter. To make our contribution to the deterrent we must ourselves possess the most up-to-date nuclear weapons, and the means of delivering them.

That is the position which the Government occupy. We are to

discuss this not only as a matter of principle; there are many practical reasons which should be given. Should war come, which God forbid, there are a large number of targets that we and the Americans must be able to strike at once. There are scores of airfields from which the Soviets could launch attacks with hydrogen bombs as soon as they have the bombers to carry them. It is essential to our deterrent policy and to our survival to have, with our American allies, the strength and numbers to be able to paralyse these potential Communist assaults in the first few hours of the war, should it come.

The House will perhaps note that I avoid using the word 'Russia' as much as possible in this discussion. I have a strong admiration for the Russian people – for their bravery, their many gifts and their kindly nature. It is the Communist dictatorship and the declared ambition of the Communist Party and their proselytizing activities that we are bound to resist, and that is what makes this great world cleavage which I mentioned when I opened my remarks.

There are also big administrative and industrial targets behind the Iron Curtain, and any effective deterrent policy must have the power to paralyse them all at the outset, or shortly after. There are also the Soviet submarine bases and other naval targets which will need early attention. Unless we make a contribution of our own – that is the point which I am pressing – we cannot be sure that in an emergency the resources of other Powers would be planned exactly as we would wish, or that the targets which would threaten us most would be given what we consider the necessary priority, or the deserved priority, in the first few hours.

These targets might be of such cardinal importance that it would really be a matter of life and death for us. All this, I think, must be borne in mind in deciding our policy about the conventional forces, to which I will come later, the existing Services.

Meanwhile, the United States has many times the nuclear power of Soviet Russia – I avoid any attempt to give exact figures – and they have, of course, far more effective means of delivery. Our moral and military support of the United States and our possession of nuclear weapons of the highest quality and on an appreciable scale, together with their means of delivery, will greatly reinforce the deterrent power of the free world, and will strengthen our influence within the free world. That, at any rate, is the policy we have decided to pursue. That is what we are now doing, and I am thankful that it is endorsed by a mass of responsible opinion on both sides of the House, and, I believe, by the great majority of the nation.

A vast quantity of information, some true, some exaggerated much out of proportion, has been published about the hydrogen bomb. The truth has inevitably been mingled with fiction, and I am glad to say that panic has not occurred. Panic would not necessarily make for peace. That is one reason why I have been most anxious that responsible discussions on this matter should not take place on the BBC or upon the television, and I thought that I was justified in submitting that view of Her Majesty's Government to the authorities, which they at once accepted – very willingly accepted.

Panic would not necessarily make for peace even in this country. There are many countries where a certain wave of opinion may arise and swing so furiously into action that decisive steps may be taken from which there is no recall. As it is, the world population goes on its daily journey despite its sombre impression and earnest longing for relief. That is the way we are going on now.

I shall content myself with saying about the power of this weapon, the hydrogen bomb, that apart from all the statements about blast and heat effects over increasingly wide areas there are now to be considered the consquences of 'fall out', as it is called, of wind-borne radio-active particles. There is both an immediate direct effect on human beings who are in the path of such a cloud and an indirect effect through animals, grass and vegetables, which pass on these contagions to human beings through food.

This would confront many who escaped the direct effects of the explosion with poisoning, or starvation, or both. Imagination stands appalled. There are, of course, the palliatives and precautions of a courageous Civil Defence, and about that the Home Secretary will be speaking later on tonight. But our best protection lies, as I am sure the House will be convinced, in successful deterrents operating from a foundation of sober, calm and tireless vigilance.

Moreover, a curious paradox has emerged. Let me put it simply. After a certain point has been passed it may be said, 'The worse things get, the better'.

The broad effect of the latest developments is to spread almost indefinitely and at least to a vast extent the area of mortal danger. This should certainly increase the deterrent upon Soviet Russia by putting her enormous spaces and scattered population on an equality or near-equality of vulnerability with our small densely populated island and with Western Europe.

I cannot regard this development as adding to our dangers. We have reached the maximum already. On the contrary, to this form of attack continents are vulnerable as well as islands. Hitherto, crowded countries, as I have said, like the United Kingdom and Western Europe, have had this outstanding vulnerability to carry. But the hydrogen bomb, with its vast range of destruction and the even wider area of contamination, would be effective also against nations whose population, hitherto, has been so widely dispersed over large land areas as to make them feel that they were not in any danger at all.

They, too, become highly vulnerable; not yet equally perhaps, but, still, highly and increasingly vulnerable. Here again we see the value of deterrents, immune against surprise and well understood by all persons on both sides – I repeat 'on both sides' – who have the power to control events. That is why I have hoped for a long time for a top-level conference where these matters could be put plainly and bluntly from one friendly visitor to the conference to another.

Then it may well be that we shall by a process of sublime irony have reached a stage in this story where safety will be the sturdy child of terror, and survival the twin brother of annihilation. Although the Americans have developed weapons capable of producing all the effects I have mentioned, we believe that the Soviets so far have tested by explosion only a type of bomb of intermediate power.

There is no reason why, however, they should not develop some time within the next four, three, or even two years more advanced weapons and full means to deliver them on North American targets. Indeed, there is every reason to believe that within that period they will. In trying to look ahead like this we must be careful ourselves to avoid the error of comparing the present state of our preparations with the stage which the Soviets may reach in three or four years' time. It is a major error of thought to contrast the Soviet position three or four years hence with our own position today. It is a mistake to do this, either in the comparatively precise details of aircraft development or in the measureless sphere of nuclear weapons.

The threat of hydrogen attack on these islands lies in the future. It is not with us now. According to the information that I have been able to obtain – I have taken every opportunity to consult all the highest authorities at our disposal – the only country which is able to deliver today a full-scale nuclear attack with hydrogen bombs at a few hours' notice is the United States. That surely is an important fact, and from some points of view and to some of us it is not entirely without comfort.

It is conceivable that Soviet Russia, fearing a nuclear attack before she has caught up with the United States and created deterrents of her own, as she might argue that they are, might attempt to bridge the gulf by a surprise attack with such nuclear weapons as she has already. American superiority in nuclear weapons, reinforced by Britain, must, therefore, be so organized as to make it clear that no such surprise attack would prevent immediate retaliation on a far larger scale. This is an essential of the deterrent policy.

For this purpose, not only must the nuclear superiority of the Western Powers be stimulated in every possible way, but their means of delivery of bombs must be expanded, improved, and varied. It is even probable, though we have not been told about it outside the NATO sphere, that a great deal of this has been already done by the United States. We should aid them in every possible way. I will not attempt to go into details, but it is known that bases have been and are being established in as many parts of the world as possible and that over all the rest the United States Strategic Air Force, which is in itself a deterrent of the highest order, is in ceaseless readiness.

The Soviet Government probably knows, in general terms, of the policy that is being pursued, and of the present United States strength and our own growing addition to it. Thus, they should be convinced that a surprise attack could not exclude immediate retaliation. As one might say to them. 'Although you might kill millions of our peoples, and cause widespread havoc by a surprise attack, we could, within a few hours of this outrage, certainly deliver several, indeed many times the weight of nuclear material which you have used, and continue retaliation on that same scale. We have', we could say, 'already hundreds of bases for attack from all angles and have made an intricate study of suitable targets.' Thus, it seems to me with some experience of wartime talks, you might go to dinner and have a friendly evening. I should not be afraid to talk things over as far as they can be. This, and the hard facts, would make the deterrent effective.

I must make one admission, and any admission is formidable. The deterrent does not cover the case of lunatics or dictators in the mood of Hitler when he found himself in his final dug-out. That is a blank. Happily, we may find methods of protecting ourselves, if we were all agreed, against that.

All these considerations lead me to believe that, on a broad view, the Soviets would be ill-advised to embark on major aggression within the next three or four years. One must always consider the interests of other people when you are facing a particular situation. Their interests may be the only guide that is available. We may calculate, therefore, that world war will not break out within that time. If, at the end of that time, there should be a supreme conflict, the weapons which I have described this afternoon would be available to both sides, and it would be folly to suppose that they would not be used. Our precautionary dispositions and preparations must, therefore, be based on the assumption that, if war should come, these weapons would be used.

I repeat, therefore, that during the next three or four years the free world should, and will, retain an overwhelming superiority in hydrogen weapons. During that period it is most unlikely that the Russians would deliberately embark on major war or attempt a suprise attack, either of which would bring down upon them at once a crushing weight of nuclear retaliation. In three or four years' time, it may be even less, the scene will be changed. The Soviets will probably stand possessed of hydrogen bombs and the means of delivering them not only on the United Kingdom but also on North American targets. They may then have reached a stage, not indeed of parity which the United States and Britain but of what is called 'saturation'.

I must explain this term of art. 'Saturation' in this connection means the point where, although one Power is stronger than the other, perhaps much stronger, both are capable of inflicting crippling or quasi-mortal injury on the other with what they have got. It does not follow, however, that the risk of war will then be greater. Indeed, it is arguable that it will be less, for both sides will then realize that global war would result in mutual annihilation.

Major war of the future will differ, therefore, from anything we have known in the past in this one significant respect, that each side, at the outset, will suffer what it dreads the most, the loss of everything that it has ever known of. The deterrents will grow continually in value. In the past, an aggressor has been tempted by the hope of snatching an early advantage. In future, he may be deterred by the knowledge that the other side has the certain power to inflict swift, inescapable and crushing retaliation.

Of course, we should all agree that a worldwide international agreement on disarmament is the goal at which we should aim. The Western democracies disarmed themselves at the end of the war. The Soviet Government did not disarm, and the Western nations were forced to rearm, though only partially, after the Soviets and Communists had dominated all China and half Europe. That is the present position. It is easy, of course, for the

348

Communists to say now, 'Let us ban all nuclear weapons'. Communist ascendancy in conventional weapons would then become overwhelming. That might bring peace, but only peace in the form of the subjugation of the Free World to the Communist system.

I shall not detain the House very much longer, and I am sorry to be so long. The topic is very intricate. I am anxious to repeat and to emphasize the one word which is the theme of my remarks, namely, 'Deterrent'. That is the main theme.

The hydrogen bomb has made an astounding incursion into the structure of our lives and thoughts. Its impact is prodigious and profound, but I do not agree with those who say, 'Let us sweep away forthwith all our existing defence services and concentrate our energy and resources on nuclear weapons and their immediate ancillaries.' The policy of the deterrent cannot rest on nuclear weapons alone. We must, together with our NATO allies, maintain the defensive shield in Western Europe.

Unless the NATO Powers had effective forces there on the ground and could make a front, there would be nothing to prevent piecemeal advance and encroachment by the Communists in this time of so-called peace. By successive infiltrations, the Communists could progressively undermine the security of Europe. Unless we were prepared to unleash a full-scale nuclear war as soon as some local incident occurs in some distant country, we must have conventional forces in readiness to deal with such situations as they arise.

We must, therefore, honour our undertaking to maintain our contribution to the NATO forces in Europe in time of peace. In war, this defensive shield would be of vital importance, for we must do our utmost to hold the Soviet and satellite forces at arms' length in order to prevent short-range air and rocket attack on these islands. Thus, substantial strength in conventional forces has still a vital part to play in the policy of the deterrent. It is perhaps of even greater importance in the cold war.

Though world war may be prevented by the deterrent power of nuclear weapons, the Communists may well resort to military

action in furtherance of their policy of infiltration and encroachment in many parts of the world. There may well be limited wars
on the Korean model, with limited objectives. We must be able
to play our part in these, if called upon by the United Nations
organization. In the conditions of today, this is also an aspect of
our Commonwealth responsibility. We shall need substantial
strength in conventional forces to fulfil our worldwide obligations in these days of uneasy peace and extreme bad temper.

To sum up this part of the argument, of course, the development of nuclear weapons will affect the shape and organization of
the Armed Forces and also of Civil Defence. We have entered a
period of transition in which the past and the future will overlap.
But it is an error to suppose that, because of these changes, our
traditional forces can be cast away or superseded. The tasks of
the Army, Navy and Air Force in this transition period are set
forth with clarity in the Defence White Paper. The means by
which these duties will be met are explained in more detail in the
Departmental Papers which have been laid before the House by
the three Service Ministers.

No doubt, nothing is perfect; certainly, nothing is complete,
but, considering that these arrangements have been made in the
first year after the apparition of the hydrogen bomb, the far-
seeing and progressive adaptability which is being displayed by
all three Services is remarkable [*Hon. Members: 'Oh'*]. I understand that there is to be a Motion of censure. Well, certainly,
nothing could be more worthy of censure than to try to use the
inevitable administrative difficulties of the transitional stage as a
utensil of party politics and would-be electioneering. I am not saying that anyone is doing it; we shall see when it comes to the vote.

The future shape of Civil Defence is also indicated in broad
outline in the Defence White Paper. This outline will be filled in
as the preparation of the new plans proceeds, but the need for an
effective system of Civil Defence is surely beyond dispute. It
presents itself today in its noblest aspect, namely, the Christian
duty of helping fellow-mortals in distress. Rescue, salvage and
ambulance work have always been the core of Civil Defence, and
no city, no family nor any honourable man or woman can

350

repudiate this duty and accept from others help which they are not prepared to fit themselves to render in return. If war comes, great numbers may be relieved of their duty by death, but none must deny it as long as they live. If they do, they might perhaps be put in what is called 'Coventry' [*laughter*]. I am speaking of the tradition, and not of any particular locality.

The argument which I have been endeavouring to unfold and consolidate gives us in this island an interlude. Let us not waste it. Let us hope we shall use it to augment or at least to prolong our security and that of mankind. But how? There are those who believe, or at any rate say, 'If we have the protection of the overwhelmingly powerful United States, we need not make the hydrogen bomb for ourselves or build a fleet of bombers for its delivery. We can leave that to our friends across the ocean. Our contribution should be criticism of any unwise policy to which they may drift or plunge. We should throw our hearts and consciences into that.'

Personally, I cannot feel that we should have much influence over their policy or actions, wise or unwise, while we are largely dependent, as we are today, upon their protection. We, too, must possess substantial deterrent power of our own. We must also never allow, above all, I hold, the growing sense of unity and brotherhood between the United Kingdom and the United States and throughout the English-speaking world to be injured or retarded. Its maintenance, its stimulation and its fortifying is one of the first duties of every person who wishes to see peace in the world and wishes to see the survival of this country.

To conclude: mercifully, there is time and hope if we combine patience and courage. All deterrents will improve and gain authority during the next ten years. By that time, the deterrent may well reach its acme and reap its final reward. The day may dawn when fair play, love for one's fellow-men, respect for justice and freedom, will enable tormented generations to march forth serene and triumphant from the hideous epoch in which we have to dwell. Meanwhile, never flinch, never weary, never despair.

Index

Index

Index

354

Index

355